THE SEVENTH GAME

The 35 World Series That Have Gone the Distance

BARRY LEVENSON

McGraw·Hill

New York   Chicago   San Francisco   Lisbon   London   Madrid   Mexico City
Milan   New Delhi   San Juan   Seoul   Singapore   Sydney   Toronto

The McGraw·Hill Companies

Library of Congress Cataloging-in-Publication Data

Levenson, Barry.
    The seventh game : the 35 world series that have gone the distance / Barry Levinson.
       p.   cm.
    Includes index.
    ISBN 0-07-141271-9
    1. World Series (Baseball)—History.   I. Title.

  GV878.4.L49   2004
  796.357'646—dc21   2003011299

1 2 3 4 5 6 7 8 9 0   AGM/AGM   3 2 1 0 9 8 7 6 5 4

ISBN 0-07-141271-9

All of the ticket stubs shown in the insert are from the author's private collection except the 1925 ticket, which is courtesy of the National Baseball Hall of Fame, and the 1912 ticket, which is an artist's modification of a Game 5 ticket stub courtesy of Mark Rucker of Transcendental Graphics.

McGraw-Hill books are available at special quantity discounts to use as premiums and sales promotions, or for use in corporate training programs. For more information, please write to the Director of Special Sales, Professional Publishing, McGraw-Hill, Two Penn Plaza, New York, NY 10121-2298. Or contact your local bookstore.

This book is printed on acid-free paper.

THE SEVENTH GAME

To My Dad

*I must have been five when you took me to our first Red Sox
game. One of the players was so angry over a called strike
that he threw his bat and I thought that was cool. When
we got home, I imitated the irate player by throwing my little
bat around the backyard. By accident (really!) I threw the
bat through my own bedroom window and shattered glass
everywhere. Mom was horrified but you saw the humor in
it and laughed.*

*Thanks for playing catch with me, even when you were so
tired and wanted to lie down.*

*Thanks for letting me stay up late to listen to the games
on the Philco.*

*Thanks for instilling in me a deep and abiding love for
the game.*

Hang in, Dad, this will be the year.

Contents

Foreword

I know that a lot of baseball fans remember me for giving up the home run to Bill Mazeroski in the Seventh Game back in 1960. There's nothing I can do about that, but I don't think they are the real fans who keep the game alive. I'm glad that this book tells another story of me and another Seventh Game.

I remember the pitch to Mazeroski. It was high—not high enough to be a ball, but right at the letters, exactly where Mazeroski liked it. I knew that he was a good high ball hitter, but I could not get the pitch down where I wanted it. After the first pitch, which was way up, Johnny Blanchard came out and told me to keep it down. Heck, I knew that. You have to remember that Casey Stengel had me warming up four or five times during the game. I was already tired when I came in to nail down the final out in the eighth inning.

No one struck out that day? That doesn't surprise me. It was definitely a day for the hitters. Almost like slow-pitch softball: *everybody* hits!

So why wasn't my roomie Ryne Duren out there instead of me? I later gave Ryne a picture of me and signed it "Where the hell were you?" [Editor's note: Ryne Duren still has that picture.] I think Casey was asking the same thing. But I was the lucky one.

I felt bad after the game, not for me but for Casey. I went into his office, and he was taking off his uniform. He asked me about the pitch. Why did I leave it up high? Didn't I know the scouting report on Mazeroski? I told Casey I knew exactly what I was supposed to do but that I just couldn't get the ball down. That was okay with Casey. "As long as you weren't goin' against the scouting report. If it was just a physical mistake, that's fine."

That's all he said. I don't think it hit me at the time, but it turned out that I was the last person to see Casey wearing the Yankee pinstripes.

I'll say this about the New York fans: they never got on me for giving up the home run. I know that in other cities the fans would have made life miserable for me, but those Yankees fans were terrific.

We won the 1961 World Series in five games with that powerhouse team led by Maris and Mantle. Then came 1962. Even though Roger and Mickey had "off years" compared with 1961, we were still a good team, and I had my career year—23 wins and a league-leading 298⅔ innings pitched. And I got my second chance.

The Giants had a great ballclub in 1962. Think of it: Willie Mays, Orlando Cepeda, Willie McCovey. Jack Sanford won 24 games; I think he should have got the Cy Young award that year. After a lot of rain, we finally got to finish the Series. Was I nervous? I guess I must have been—I wanted to win that game so bad. But I had a job to do, so I really didn't have time to be nervous.

I slept like a baby the night before. We were playing poker that night—Yogi, Hector Lopez, Ellie Howard, maybe a few others. Yogi had a lot of money and was always trying to buy the pot. I remember the last hand: I drew the ace of clubs to give me a flush and beat Yogi's king-high heart flush—$350! I got up from the table and just said "Good night, boys!" Yogi couldn't believe it.

On the bus to Candlestick Park we were listening to Joe Garagiola on the radio. He predicted that I would choke and that the Giants would win. I saw Joe at the park and asked him why he would say that. At first he denied saying it, but when I told him we all heard it on the way over to the game, he laughed it off with, "Well, you know, I had to say something."

I was psyched. I think it took me only ten warm-up pitches to get ready. Jim Bouton was a rookie with the Yankees that year and was probably more nervous than I was. He says that I told him, "Hey kid, win or lose, two hundred million Chinese communists won't give a [bleep]." Did I really say that? You bet I did!

The field was in rough shape. The outfield and the base paths were still soggy from several days of hard rain. I had good stuff, real good stuff. Sure, I knew that I had a perfect game into the sixth. Then I threw a fastball to Jack Sanford. The pitcher, of all players, broke up the perfect game. It was a mistake pitch, and Sanford hit it. Remember, though, all the pitchers back then had to hit for themselves, and Sanford was not a bad hitter. He had three hits in seven at-bats during the series. That was two more than I got!

I never figured the one run we scored in the fifth on Tony Kubek's double play grounder would hold up. With all the great hitters in the lineup on both sides and the good scoring chances that we had, I figure it should have been maybe a 5–2 game.

So it came down to the bottom of the ninth. That was some play Maris made to hold Alou [Matty] at third on that slicing double down the right-field line by Mays—especially with the field in as rough shape as it was. Even with runners on second and third, there was no way I was coming out of the game. We didn't have a Mariano Rivera to nail it down. Our relievers that year were not that great. So why did I pitch to McCovey, a left-handed batter, with first base open and the righty Cepeda on deck?

I'm sure that if McCovey's line drive went through for a hit they'd be criticizing Ralph Houk today. Here's the truth: I tried to pitch around McCovey. I knew he had tripled off me in the seventh. I was hoping to get him to chase a bad pitch. Instead, he chased one that was a little too good.

I knew that McCovey's run meant nothing and some might say we should have walked him to face Cepeda. Now, after reading *The Seventh Game*, I find out that Cepeda holds the record for most seventh-game plate appearances without a hit: 11. Of course, I had no way of knowing that then, and we considered him one of their most dangerous hitters. I did not want to face him with the bases jammed.

You walk someone to load the bases and there's always the risk of walking in a run. Sure, I had great control. Did you know I walked only two batters in 25 innings in the '62 World Series? But I was in a National League park, and a National League umpire was behind the plate. Nothing against Stan Landis—he called a great game (I think he missed one pitch the whole day)—but I wasn't interested in pitching to anyone with the bases loaded.

McCovey sure tagged that one, didn't he? He hit it so hard I didn't even have time to think that we might lose. All I knew is that we had Bobby Richardson placed well around toward first, kind of like a shift. The next thing I knew Bobby had it and we were the champs. Oh yes, it felt good!

It still feels good. I'm in good company, aren't I? A seventh-game shutout is special, and I'm proud of what I did that day. Only Jack Morris and I can claim 1–0 shutouts in seventh games; but mine is the only one pitched on the road. Does it make up for the Mazeroski home run? It's not a matter of "making up" for it. I'm just happy that I got a second chance and pitched well. Of course I'm even happier that I won.

This book puts into perspective what it's like to play in a seventh game. I guess I know, more than anyone, both the lows and the highs. If a World Series is the icing on the cake of a good season, think of what that makes the Seventh Game. I'm lucky. I figured prominently in two Seventh Games. Not a lot of players can say that.

I know that my Yankees teammates will enjoy reading this book, as will the players from all the other teams who were fortunate enough to play in those exciting seventh games. Barry Levenson has done a fabulous job in capturing the feel of those unforgettable games. For all of the players and all of the fans, thank you, Barry, for making the magic come alive again.

At least one thing has changed since 1962. With the Internet and everything else bringing the world closer together, I suspect that two hundred million Chinese communists—maybe even more today—*would* give a [bleep] today.

Ralph Terry
Larned, Kansas
November 2003

Preface

It was the bottom of the ninth inning of the Seventh Game of the World Series. The bases were loaded. My team was down by three runs and there were two outs. I was facing the toughest pitcher in all of baseball and he had two strikes on me. I gritted my teeth, concentrated on the ball coming at me at more than a hundred miles an hour, and let loose with my best swing. I made contact and watched as the ball soared majestically over the left-field wall. I had hit a grand-slam home run to win the World Series. I was the greatest hero in all of baseball.

I was on the mound in the bottom of the ninth inning of the Seventh Game of the World Series, facing the best hitter in all of baseball. The bases were loaded with two outs. I was protecting a one-run lead, but a walk would tie it and a hit would lose it for my team. I could see the determination in the batter's eyes, the flexing of the muscles in his arms, and the twitch that seemed always to precede a mighty hit from his bat. The count was full. I reared back and fired a fastball by him for strike three. I was the greatest hero in all of baseball.

I was in left field in the bottom of the ninth inning of the Seventh Game of the World Series, when the best hitter in all of baseball came to bat. There were two outs. My team was ahead by a run but the opposition had the bases loaded. A hit would win it for them. He nailed the pitch deep to left center and it seemed like a sure hit. I ran as hard as I could and at the last second leapt high against the wall to snag the ball in the webbing of my glove. I was the greatest hero in all of baseball.

I performed all of these heroic acts at the age of ten. And I was not alone in coming through with the big hit, the dramatic strikeout, and the amazing catch. Millions of other boys and girls did the same to win the Seventh Game of the World Series. We did it over and over in the sandlots, schoolyards, pastures, fields, and playgrounds of our minds.

The Seventh Game of the World Series is the pinnacle of baseball tension and excitement. A World Series that ends in four, five, or six games is like a gourmet meal without a great dessert. It may be satisfying in its own right, but it is not the complete dining experience. The sportswriters haul out all the clichés. *There's no tomorrow. The seventh and deciding game. It's sudden death. The players have all winter to rest up.* Language tries but often fails to describe the tension and drama of these games. For the baseball aficionado, the Seventh Game is the ultimate thrill.

My first memory of a Seventh Game goes back to 1955, when the Dodgers finally beat the Yankees. I was nearly seven but already an incurable baseball fan. Although I was a Red Sox fan, my father made sure I appreciated the beauty of the game no matter who played, especially when it was World Series time. I remember little of the 1955 Seventh Game except that someone finally beat the Yankees. As a Boston fan, that was second best to the Sox winning the World Series—an unlikely event, my dad explained.

I remember more vividly the Seventh Games between the Braves and the Yankees in 1957 and 1958. The 1960 Seventh Game between the Yankees and Pirates seems like only yesterday. I fancied myself the next Bill Mazeroski. A few years later I imagined myself as the next Sandy Koufax. Was that so far-fetched? Sandy and I had so much in common: we shared the same birthday, neither one of us worked on Yom Kippur, and we both loved to play baseball. Sandy may have had a little more zip on his fastball and a sharper break on his curve, but those were trivial details. I was so proud of us—of him—when he won the Seventh Game of the 1965 World Series.

When the Red Sox won the pennant in 1967, I watched all the games with my dad. The Seventh Game was one of those unique bonding moments between father and son, when we shared the pride of the "Impossible Dream" season and the disappointment of coming up one game short.

When Carlton Fisk's Game Six home run in 1975 made another Red Sox Seventh Game possible, I could barely sleep in anticipation of the climax to that marvelous Series. I wondered: if I'm so nervous about the Seventh Game, how are the players handling it? Yes, they lost and I was sad for days.

More Seventh Games blessed us, and I watched them all. In 1986, the Red Sox were in one more Seventh Game, although I blamed myself for their not winning the Sixth Game. With two outs in the bottom of the tenth inning of Game Six and the Red Sox leading the Mets by two runs,

I was so sure that victory was at hand that I opened a half-bottle of champagne to get a jump on the celebration. I was a lawyer in Madison, Wisconsin, but I had to share the moment with my father. I called him at my boyhood home in Worcester, Massachusetts, and we watched together as the Red Sox snatched defeat from the jaws of victory. I am certain that I jinxed them by popping the cork prematurely.

I watched the 1986 Game Seven alone, expecting the worst and getting it. I was so depressed about the loss that I could not sleep. At two o'clock in the morning, I went to an all-night grocery to walk away my sorrows. I realized that it was not good for a grown man to be so despondent over a lost baseball game. I decided to engage in some hobby, some constructive leisure pursuit that would take my mind off baseball. I was walking down the condiment aisle at the time and decided to collect jars of mustard.

I continued to collect jars of mustard and left my job as a Wisconsin assistant attorney general in 1991 to open the Mount Horeb Mustard Museum, home today of the world's largest collection of mustards and mustard memorabilia. And all because the Red Sox lost a Seventh Game of the World Series.

The truth is, though, that my mustard obsession did not cure me. I still love baseball, still yearn for the day the Red Sox will win it all, and still savor every Seventh Game of the World Series.

I came to realize that every Game Seven produces both jubilation and despair, even more so than World Series that are resolved in fewer games. Maybe it is because fans of the two teams understand that they have come to the brink of baseball drama, that there is nothing more that the game can give. As I relished each Seventh Game after 1986, I also looked back at older Seventh Games to comprehend the depth of those feelings. I fell in love with every one of them.

So here I am, describing a love affair, with all the passion and fervor and excitement that every lover has felt about the objects of his affection. Can a lover really share those feelings? I hope I can do that, bring the flavor of those magical thirty-five Seventh Games to you. This love story is not just about events but also about people, because that is what makes baseball such a personal endeavor. We love the game because we love the players. Although more than 100,000 men have played in the major leagues since the beginning of the modern baseball era in 1901, only a select few—743 to be exact—have appeared in this narrow universe of games. This book is their story.

Baseball has its own language, its own lingo, and I will be using it to describe the magic of these Seventh Games. I promise, though, that I will do my best to avoid the trite and hackneyed expressions that can make sportswriting tedious and corny.

I have also ranked each Seventh Game, from worst to best. You will undoubtedly disagree with my opinions, especially when it comes to my view of the all-time best Seventh Games. That's what makes baseball the great American game that it is. We love to play it (as best we can), watch it, and argue about it.

I want to thank the many people who have encouraged me to write this book and helped make it happen. The staff at the research library at the Baseball Hall of Fame in Cooperstown, New York, generously opened up their archives and resources to me for material that would have been otherwise unavailable. My persistent agents, Jane Dystel and Miriam Goderich, have believed in this idea from the first day I presented it to them. Even though Miriam is a true-blue Yankees fan, I love her dearly.

Thank you, Mark Rinaldi, president of Miller Associates, creators of the APBA baseball simulation game, for providing me with the software and data disks for the thirty-five Seventh Game seasons. His generosity made it possible to experience anew the thrills of each of those enchanting games. I hope you enjoy reading about the results of those replays in Chapter 41.

Thank you, Patti, my patient and attentive wife, for proofreading a lot of what must have seemed like gibberish to her. She likes baseball but is not the fanatic that her husband is. She was at the 1985 Seventh Game between the Royals and the Cardinals. I asked her if she had saved the ticket stub. "What ticket stub?" she asked. "I snuck in with a friend and spent most of the game moving around in the seats behind first base trying to avoid the commissioner."

Thanks also to my mustard-loving friend, Barry Seifert, for reading the manuscript and giving me hundreds of helpful suggestions and insights. His careful eye has made this book so much better. There are many facts and statistics in this book. I have tried to double- and triple-check their accuracy. I accept full responsibility for any errors or omissions.

Finally, thank you to the men who batted, pitched, ran, and fielded in these games. I admire all of you and would give the rarest jar of mustard in my collection to have been in your cleats when you played in your Seventh Games. Please do not take personally any criticism that you think I have intended about your play. You are my heroes, and the heroes of millions.

Before We Get Started

Warming Up—a Test of Your Seventh-Game Knowledge

Here are fifty questions to test your knowledge of the World Series Seventh Games. (Answers begin on page xxii.)

1. The record for most career Seventh Game stolen bases is three, held by two ex-Cardinals. Who are they?
2. Who holds the record for most total bases in a single Seventh Game?
3. Who was the last player to collect four hits in a Seventh Game?
4. True or False: "Mr. October," Reggie Jackson, never hit a Seventh Game home run.
5. Four players have hit more than one career Seventh Game home run, but only one did so in consecutive years. Who was this Braves slugger?
6. Who is the only pitcher to hit a Seventh Game home run?
7. Who hit the first home run in a Seventh Game?
8. Who hit the first Yankees Seventh Game home run?
9. Who is the only player to end a Seventh Game by being caught stealing?
10. There has been only one player with a last name beginning with the letter "Q" to appear in a Seventh Game. Who was he?
11. Only one Red Sox player has ever tripled in a Seventh Game. Who was he? Hint: he was not known for his speed on the base paths.
12. How many of the famed Alou family have appeared in Seventh Games?
13. Who holds the unenviable record for most career Seventh Game official at-bats without a hit? By the way, he is in the Hall of Fame with a career batting average of .297 and more than 375 home runs.

14. He appeared in two Seventh Games, fourteen years apart, and distinguished himself by collecting four hits in nine at-bats. Who was he?

15. What pitcher not only hurled a shutout in his only Seventh Game appearance but also collected two hits as a batter in one inning?

16. Which DiMaggio has more career Seventh Game hits, Joe or Dom?

17. There have been only 13 triples in the thirty-five Seventh Games. Honus Wagner hit the first. Who has the most recent?

18. He played in the 1991, 1997, and 2001 Seventh Games, all on different losing teams. Who is he?

19. Who is the only pitcher to have thrown a Seventh Game shutout without having a career winning record?

20. Whitey Ford holds the record for most World Series appearances by a pitcher (also most World Series wins), but what was his record in Seventh Games?

21. Two players are tied for most career Seventh Game hits. One is in the Hall of Fame, the other isn't. Name these two Yankees.

22. Goose Goslin was the first to do it and Marty Barrett was the last. In between, Jackie Robinson, Bob Allison, and George Scott did it. What Seventh Game distinction is it? Hint: it can be done only once in any Seventh Game.

23. This weak-hitting catcher (career batting average of .227) went on to be a big-league manager but in his only Seventh Game appearance knocked the cover off the ball with a pair of doubles and four RBIs. Who is he?

24. What Hall of Famer is the last catcher to steal a base in a Seventh Game?

25. The record for most pitchers used by both teams in a Seventh Game is twelve. In what World Series did this equal-opportunity pitching carnival take place? (Bonus: front-row seats behind the first-base dugout if you can name all twelve pitchers!)

26. Who is the only player to end a Seventh Game by grounding into a double play?

27. Hall of Famers Carlton Fisk, Mickey Mantle, and Hank Greenberg are among the seven players to share this dubious record (along with Wayne Garrett, David Justice, Tony Lazzeri, and Ernie Orsatti)—what "record" is it?

28. There have been nine Seventh Game shutouts. Who pitched the last one?
29. Who is credited with the first Seventh Game save?
30. What Seventh Game holds the record for largest attendance?
31. Who has hit the only grand-slam home run in Seventh Game history?
32. In which Seventh Game did no one strike out?
33. What pitcher holds the Seventh Game record for most earned runs allowed without recording a single out?
34. What two brothers, playing on opposing teams, hit home runs in the same Seventh Game?
35. When Roger Clemens struck out ten Arizona Diamondbacks in 2001, he joined what three Hall of Famers in holding the record for most strikeouts in a Seventh Game?
36. What Hall of Fame pitcher holds the record for most hits allowed in a Seventh Game?
37. Only two players went 0 for 6 in a Seventh Game. One did it in 1924, the other did it in 1997. Who were they?
38. What Seventh Game fielding "feat" did Larry Gardner, Denny Doyle, Ossie Bluege, Frank Torre, Travis Jackson, Roger Peckin-paugh, and Gil McDougald accomplish?
39. Barry Bonds set a major-league record when he walked 198 times during the 2002 season. How many times did the Anaheim Angels walk him in the Seventh Game of the 2002 World Series?
40. What team is undefeated in five Seventh Game appearances?
41. The New York Yankees have won more World Series titles than any other team. But what is their record in their eleven Seventh Game appearances?
42. Which league holds the edge in Seventh Game play?
43. In only two Seventh Games did both starting pitchers hurl complete games. Name the years of these pitching gems and name the pitchers.
44. Several Seventh Game pitchers have given up earned runs without being credited with an out, giving them an earned run average of "infinity." Who has the distinction of having the highest real-number Seventh Game ERA of 360.00 (four earned runs in one-third of an inning)?

45. What pitcher has started the most Seventh Games?
46. Only two pitchers have pitched more than nine innings in a single Seventh Game. Name them.
47. What hitter has appeared in the most Seventh Games?
48. While thirty-three batters have appeared in three or more Seventh Games, only two pitchers have done so. They are both named Bob. Who are they?
49. What team holds the record for most errors committed in a Seventh Game?
50. Only four of the thirty-five Seventh Games have been error-free. When was the last of these fielding-perfect matches?

ANSWERS

1. Pepper Martin (1934) and Lou Brock (1967)
2. Willie Stargell (1979 Pirates) had nine total bases (one single, two doubles, and one home run).
3. George Brett (1985 Royals)
4. False. In his only Seventh Game (1973), Reggie went one for four, and that hit was a home run.
5. Del Crandall (1957 and 1958)
6. Bob Gibson
7. Bucky Harris
8. Babe Ruth
9. Babe Ruth
10. Frank Quillici (1965 Twins)
11. George "The Boomer" Scott (1967)
12. All four Alous—Jesus, Felipe, Matty, and Moises—have made Seventh Game appearances.
13. Orlando Cepeda went 0 for 11 in three Seventh Games.
14. Doc Cramer
15. Dizzy Dean
16. Dom DiMaggio got one hit in the 1946 Seventh Game, while brother Joe went hitless in 1947.
17. Jim Northrup (1968)
18. David Justice

19. Johnny Kucks (1956 Yankees)
20. Whitey Ford never appeared in a Seventh Game.
21. Mickey Mantle and Gil McDougald each had nine Seventh Game hits.
22. They all struck out to end a Seventh Game.
23. Paul Richards (1945 Tigers)
24. Johnny Bench (1972 Reds). If you thought the answer was Tony Pena (who stole a base in 1987), you are wrong because Pena was the designated hitter in that game.
25. In the 1997 Seventh Game between the Cleveland Indians and the Florida Marlins, each team used six pitchers. For Cleveland: Jared Wright, Paul Assenmacher, Mike Jackson, Brian Anderson, Jose Mesa, and Charles Nagy. For Florida: Al Leiter, Dennis Cook, Antonio Alfonseca, Felix Heredia, Robb Nen, and Jay Powell.
26. Bruce Edwards, playing for the Brooklyn Dodgers in the 1947 World Series, was the victim.
27. Most strikeouts in a single Seventh Game by a non-pitcher—three
28. Jack Morris (1991 Twins)
29. Red Oldham (1925 Pirates)
30. The 1947 Seventh Game at Yankee Stadium drew a crowd of 71,548.
31. Bill Skowron (1956 Yankees)
32. No one struck out in the 1960 slugfest between the Yankees and the Pirates.
33. Roger Craig (1956 Dodgers) gave up four earned runs without recording an out.
34. Brothers Ken (St. Louis Cardinals) and Cletis (New York Yankees) Boyer homered in the 1964 Seventh Game.
35. Bob Gibson, Sandy Koufax, and Hal Newhouser
36. Walter Johnson (1925 Senators) gave up 15 hits to the Pirates; he lost.
37. Travis Jackson (1924 Giants) and Devon White (1997 Marlins)
38. They are the only players to commit two errors in a single Seventh Game.
39. Barry walked once in the 2002 Seventh Game.
40. The Pittsburgh Pirates have won all five of their Seventh Games (1909, 1925, 1960, 1971, and 1979).
41. The Yankees have won five and lost six Seventh Games.

42. The American League leads, 18 to 17.
43. In 1940 Paul Derringer outdueled Bobo Newsom, and in 1968 Mickey Lolich beat Bob Gibson, with all four pitchers going the distance.
44. Vic Aldridge (1925 Pirates)
45. Bob Gibson
46. Christy Mathewson (1912 Giants) and Jack Morris (1991 Twins)
47. Mickey Mantle appeared in eight Seventh Games between 1952 and 1964.
48. Bob Gibson (St. Louis Cardinals) and Bob Turley (New York Yankees)
49. The 1912 Red Sox committed five errors but still won the game.
50. There were no errors in the 2002 Seventh Game between the Anaheim Angels and the San Francisco Giants.

So how did you do? Here's how we rate your knowledge, based on the number of correct answers:

45–50   You are a baseball genius and we hereby enshrine you in the Hall of Fame.

35–44   Very impressive. You are more than qualified to be the next commissioner of baseball.

25–34   That's good, really. These are tough questions and you may buy yourself an extra hot dog at the ballpark next summer. Don't forget the mustard.

15–24   Don't be discouraged. Even the best hitters make outs two-thirds of the time.

5–14   You will learn a lot from reading this book. Just pay attention.

0–4   They say that Einstein was a terrible test taker. Enjoy the book.

For more Seventh Game trivia, visit www.theseventhgame.com.

Introduction

The Magic of Seven—the Story Behind the Seven-Game World Series

They were the best of games, they were the worst of games. They were games of skillful hitting, they were games of missed opportunities. They were matches of dominating pitching, they were contests of inexplicable lapses of fielding. They were the thirty-five Seventh Games of baseball's World Series.

The World Series has gone to a Seventh Game thirty-five times. The first Seventh Game, between the Detroit Tigers and the Pittsburgh Pirates, unfolded before a crowd of 17,562 fans in Detroit on October 16, 1909, in cold weather, under dark and threatening clouds. The most recent Seventh Game, between the San Francisco Giants and the Anaheim Angels, was played in the warmth of a southern California night on October 27, 2002, before 44,598 fans and enjoyed by countless millions around the globe on radio and television.

Since 1903, and with only two minor exceptions, the championship of professional baseball in North America has been determined by a seven-game series between the pennant winners of two rival leagues, the National League and the American League. It has always been called the "World Series," even though the distinctly American game of baseball is now played around the world and teams from other leagues and other countries do not participate in this championship tournament.

Why seven games? What is the magic of a "best-of-seven" format? Why has baseball adopted the tradition of proclaiming a champion when one team is the first to defeat its rival four times? Would not a single championship game, winner-take-all, be more exciting? That is how professional football determines its champion in the "Super Bowl."

Those who understand baseball know that the measure of a team cannot be determined by a single game. Because every team plays its regular-season games with several pitchers to start the games, a single-game championship would unduly reward the team with one shining star pitcher and could unfairly penalize the team with an overall better pitching staff. Football, where every player is expected to perform in every game and teams rest a week between games, is a sprint. Baseball, where pitchers do not appear in every game and teams often play day after day without a break, is a marathon. One game cannot be a valid sampling of one team's superiority. But why seven?

The answer to why baseball plays a seven-game World Series, in which the first team to win four games is the champion, may be found in the Broadway musical *Fiddler on the Roof*. When Tevye asks why they do things a certain way in their little village of Anatevke, he answers: "Tradition!"

A best-of-five World Series would allow for the expected statistical variations in player performances that seem to even out in a multi-game series. Why not five? But that logic would seem to favor an even longer series, best-of-nine or best-of-eleven, etc., to prove that the winner is not just a fluke of a short series. That logic, of course, loses itself in the obvious. At some point, you need to draw a line or else you are committed to playing an entire season all over again.

It is seven because seven fits. Seven is comfortable. Baseball experimented with a best-of-nine format from 1919 through 1922 and, like Goldilocks trying out Papa Bear's bed, found that it was too big. The cliché about it not being possible to be too rich or too thin does not apply to the number of games in a World Series. Just because the fans love a seven-game series does not mean that they will love a longer series even more. It took baseball a few years to figure that out.

The four-year flirtation with a best-of-nine format was one exception. The first World Series, another best-of-nine, was the other. In 1903, professional baseball was played by two separate and distinct groups, the older and more established National League and the younger and less established American League. They saw each other as fierce rivals in a limited market for the sport. The Boston Pilgrims (now the Red Sox) beat the Pittsburgh Pirates, five games to three, and the seeds for an annual World Series had been sown. There was no World Series in 1904 because John McGraw, the arrogant manager of the National League New York Giants, refused to bring his team down to the level of what he considered to be the obviously inferior American League.

The rival leagues made peace and in 1905 baseball's World Series became an annual event. Not even the horrors of two world wars would stop the playing of the World Series. The only year without any World Series was 1994, when a labor dispute cancelled the World Series and threatened to destroy the game itself.

About one-third of all World Series have ended with Seventh Games. The first two Game Sevens were in 1909 and 1912, and it was another twelve years before baseball saw its next Game Seven, beginning a streak of three in three years. The longest streak of Seventh Games took place between 1955 and 1958, four years in a row and all involving the New York Yankees.

Seven is a lucky number. We speak of the Seven Wonders of the World, the Seven Seas, and the Seven Deadly Sins. Hawthorne found poetry in his title *The House of the Seven Gables*. There is ringing symmetry to the names of films like *Seven Days in May*, *Seven Brides for Seven Brothers*, and *The Seven Samurai*. Although effective people probably have dozens of good habits, Steven Covey found it advantageous to write his bestseller about *The Seven Habits of Highly Effective People*.

The Seventh Game of the World Series is the Seventh Wonder of the baseball world. No other number would do justice to the game.

Each Seventh Game is a saga that has already been told by countless thousands who have cherished the game of baseball and have shown their affection by retelling it to their children and grandchildren. For the old games, before the invention of television and video technology, these memories have been kept alive through the oral tradition and the written word.

Even the more recent games, available on VHS and DVD and the newest image technology, need to be told so that the drama can unfold slowly and at the pace that has always suited the game of baseball. Each game needs perspective so that we can immerse ourselves in the moment. For that reason, in Part 1, telling the story of each of the thirty-five World Series that reached a Seventh Game, each chapter begins with a glimpse into the culture that surrounded the playing of the game—a song, a movie, a scientific achievement, a historic event—something that brings us back to the era.

Because no Seventh Game took place in a baseball vacuum, each chapter contains as much information about the teams as is required to appreciate the character of those notable contests. Obviously, the Seventh

Games came after the teams played six games, each winning three, so as much information about these preceding games as is necessary to understand the full context of Game Seven is briefly presented. Some of these games may have been historic in their own right, but they will be only briefly noted. We are here to appreciate the wonder of these final games and how baseball has delivered on its promise to mete out Seventh Games, good and great, when America has needed them.

In each chapter there is a sidebar of baseball facts that relate to the specific season. This "Around the Horn" feature adds a few more juicy details to further bring out the flavor of baseball when these Seventh Games unfolded.

In Part 2, Chapters 36 through 39 are for the baseball fanatic. They examine the trends, numbers, and statistics that baseball enthusiasts devour for breakfast, lunch, and dinner. Each Seventh Game has generated hundreds of bits of information that casual fans may find tedious but those addicted to the game will find both fascinating and enlightening.

If you want to know how the hitters in Seventh Games did compared with the hitters in Games One through Six, read Part 2. If you want to know how Hall of Famers have done compared with the more "ordinary" players, keep going. If you are curious as to which teams have done well and which have done poorly in Seventh Games, these chapters are for you. If you are interested in the significance of pitching versus hitting, keep reading.

If you want to bypass these analyses and go right to the selection of the greatest Seventh Game ever played (Chapter 40), you will not hurt the author's feelings.

If you have wondered, as baseball fans often do, what if the teams had a chance to replay these historic games, then Chapter 41 is for you. With the help of simple but elegant computer simulation, I have "replayed" each of the Seventh Games. The results may surprise you.

If you want a handy reference to all Seventh Games in one place, you need look no further than the Appendix. If you're looking for even more nitty-gritty information, such as the lifetime statistics of every hitter and pitcher to appear in the thirty-five Seventh Games, then go to this book's companion website, www.theseventhgame.com.

Play ball!

Part 1

The Seventh Games

1909

The Original Babe

Pittsburgh Pirates   8
Detroit Tigers   0

It was a year of monumental firsts. The Lincoln-head penny made its debut in 1909, when a penny could actually buy something. Standard Oil's John D. Rockefeller became the world's first billionaire, when a billion dollars also could buy something.

A typical American worker made thirteen dollars a week for fifty-nine hours of hard labor. Wintergreen won the Kentucky Derby and Yale was the toast of college football. We tapped our toes and hummed the words to the popular songs of the day, like "I've Rings on My Fingers," "Casey Jones," and "By the Light of the Silvery Moon." Dr. Sigmund Freud was lecturing on a wild new craze called "psychoanalysis," but feisty Alice Ramsey had no use for Dr. Freud's services as she happily drove coast-to-coast in her Maxwell, a fifty-nine-day trip from New York to San Francisco.

It was an exciting year for everything, especially baseball. Home runs were a rarity, as teams continued to rely on pitching, speed, and defense. The Chicago White Sox managed only four home runs the entire season, an absurdly low number but one more than they had hit in 1908. Sluggers were defined not by the number of home runs they could smash but by the doubles and triples they could fabricate, more through speed and guile than raw power.

Around the Horn in 1909

- ↷ The Boston Braves finished 65½ games behind the Pirates in the National League. It could have been worse: the Braves finished 66½ out in 1906.
- ↷ The Washington Senators had two pitchers who each lost 25 or more games, a record that still stands today. They were Bob Groom (26 losses) and Walter Johnson (25).
- ↷ Cleveland's Neal Ball recorded baseball's first unassisted triple play on July 19 against Boston.

The best hitter in the American League was young Ty Cobb, only twenty-two in 1909, of the Detroit Tigers. The "Georgia Peach" won his third consecutive batting title with a .377 average and led the league in hits, slugging percentage, runs batted in, home runs (nine), and, of course, stolen bases.

The National League's best hitter was the veteran Honus Wagner of the Pittsburgh Pirates. The "Flying Dutchman" won his fourth straight batting title with a .339 average and led the league in slugging percentage, runs batted in, and doubles.

Fan interest in the game was high, in large part due to the performances of Cobb and Wagner in leading their teams to victory in their respective leagues. Which player was better? Their teams would have to meet in a World Series that went to the limit in order to give these Herculean heroes the fullest of opportunities to settle the argument.

It had been business as usual for the Detroit Tigers in 1909, as they won their third consecutive American League pennant. It was not an easy struggle, as a mid-season slump put the issue in jeopardy until a late August surge led Detroit past Connie Mack's Philadelphia Athletics.

The Pittsburgh Pirates mastered the National League with surprising ease, winning 110 games and losing only 42. The Chicago Cubs won 104 games, good enough for a pennant in almost any other year, but not in 1909.

Although neither team's pitching staff could boast of future Hall of Fame legends, each club had two 20-game winners and a 19-game winner.

The Tigers were led by George Mullin (29 wins), Ed Willett (22), and Ed Summers (19), while the Pirates relied on Howie Camnitz (25 wins), Vic Willis (22), and Lefty Leifeld (19). The Pirates also had a rookie by the name of Charles Benjamin "Babe" Adams, who won 12 games with a sparkling 1.11 earned run average, but few expected this youngster to figure prominently in the World Series.

The teams alternated wins in the first four games of the Series. The pivotal fifth game went to the Pirates, who broke a 3–3 tie with four runs in the sixth inning and held on to win, 8–4. The Series moved to Detroit for Game Six and, if necessary, Game Seven.

The Pirates jumped on Tigers ace George Mullin for three runs in the first inning of Game Six but the Tigers chipped away for five runs against Vic Willis and Howie Camnitz. Detroit fought off a furious ninth-inning Pirates rally—the first three Pirates reached safely—to hold on to a 5–4 win (the only one-run game of the Series) and force the first Seventh Game in the history of the World Series.

Saturday, October 16, 1909, was cold and blustery in Detroit. Before the game started, a group of appreciative Tigers fans presented pitcher George Mullin with a purse filled with money. Law enforcement authorities from Cleveland made a different kind of presentation—they served Michigan Governor Warren with a request to turn over the person of one Ty Cobb, wanted in Ohio on a charge of assault with intent to kill; the governor denied the request. That explains why Cobb did not travel with the team between Pittsburgh and Detroit; he avoided Ohio altogether by taking the longer route through Buffalo and entering Detroit through Windsor, Ontario. It also tells us a lot about Ty Cobb.

As for his National League superstar rival, Honus Wagner also had other things on his mind. It was in 1909 that Wagner demanded that the American Tobacco Company take his picture off the trading cards that went into "Sweet Caporal" tobacco, for fear they might be inducing children to smoke. That tells us a lot about Honus Wagner and also explains why a T206 Honus Wagner baseball card is the most valuable baseball card on the planet; only a few were released before Wagner could bar their distribution.

During the first six games of the World Series, Pirates player-manager Fred Clarke had little success with his frontline pitchers. He surprised everyone by starting the unheralded rookie Babe Adams in the opener.

Clarke emerged a genius, as Adams won not only Game One but also shocked everyone by winning Game Five. Veteran Deacon Phillippe, who had won three games in the 1903 Series, begged manager Clarke to let him start the Seventh Game but Clarke called on Adams to pitch the final game of the 1909 World Series.

Tigers manager Hughie Jennings went with his veteran, Wild Bill Donovan, winner of only eight games during the regular season. Donovan had pitched a strong complete-game win in Game Two, so the choice of the well-rested Donovan was hard to criticize. George Mullin, who had won Game Six for Detroit (a complete game), stood ready to throw should Donovan falter. Falter he did, as Wild Bill lived up to his name early and often.

Pirates third baseman Bobby Byrne was the first batter of the Seventh Game and Wild Bill Donovan hit him with a pitch. Byrne took second on a bunt and tried to steal third. Tigers catcher Boss Schmidt nailed Byrne with a perfect throw and Tigers third baseman George Moriarty added injury to insult by spiking Byrne. The next two Pirates walked but could not score. Nevertheless, Donovan's early and continuing wildness would prove to be his and the Tigers' undoing.

The Pirates scored two runs in their second inning, without a hit. Bill Abstein walked, stole second, and took third on Owen Wilson's sacrifice bunt; Wilson was safe at first on the late throw. After George Gibson popped out, pitcher Babe Adams drew an unexpected walk from Donovan, loading the bases. A sacrifice fly plated the first run of the inning and two more walks brought in another. It was all that Babe Adams would need.

The Tigers threatened in the second inning, as a one-out walk and a double put runners into scoring position. Adams snuffed the rally and the Tigers would growl no further. Wild Bill Donovan was gone by the fourth inning and the Pirates feasted on the offerings of an obviously tired George Mullin for six more runs.

As for the marquee matchup of Cobb versus Wagner, it was no contest. Cobb went hitless in four trips, while Wagner tripled in three official plate appearances, knocking in two runs. Over the course of the seven games, Cobb gathered six hits for an anemic .231 showing. Wagner's Series average was a robust .333. Wagner also won the battle of grace and manners when he declared Cobb "the most finished player in the profession."

Player-manager Fred Clarke, who led the National League in walks, was the master of patience, coaxing four walks off Detroit pitchers in the finale. It was a Seventh Game record he would ultimately share with Ross Youngs and Babe Ruth.

The Pirates outhit the Tigers in Game Seven by only one, 7–6, but trounced them by an 8–0 score. The difference was defense (three Tigers errors) and control: the 10 walks given up by Detroit remain a Seventh Game record.

It was a bitter defeat for Detroit, their third World Series loss in as many years. Although Ty Cobb would win eight more American League batting titles, he would never again appear in a World Series. Honus Wagner, too, had seen his last World Series; he would play another eight seasons for Pittsburgh, win one more batting crown, but never again play for the championship.

Babe Adams took home the princely sum of $3,117 for his efforts. Only $1,853 was his World Series "share." The rest was made up from donations by fans back in Pittsburgh and his grateful teammates, who kicked in twenty-five dollars each for the young hero. It was Babe's finest hour, although he pitched another sixteen seasons for the Pirates. Over the course of his career, Babe Adams had two 20-win seasons and retired with a record of 194–140, an ERA of 2.76, and 47 career shutouts. He had more career wins and shutouts than Dizzy Dean or Sandy Koufax, but Babe Adams is the only one of the three not in the Hall of Fame. He saw one more World Series, pitching one scoreless inning in the fourth game in 1925. Babe Adams died in 1968. Loving Pirates fans will always remember him, for a masterful performance on October 16, 1909, and a noble and loyal career.

As Seventh Games go, the 1909 finale had little excitement to offer the baseball aficionado. The anticipated showdown between Cobb and Wagner never materialized. Francis C. Richter, writing in *The Sporting Life* shortly after the Series ended, had no trouble heaping blame on the Detroit manager:

> But manager Jennings' crowning blunder, which showed lack of moral courage, was to put Donovan in, on a cold day, for the final game, when practice showed that the veteran "had nothing," and to

keep him in when the opening inning proved that he utterly lacked control—a condition which was bound to hearten the opposition and dishearten his own team at the very outset of the game, in which mistakes would count without any hope of recall. As the Tigers were shut out, they probably could not have won under any conditions, but the selection of Donovan, out of form, made all the conditions favorable for the Pittsburg [sic] pitcher and foredoomed Detroit to defeat and to the loss of the Series.

October 16, 1909

	1	2	3	4	5	6	7	8	9	R	H	E
PITTSBURGH (NL)	0	2	0	2	0	3	0	1	0	8	7	0
DETROIT (AL)	0	0	0	0	0	0	0	0	0	0	6	3

PITCHERS: PGH: Adams (W); DET: Donovan (L), Mullin

DOUBLES: Abstein, Delahanty, Gibson, Leach, Moriarty, Schmidt

TRIPLES: Wagner

HOME RUNS: None

ATTENDANCE: 17,562

TIME OF GAME: 2:10

1912

Giant Blunders

New York Giants   2
Boston Red Sox   3 (10 Innings)

Red Sox fans claim to know the true meaning of cosmic suffering, an affliction ripened by four consecutive World Series appearances in which they lost the Seventh Game. They forget that their beloved team once won a seventh and deciding game. The year was 1912.

It was the inaugural season of Fenway Park. The cost of mailing a first-class letter was two cents. W. C. Handy published his "Memphis Blues." The world wondered how a ship as sturdy and unsinkable as the *Titanic* could go down. William H. Taft was in the White House, presiding over a government spending 690 million dollars. Italian-American crooner Perry Como was born, as was Jackson Beck, the raspy voice of Bluto, Popeye's archenemy. Jim Thorpe starred at the Olympic Games in Stockholm, Sweden. Americans had their first taste of "Oreo Biscuits" and "Lorna Doones," but it was the taste of baseball that they savored most, especially in the fall.

John McGraw's New York Giants were the class of the National League. They did it the old-fashioned way, with pitching, speed, and defense. Christy Mathewson and Rube Marquard combined to win 49 of the Giants' 103 victories. Marquard had put together a string of 19 consecutive wins. To no one's surprise, the team led the league in batting average and stolen bases and finished a comfortable 10 games ahead of their nearest rivals, the Chicago Cubs.

Few picked the Boston Red Sox to win the American League pennant, and certainly not by 14 games. Connie Mack's Philadelphia A's, winners in 1910 and 1911, were strong on paper but weak in their execution.

Boston fans sometimes engage in the pointless debate over which Red Sox pitcher put together the best single season, Roger Clemens or Pedro Martinez. It's neither. Young Smokey Joe Wood carried the 1912 team, winning 34 games, 10 by shutout. Leading the offense was future Hall of Famer Tris Speaker, who hit .383 with 53 doubles, 52 stolen bases, and 136 runs scored. Speaker, along with Duffy Lewis and Harry Hooper, combined to form arguably the best defensive outfield in baseball history.

The Red Sox had one more element in their favor: the Royal Rooters. These three hundred loyal fans were cheerleaders of the most peculiar and eccentric sort. They dressed in red and were known to follow a marching brass band. They sang and hooted and cheered their beloved team on to victory. When the World Series opened in New York, the Giants' management allowed the Royal Rooters to parade across the Polo Grounds to a section reserved just for them. The pageantry continued as Boston Mayor John "Honey Fitz" Fitzgerald greeted the Red Sox as they entered from a gate in right field.

Manager John McGraw held back his aces Mathewson and Marquard in Game One, giving the nod to rookie Jeff Tesreau. Tesreau had led the league with his 1.96 ERA and won 16 games but he was up against the Boston Red Sox and their superstar Smokey Joe Wood. Was McGraw so fearful of Wood that he did not dare to use his best pitchers against him? Whatever the reason, Boston won the first game, 4–3.

With Mathewson on the mound in Game Two in Boston, the Giants were favored to tie the series. Mathewson pitched well but five Giants errors allowed the Red Sox to stay close enough that the game ended in a 6–6 tie, called after 11 innings because of darkness.

The tie game meant that the Giants had squandered their ace and would have to make up ground with their other pitchers. But Rube Marquard won the next game to tie the series at one game apiece.

Boston took the next two games behind Wood and Hugh Bedient and needed only one more win for the championship. It would not come easy. The Giants won the next game behind Marquard but would have to beat Smokey Joe Wood in order to force a final game. And beat Wood they did,

Around the Horn in 1912

- ɔ Owen Wilson set the major-league record for most triples in a season with 36; to this date, no other player has notched even 30 in a season.
- ɔ Casey Stengel made his major-league debut as an outfielder with the Brooklyn Robins.
- ɔ Ty Cobb batted .410 but the Tigers still finished in sixth place.

scoring six runs in the first inning en route to an 11–4 thrashing before an angry throng at Fenway. The crowd was furious because Red Sox management betrayed the Royal Rooters by selling their seats out from under them to visiting dignitaries and VIPs.

October 16, 1912, was a cold and damp day at Fenway Park. Only 17,034 fans showed up, the smallest crowd in Seventh Game history. As foul as the weather was, not a soul more would have showed up if the weather had been warm and sunny. Thousands boycotted the game because of the shoddy treatment given the faithful Royal Rooters the game before.

The Giants were confident because they finally had the pitching matchup they wanted. On the mound for John McGraw's team was the legendary Christy Mathewson. The Red Sox sent out Hugh Bedient, a 20-game winner during the regular season, but not one to instill fear in the hearts of the Giants' batters.

The Giants scored first, when Red Murray doubled home Josh Devore in the third inning. New York threatened in the fourth and fifth, but squandered opportunities that would later haunt them. In the fourth inning, Buck Herzog doubled, went to third on a sacrifice bunt, and died there. In the fifth, Hick Cady nailed Josh Devore trying to steal and Harry Hooper robbed Larry Doyle of a home run with a leaping catch at the right-field stands.

Christy Mathewson held the Red Sox in check until the seventh inning, when Jake Stahl blooped a one-out single and moved to second on a rare walk off of Mathewson. After Cady made the second out, Olaf Henriksen pinch-hit for Bedient and tied the score with a double down the left-field line.

With Bedient gone from the game, the Red Sox brought in Smokey Joe Wood, only a day after the Giants had punished him with an uncharacteristic offensive barrage. The Giants knew that they could score off Wood; it was only a matter of time.

Neither team scored in the eighth or ninth inning, and for the first time a Seventh Game would need extra innings. With one out in the tenth, Red Murray doubled and Fred Merkle singled home the lead run for the Giants. The final out in the Giants' half of the tenth proved to be of great consequence: Chief Meyers lined a shot back to the mound. Wood stopped it and threw out Meyers at first but the force of the line drive was so great that Wood could no longer continue. At the time, it seemed unimportant because all Christy Mathewson had to do was retire the Red Sox in the bottom of the tenth and the championship would be New York's.

Wood was scheduled to lead off the Red Sox tenth. Although he was a pitcher, his hitting prowess was well known. During the season, he batted .290 with 15 extra-base hits. He would surely have batted for himself if he had not been hurt by the Meyers line drive. In his place came Clyde Engle. During the regular season Engle batted .234 with only 8 extra-base hits. He was certainly no Tris Speaker and he wasn't even a Smokey Joe Wood. The Giants had seemingly caught a break.

Engle led off with an easy fly to center field. Fred Snodgrass played the ball perfectly but inexplicably dropped it. The Giants had given away the first out and Clyde Engle stood at second base. Harry Hooper stepped in against Mathewson and ripped a drive to center. To his credit, Snodgrass did not let his miscue of moments earlier dissipate his resolve and he made a sensational catch to rob Hooper of an apparent double. Engle, though, took third base after the catch.

Boston had the tying run at third and its weakest hitter at the plate. Steve Yerkes had batted only .252 during the regular season. Mathewson, known for his pinpoint control over the course of his career, walked Yerkes. Did Matty's frustration over the Snodgrass muff finally get the best of him?

Boston's top hitter, Tris Speaker, stepped in. Speaker swung at the first pitch and the advantage shifted back to New York. It was a routine foul fly in the direction of first baseman Fred Merkle. For reasons we will never know, Merkle did not move for the ball; perhaps he was basking in the glory of his RBI single in the top of the inning. Some say that Matty himself called for the catcher to make the play. No matter, the foul fly dropped harmlessly for a strike. It should have been the third out of the inning (the Snodgrass muff should have been the first and his great catch should have been out number two).

By some accounts, Speaker pointed at Mathewson and told him that he would pay dearly for the Giants' bad fielding. Mathewson had done the unthinkable: he had given Boston's best hitter a second chance. Speaker promptly singled to right, scoring Engle with the tying run and sending Yerkes to third. Speaker took second on the unsuccessful throw to third. The Giants had no choice but to walk Duffy Lewis to set up a force play.

With one out and the bases loaded, Larry Gardner lifted a fly ball to Josh Devore in right field, deep enough to score Yerkes with the winning run.

Spalding's Official Base Ball Guide of the day summarized the game:

> The New York players unquestionably had the championship won for nine and one half innings of the final game and then, by the simplest of errors, overturned all of the good which they had accomplished in their wonderful rally of the two days preceding. After outplaying the Bostons in a manner which showed some thing of the caliber of the teams when both were going at top speed, the New York team stopped short. As one wit dryly put it: "Boston did not win the championship, but New York lost it."

Fred Snodgrass played professional baseball for four more years. He moved on to become mayor of Oxnard, California, as well as a respected rancher and businessman. When he passed away in 1974, the *New York Times* obituary heading remembered only the dropped fly ball: "Fred Snodgrass, 86, Dead; Ballplayer Muffed 1912 Fly."

For the few Red Sox fans who witnessed the final game of the 1912 World Series, their team's victory was a thrill they would never experience again, unless they were very young in 1912, are lucky enough to still be alive, and the Red Sox win again very soon. Boston would appear in four more World Series Seventh Games over the next seventy-four years and lose them all.

Boston fans point to the "Curse of the Bambino" for their woes, blaming it all on the sale of Babe Ruth to the Yankees after the 1919 season. Perhaps the true curse arises from the way Red Sox management treated their most loyal fans, the Royal Rooters, in 1912.

The final game of the 1912 World Series was the only Seventh Game in which the visiting team scored in an extra inning only to see the home team come back to win the championship. That hardly tells the story of this most improbable finish, a heartbreaking one for Giants fans. The Giants would return to the Seventh Game in 1924, in 1962, and finally in 2002; they would lose them all, to have a perfect 0–4 record in World Series Seventh Games.

At least the fans of Boston can point to one Seventh Game victory, far beyond their own memories, to go with the four consecutive Seventh Game defeats that they blame on the Curse. If you consider the tie game (called because of darkness), some Boston cynics may argue that the Sox never really have won a "seventh" game, only an "eighth" game.

October 16, 1912

	1	2	3	4	5	6	7	8	9	10	R	H	E
NEW YORK (NL)	0	0	1	0	0	0	0	0	0	1	2	9	2
BOSTON (AL)	0	0	0	0	0	0	1	0	0	2	3	8	5

PITCHERS: NYG: Mathewson (L); BOS: Bedient, Wood (W)

DOUBLES: Gardner, Henriksen, Herzog, Murray (2), Stahl

TRIPLES: None

HOME RUNS: None

ATTENDANCE: 17,034

TIME OF GAME: 2:37

1924

An Unlikely Bounce

New York Giants	3
Washington Senators	4 (12 Innings)

The twenties were roaring with prosperity and excitement. Calvin Coolidge had ascended to the presidency upon the death of Warren Harding in 1923 and then mounted his own campaign in 1924 with the slogan "Keep Cool with Coolidge." He won.

Life was good in 1924. The Savage Arms Corporation invented the spin dryer and the nickel Hershey bar increased in size from one ounce to one and three-eighths ounces without any increase in price. It was the debut of fruit-flavored Life Savers and George Gershwin's "Rhapsody in Blue." Al Jolson was the most popular voice in America; everyone was humming "California, Here I Come!"

On the sporting scene, Paris hosted the Summer Olympics, where Paavo Nurmi of Finland won Gold Medals in both the 1,500 and 5,000 meter runs. Eric Liddell won at 400 meters and Harold Abrahams won at 100 meters; they would be immortalized in the 1981 film *Chariots of Fire*. Ottavio Bottecchia won the Tour de France bicycle race and would repeat his triumph in 1925.

Baseball had gone a dozen years without a seventh *and deciding* game in the World Series. There had been "seventh games" in 1919, 1920, and 1921, when the Series was expanded to a best-of-nine format, but these

Around the Horn in 1924

- ➔ Eddie Collins of the White Sox became the first player on a last-place team to lead his league in stolen bases.
- ➔ Rogers Hornsby set the standard of excellence in batting, hitting .424 for the Cardinals.
- ➔ Al Yeargen went 1–11 with the Boston Braves and immediately quit major-league baseball with a lifetime 1–12 record.

"seventh games" are not the games that concern us. Not once did a nine-game World Series go to a final and decisive ninth game, so it was clear to all that the seven-game World Series should be restored.

The stain of the 1919 World Series scandal, when gamblers induced members of the heavily favored Chicago White Sox to throw the Series (they lost, five games to three), was finally dissolving. Babe Ruth was not only the brightest star in the baseball galaxy but the most celebrated figure on the American scene. As fantastic as his numbers were in his first three seasons, the Yankees had two league pennants but no world championship to show for their investment. They finally won it all in 1923, beating the Giants four games to two. They looked unbeatable in 1924.

So it was the biggest surprise in baseball in 1924 when the New York Yankees did not win the American League flag. Babe Ruth produced another "Ruthian" performance (although that adjective had yet to be born), leading the league in home runs (46) and batting average (.378), but the rest of the team faltered. Faltered? Only by comparison with the past three seasons, because the truth is that a better team beat them.

Charley Dryden, sports editor of the *San Francisco Chronicle*, had made the Senators the butt of many a joke when he described Washington as "first in war, first in peace, last in the American League." Not so in 1924.

For the first time in their history, the Washington Senators won the American League. Walter Johnson was a living legend in Washington, having already won 350 games before the season started, but in 1924 he had help from his teammates. Joe Judge, Sam Rice, and Goose Goslin all hit above .320 and player-manager Bucky Harris—at the age of twenty-seven—blended speed, pitching, and timely hitting into a pennant, beating the Yankees by two games.

There was no change at the top of the National League in 1924. The New York Giants won the pennant on the strength of a lineup that showed its opposition no mercy. Six of the eight regulars batted over .300. We can only drool at the embarrassment of riches who played for manager John McGraw that year—no fewer than six future Hall of Famers: George Kelly, Frankie Frisch, Travis Jackson, Ross Youngs, Bill Terry, and Hack Wilson.

Game One of the 1924 World Series saw the Giants edge the Senators and Walter Johnson by a score of 4–3 in twelve innings. (For those of you who already know the score of the Seventh Game, that is not a misprint.) The Senators came back and beat the Giants by the same score in Game Two, scoring the winning run in the bottom of the ninth inning on Roger Peckinpaugh's double. When the Giants took two of the next three games, the Senators faced the burdensome task of winning the final two games against John McGraw's surging Giants.

At least the Senators were back home for Game Six and, if they could survive the Giants' attack, for Game Seven. In the sixth game, Washington could muster only four hits against Giants pitchers Art Nehf and Rosy Ryan, but they made them count, as boy wonder Bucky Harris delivered a clutch two-run single in the sixth inning. Pitcher Tom Zachary survived a shaky first inning and held the Giants to only one run to force the first real Seventh Game in a dozen years.

Game Seven was all about strategy. Lest we think that the ploy that managers use to gain an advantage by bringing in a left-handed pitcher to face a dangerous left-handed batter (or righty versus righty) is some new insight into how baseball works, we would do well to consult history. As early as 1914, George Stallings managed his miracle Boston Braves with that strategy in mind. John McGraw, the feisty manager of the New York Giants, ascribed to that strategy, too. And so did Washington manager Bucky Harris, who surprised everyone by naming Curly Ogden to start Game Seven.

It was, of course, a ruse. Harris had no intention of using Curly for more than a few batters. He wanted to induce John McGraw into starting his left-handed lineup against the right-handed Ogden and then pull the proverbial fast one by yanking Ogden in favor of his lefty, George Mogridge, the man whom Bucky Harris had chosen to start in the first place. The irony of all this is that Ogden, an early season acquisition from Connie Mack's A's, actually had at least as good a season as did Mogridge and even had a much lower earned run average. Though it was Ogden's only appearance of the Series, it was a credible move and there was no way that John McGraw could have known that Curly was only starting as a decoy.

Ogden surprised his own manager when he struck out New York's Freddie Lindstrom to start the game. Three pitches, three strikes. Maybe Curly was the pitcher who should be in there after all, and Harris let Ogden pitch to the next batter, Frankie Frisch. The lefty-lefty, righty-righty strategy didn't apply to Frisch because he was a switch-hitter and always had the theoretical edge. Frisch walked and Bucky Harris made the switch. He brought in the slender Mogridge to face the lefty Ross Youngs. Youngs struck out and George Kelly ended the inning with a harmless ground ball back to Mogridge. For the moment, Bucky Harris was a genius.

As for Curly Ogden, he may forever be remembered as the snare, the trap, and the bait, but he got into a Seventh Game and no one has ever bettered his earned run average of 0.00. He even struck out a future Hall of Famer. He did his job. After two more seasons of limited work with the Senators, Curly was gone from the big leagues.

Virgil Barnes, John McGraw's talented 16-game winner during the regular season, was the Giants' starter for real. The Senators had roughed up Barnes in Game Four, scoring five runs in five innings and saddling him with the loss. McGraw hoped for a better game from "Zeke" Barnes this time but had the entire staff ready for work in case he faltered. Through the first three innings, Barnes was tough. He retired the first nine Senators to face him, four by strikeout. Meanwhile, the Giants were having no success against Mogridge. They put together two singles and were the beneficiaries of an error but the game was scoreless going into the bottom of the fourth inning. That was when manager Bucky Harris took matters into his own hands.

After Earl McNeely struck out to start the Washington fourth, Bucky Harris nailed one of Virgil Barnes's prime offerings for a home run over the left-field wall. It was the first hit off Barnes, the first run of the game, and the first home run in Seventh Game history. Barnes settled down to retire the side without further scoring but the Senators had the lead. George Mogridge gave up a two-out double to Fred Lindstrom in the fifth inning but nothing came of it. Barnes put down Washington in the home half of the fifth inning and Mogridge came out for the sixth inning, clinging to a one-run lead.

It was time for the slumbering Giants to awaken. Ross Youngs walked and George Kelly followed with a single, sending Youngs to third. The next batter was a lefty, Bill Terry. This was Terry's second year in the big leagues and he had not yet become the feared hitter that would hit over .300 in ten straight seasons. He had promise but was just another left-handed bat in John McGraw's stable. McGraw played the percentages and lifted Terry for a right-handed hitter, Emil "Irish" Meusel. Meusel was an accomplished .300 hitter and must have been eager to try the left-handed offerings of George Mogridge. Bucky Harris countered the ploy and regained the advantage by removing Mogridge in favor of a righty, Frederick "Firpo" Marberry. Firpo was a pitcher ahead of his time, a relief specialist who had just set the major-league record for saves with 15. Firpo had already saved Games Two and Four and had been tough on the Giants.

The best Irish Meusel could do against Marberry was a fly ball to right, scoring Youngs with the tying run. Hack Wilson, in only his first full season in the big leagues and with his best years ahead of him, singled to send Kelly to third. Marberry stiffened but his defense let him down. Errors by Joe Judge and Ossie Bluege brought home two more Giants runs and New York took a 3–1 lead into the bottom of the sixth inning. The Senators could not get through to Virgil Barnes and the crowd grew restless. They squandered a pair of singles in the seventh and were still down by two. Marberry kept the Giants from scoring any more runs but Washington was running out of outs.

In the bottom of the eighth, Ossie Bluege fouled out to catcher Hank Gowdy for the first out. Barnes was in control and needed just five more outs. The veteran Nemo Leibold batted for Tommy Taylor and slapped a double down the left-field line. Nemo was near the end of his career and never had so big a hit as that opposite-field two-bagger. The crowd groaned, though, when the Washington catcher, Herold Domonic "Muddy" Ruel stepped to the plate. Muddy had gone 0 for 18 through the Series and prospects for a hit were bleak. Muddy stunned the crowd with a single off the glove of George Kelly. Leibold went to third and out came another pinch hitter, Bennie Tate, to bat for Marberry.

It was Bennie Tate's first year in the big leagues. He had only 13 hits during the season, but he squeezed a walk out of Virgil Barnes to load the bases with one out. The tying run moved to second base on the slow, heavy legs of Muddy Ruel. Earl McNeely flied to short left field and the runners had to hold. It was up to Bucky Harris, player-manager wunderkind, who had made all the moves he could. Now it came down to Bucky as player. If he were to lead his team to victory, it would have to be through his bat.

Harris singled over Freddie Lindstrom, scoring Leibold and the nearly out-of-breath Ruel. The Senators had wiped out the deficit and tied the game. Artie Nehf relieved Barnes to get the third out. Washington was now buzzing with excitement and hope. But they needed a pitcher.

With mixed emotions, the crowd greeted their favorite player, the already legendary Walter Johnson. They called him "Barney" and "the Big Train" and he had been the most dominating pitcher in baseball since Cy Young. Even at the age of thirty-six, he led the American League in wins and earned run average. But the 1924 World Series had not been kind to Johnson. He pitched all twelve innings in the opener, only to lose, 4–3. He started Game Five and allowed 13 hits and six runs in his second loss of the Series. The hopes of the Senators now rested on the best pitcher in baseball, tired as he might have been.

After Fred Lindstrom popped to third, Frankie Frisch tripled to deep center field. The Big Train was now in big trouble. He intentionally walked Youngs to set up a possible double play and to avoid the Giants' most dangerous left-handed hitter. George Kelly, New York's slugging first baseman, stood in against Johnson, the future Hall of Fame hitter facing the future Hall of Fame pitcher. Johnson won the battle, striking out Kelly on three pitches. It was the Walter Johnson of old back on the mound. He retired Irish Meusel on a grounder to third and the Senators came up in the bottom of the ninth with a chance to win their first-ever world championship.

When Joe Judge singled and Ossie Bluege reached on Travis Jackson's error, the skies looked bright in the nation's capital. With only one hit, the new third baseman, Ralph Miller, had a chance to be a hero. And if Miller could not deliver, Muddy Ruel might do it again. John McGraw decided it was time for a new pitcher and he summoned Hugh McQuillan.

"Handsome Hugh" McQuillan had come off his best year in baseball, winning 14 games for the Giants, and he had pitched well in his two earlier Series appearances. Ralph Miller had come off his third and last year in the big leagues, seeing limited action that allowed him to produce only a pair of singles in 15 at-bats. But he had twice before come through with run-scoring singles during the World Series. One more was all the Senators needed.

It was not Ralph Miller's finest hour. He grounded into a double play to end the threat and send the game into extra innings.

Neither team threatened in the tenth inning, as the crowd settled in for a late afternoon of classic pitching. In the top of the eleventh, Heinie Groh pinch-hit for McQuillan and singled. Freddie Lindstrom sacrificed the pinch runner, Billy Southworth, to second. Frankie Frisch, who had tripled against Johnson only two innings earlier, faced him now with the go-ahead run in scoring position. This time Johnson won the duel, striking out Frisch. Repeating the script from the ninth inning, Johnson intentionally walked Ross Youngs (his fourth base on balls of the game) to face George Kelly. Once again, the Big Train subjugated "Highpockets" Kelly—he struck him out to end the threat.

John McGraw called on his ace starter, Jack Bentley, to continue the battle. Bentley was coming off his best year in baseball, winning 16 games for New York and pitching well in his two World Series starts. With two outs, Goose Goslin doubled. The winning run was at second base. On orders from McGraw, Bentley walked Joe Judge and took his chances against Ossie Bluege. Bluege had been hitless in four previous trips and had botched a couple of ground balls. With only five hits all Series, Oswald Bluege must have sensed an enormous weight on his young shoulders, then massive disappointment when he ended the scoring chance on a weak ground ball. It was not Ossie's day but he would have more; he went on to play fifteen more seasons with Washington.

The game entered the twelfth inning. How long could Johnson and Bentley hold the opposition? Irish Meusel singled off Johnson to begin the Giants' half of the inning but Walter ended the threat by striking out Hack Wilson, getting Travis Jackson on a force play, and inducing a harmless fly off the bat of Hank Gowdy.

Ralph Miller opened the bottom of the twelfth by grounding out. A thirteenth inning seemed inevitable, as Bentley needed only to face the struggling Muddy Ruel and then the pitcher, Walter Johnson. When Ruel hit a pop-up behind home plate, out number two seemed assured. But the fates smiled on Washington. Hank Gowdy threw off his mask, as catchers are supposed to do when they go after pop foul flies, but then stepped on it. The ball fell to the ground. It was only a foul strike and gave Muddy Ruel a second chance. As difficult a Series as Ruel was having, he took advantage of his stay of execution and rifled a double down the left-field line.

That brought Walter Johnson to the plate. There was no reason for Bucky Harris to even consider pinch-hitting for Johnson. First, no one was left on the Washington bench to hit for Walter, at least no one who could hit better than the veteran pitcher. Second, Johnson was the best pitcher Harris had and there was no one he wanted to bring in against New York should the game go into the thirteenth inning. Third, Walter was an excellent hitter in his own right. During the regular season he batted .283 with 10 extra-base hits. Walter Johnson could take care of himself at home plate. How sweet it would have been for the beloved Walter Johnson to win his own game with a hit! But that's not what happened. He bounced the ball to the shortstop . . . but the fates smiled again. Travis Jackson booted the grounder and Johnson was safe. It was the end, or nearly the end, of a perfectly awful day for future Hall of Fame shortstop Travis Jackson. He committed two errors and went hitless in his six trips to the plate.

Earl McNeely, the rookie center fielder, came to bat and gloom fell upon Clark Griffith Stadium as McNeely grounded to third. When the ball left the bat, it looked like a probable double play. But the fates smiled one last time on the Senators. McNeely's grounder struck a pebble and the ball deflected over Fred Lindstrom's head into left field. Muddy Ruel raced home with the winning run. As in Game One, the score was 4–3, in twelve innings. But this time, when it meant the championship, the Senators prevailed. The city of Washington was in a frenzied state of utter jubilation. Bucky Harris had delivered key hits and made all the right moves.

Sportswriter Fred Lieb visited baseball commissioner Judge Kenesaw Landis shortly after the game and recalled how happy the judge was that night. Judge Landis thought that they might have been experiencing the absolute zenith, the highest point, of professional baseball. For the patient and grateful fans of the Washington Senators, it was the best that it would ever be.

October 10, 1924

	1	2	3	4	5	6	7	8	9	10	11	12	R	H	E
NEW YORK (NL)	0	0	0	0	0	3	0	0	0	0	0	0	3	8	3
WASHINGTON (AL)	0	0	0	1	0	0	0	2	0	0	0	1	4	10	4

PITCHERS: NYG: Barnes, Nehf, McQuillan, Bentley (L); WAS: Ogden, Mogridge, Marberry, Johnson (W)
DOUBLES: Goslin, Leibold, Lindstrom, McNeely, Ruel
TRIPLES: Frisch
HOME RUNS: Harris
ATTENDANCE: 31,667
TIME OF GAME: 3:00

1925

The Miracle in Pittsburgh

Washington Senators	7
Pittsburgh Pirates	9

In 1925, a high school teacher in Dayton, Tennessee, went on trial for teaching the radical theory of evolution, but the "Scopes Monkey Trial" was only one of many contests that captured the imagination of the American public. Tennis star Bill Tilden won the United States Open and Jack Dempsey was the heavyweight champion of the world. It was a good year for literature, then and for the future, as F. Scott Fitzgerald wrote *The Great Gatsby* and mystery writer Elmore Leonard was born.

America saw Lon Chaney in *The Phantom of the Opera* but did not hear his voice because it was the golden age of silent movies. But everyone was singing "Yes, Sir! That's My Baby!" and "When My Sugar Walks Down the Street." Mr. Goodbar made his debut at the candy store. At the Indianapolis 500, Peter DePaolo and his Dusenberg took the checkered flag with an average speed of 101.27 miles per hour. It was the first time anyone had cracked the 100-mph mark at Indy, but major-league batters were unimpressed. Although no one was clocking the speed of pitchers in 1925, everyone was sure that Walter Johnson, even at the age of thirty-seven, was throwing his fastballs at speeds far greater than that.

It was a phrase that seemed like a dream to the fans in the nation's capital: "The World Champion Washington Senators." Few believed they would even repeat as pennant winners but the Senators surprised them all

Around the Horn in 1925

- For the first time, but not the last, the Chicago Cubs finished in last place.
- Rogers Hornsby won his second Triple Crown for leading his league in batting average, home runs, and RBIs. Only Ted Williams would ever match that distinction.
- Pitcher Lefty Grove of the Philadelphia A's led the American League in both walks and strikeouts.

with great pitching, consistent hitting, and plenty of team speed. Babe Ruth's intestinal abscess took the Bambino out of play until June and the rest of the Yankees were so bad that the team ended up with a losing record, a shame that would not repeat itself in the Bronx for more than forty years.

The Senators changed little from 1924 to 1925. Goose Goslin was back, and so were Joe Judge, Bucky Harris, Muddy Ruel, and the others, especially Roger Peckinpaugh. Their outstanding shortstop had missed the 1924 Seventh Game win when he suffered a severe leg injury at the end of Game Six but enjoyed an MVP season in 1925. Walter Johnson was a year older but still won 20 games. This time he had even more help. Washington acquired the veteran spitballer Stan Coveleski from Cleveland and Stan notched 20 wins. Firpo Marberry remained the game's premier relief specialist, tying his own major-league record with 15 saves.

The news from the National League was that someone had finally unseated the New York Giants from first place. After four straight pennants, John McGraw's squad finished second behind Bill McKechnie's high-flying, high-octane Pittsburgh Pirates. The Pirates team batted .307 and the eight regulars batted nearly .325. They terrorized opposing teams with daring speed on the bases, leading the league in doubles, triples, and stolen bases. Home runs? Let the lesser teams hit those things!

When a team's weakest regular hits .298 it is difficult to pinpoint a few stars, but future Hall of Famers Max Carey and Kiki Cuyler were hard to miss. With their averages of .343 and .357, they ignited the most potent offense in baseball. As for pitching, the Pirates had no standout name stars to rival the dual aces of the Senators but they pitched well enough to win. Even forty-three-year-old Babe Adams, star of the Seventh Game back in 1909, found time to win six games and save three for the Bucs.

The teams split the first two games at Forbes Field in Pittsburgh. Walter Johnson won the opener, allowing only one run and striking out ten to lead the Senators past the Pirates, 4–1. Vic Aldridge outdueled Stan Coveleski in Game Two, 3–2, as the Series moved to Washington for heroics, good play, and lasting controversy.

In Game Three, the Senators were leading by a run in the top of the eighth. With two out, Pirates catcher Earl Smith ripped a Firpo Marberry pitch deep to right field. Sam Rice jumped up against the temporary bleachers and seemingly caught the ball but silently disappeared into the friendly hometown crowd. Umpire Charlie Rigler ruled an out and the inning was over. When Rice finally emerged from the crowd—with the ball, of course —the Pirates were livid in their protest that Rice never had possession of the ball. No matter, the ruling stood and the Pirates lost.

Controversy swirled across Washington that night. Dozens of angry Pittsburgh fans claimed they could produce sworn affidavits of people who would say that Rice never caught the ball. One ardent fan sent the commissioner a letter claiming knowledge of a "colored man" who handed the ball to Rice (the letter is in the archives of the Baseball Hall of Fame). Even though the commissioner was not about to reverse the umpire's call, he took Rice aside the next day and asked him if he really had made the catch. Sam answered, "The umpire said I did." And that was that.

For years after, writers and commentators would ask Sam Rice about the catch and Sam would smile and let everyone wonder. When he passed away in 1974, the Hall of Fame opened a sealed envelope that Rice had left, to be opened only after his death. It read, "At no time did I lose possession of the ball." Wily old Sam never did say when he first got possession of the ball, did he?

The fans packed Clark Griffith Stadium to see Walter Johnson shut out the discouraged Pirates, 4–0, in Game Four. The good news for Pittsburgh was that they could finally hit Walter's fastballs—he struck out only two—but the bad news was that they couldn't hit them anywhere that did them any good. The Pirates were down three games to one, and no team in history had ever come back from such a deficit.

Washington fans sensed another championship, especially when Goose Goslin doubled home Sam Rice in the first inning of Game Five. But the Pirates came back and won, 6–3. Starter Vic Aldridge won his second game for Pittsburgh and though they were down, they were not out. And they were going home to Forbes Field.

Washington struck early against Ray Kremer in Game Six. Goose Goslin hit his third home run of the Series in the first inning and Roger Peckinpaugh doubled home another Washington run in the second to give the Senators an early lead. Pittsburgh came back to tie the game in the third and took the lead on Eddie Moore's solo homer in the fifth. The Pirates held on to force a Seventh Game.

The weather in Pittsburgh on October 15, 1925, was horrible. It had misted and rained for several days, even during the Sixth Game, but it was worse for Game Seven. The field was wet and visibility was near zero. But they played. In fog and drizzle and in a thick unholy soup they played the Seventh Game.

Walter Johnson, winner of two games already, was on the hill for Washington. In his two complete-game victories, the Big Train had allowed the Pirates only one run. How discouraging it must have been for the Pirates to peer into the mist and see the game's most dominating pitcher ready to mow them down again. It was hard enough to see Johnson's fastball on a clear day.

The Pirates called on Vic Aldridge to continue his good work. He was no Walter Johnson but had pitched two strong complete games in winning a pair himself. Vic had broken in with the Chicago Cubs and come to Pittsburgh for the 1925 season, just in time to win 15 games and solidify the starting rotation. He was ready to pitch. The only problem for Vic was that the Senators were ready for him.

Washington hammered Vic Aldridge in the first inning. Sam Rice singled to start the assault. After Bucky Harris flied out, Aldridge uncorked a wild pitch and walked Goose Goslin. Another wild pitch advanced the runners and Joe Harris drew a walk to load the bases. Aldridge filled the count to Joe Judge and lost him, walking in a run. Ossie Bluege followed with a single, scoring another run and bringing manager Bill McKechnie out to relieve the shell-shocked Vic Aldridge. It would go down as the worst start in Seventh Game history: two hits and three walks in only one-third of an inning. Into the abyss came Johnny Morrison to face Roger Peckinpaugh with the bases loaded and only one out. They called him "Jughandle Johnny" because he had a fine sweeping curveball and he made a great pitch to Peck, getting Peck to tap an easy infield grounder. But the umpire ruled that the Pirates' catcher had interfered with Peckinpaugh's swing. Peck was awarded first base and a run came home, making it 3–0. Second baseman Eddie Moore fumbled Muddy Ruel's grounder and a fourth run came across. The Pirates were falling apart. Morrison got out of the inning without further damage but the prospects for Pittsburgh were as bleak as they could be. They were down four runs and facing Walter Johnson.

Johnson gave up a one-out double to Max Carey in the bottom of the first but struck out both Kiki Cuyler and Clyde Barnhart. When the Senators did not score in the top of the second and the Pirates put runners on first and second with only one out, there was cause for optimism in the Pittsburgh dugout. No problem for Walter Johnson, however, as he quickly dashed the hometown hopes by sweet-talking Earl Smith into an inning-ending double play.

Johnny Morrison kept the Senators off the board in the third and the Pirates got some help from an unexpected source—Jughandle Johnny himself. Even though manager McKechnie had plenty of pinch hitters on the bench, he stayed with Morrison to lead off the bottom of the third. It was hardly the strategy of a manager itching to get his team back into the game. Was McKechnie so discouraged he didn't think it was worth a pinch hitter? Johnny Morrison was certainly not an accomplished hitter; he never hit over .200 in his career and managed to hit his weight, 188 pounds of Kentucky real estate, only once. But luck was with Jughandle that day. He blooped a single to center.

Eddie Moore broke the scoring ice with a long double to the fence in left center and the Pirates had finally scored on Walter Johnson, the first run in 15 innings off the old master. Max Carey singled to bring home Moore and it was now a two-run game. Carey moved to second on a groundout and stole third base. That was no surprise to the fans in Pittsburgh because Scoops Carey was the best base stealer of his day; he led the National League in steals ten times. When Clyde Barnhart singled, the Pirates were right back in the game. Johnson set down Pie Traynor and Glenn Wright but the Senators were shaken. Not for long, though.

In the Washington fourth, Joe Harris doubled home a pair of runs to lengthen the Senators' lead back to three runs. Jughandle Johnny was through, as George Grantham pinch-hit for him in the bottom of the inning. Maybe they should have let Morrison hit for himself, because Grantham and the Pirates could do nothing with Johnson in the fourth. There would be plenty of time to rest over the winter, so Bill McKechnie brought in sixth game starter and winner Ray Kremer to hold the fort. Kremer picked up where he left off in Game Six, giving the Senators nothing to hit but air. The Senators went down in order in the fifth, sixth, and seventh innings.

Meanwhile, the Pirates were busy figuring out how to get to Walter Johnson.

Pittsburgh inched closer with a run in the bottom of the fifth on back-to-back doubles by Carey and Cuyler. Johnson stayed in the game and retired the Pirates in order in the sixth. Then came the seventh inning, which started out as innocently as most Walter Johnson innings usually started. Eddie Moore lifted an easy pop fly to Roger Peckinpaugh, the American League's Most Valuable Player and the man deemed by most to be the best shortstop of his day. But it had been a difficult Series for Roger. He had already committed six errors, though only one had proved costly (his Game Two error was, in retrospect, the difference in the one-run game). Now it was *seven* errors, this one a dropped fly ball that put Moore on second base. Next to bat was Max Carey, who had already found Johnson an easy mark with three hits. Carey smacked his fourth hit and third double of the game, driving home Moore and cutting the Senators' lead to one run. After Kiki Cuyler sacrificed Carey to third and Clyde Barnhart went out, it looked as if Johnson might get out of the inning with a lead. But he had to face Pie Traynor.

Baseball memory is a strange phenomenon. We often remember players for some very good reasons but forget them for others. When Brooks Robinson was earning his reputation as the "Human Vacuum Cleaner" for his brilliant defensive work as third baseman for the Baltimore Orioles in the 1960s and 1970s, old-timers were quick to point out that he was *almost* as good as Pie Traynor. So the debate rages on—who was the best defensive third baseman of all time, Pie Traynor or Brooks Robinson? Of course, they both were, but everyone forgot something about Pie. The man could hit!

Pie Traynor hit over .300 ten times in his career and retired with a lifetime batting average of .320, putting him in the top fifty of the all-time best hitters. Walter Johnson knew that Pie Traynor could hit. He had homered off Johnson in Game One, the only run scored off Johnson in his first 20 innings of work in the Series. Now it was Johnson versus Traynor, with the tying run at third base and two outs in Game Seven. Thwack! Pie slammed the ball to deep right-center field and the game was tied. The ball bounced against the wall and Traynor kept running. Second base was a cinch and so was third. It would take a strong throw from outfielder Joe Harris and an accurate relay from Bucky Harris to prevent Traynor from an inside-the-park home run. Pie turned on the speed but catcher Muddy Ruel tagged him out as he slid into home plate. So close! But the game was tied, 6–6. The Peckinpaugh error took on a horrifying edge for Washington and Peckinpaugh knew it.

Ossie Bluege grounded out to start the Washington eighth. The next batter was Roger Peckinpaugh, who desperately needed to atone for his seven deadly sins, his record-setting seven errors. Peck, the consummate professional, brushed aside his fielding lapses and lined a shot over the left-field fence. From goat to hero in a Pennsylvania minute! The Senators had reclaimed the lead and needed only six outs to take the championship back to Washington.

Glenn Wright and Stuffy McInnis were the first two batters in the bottom of the eighth and they were no match for Johnson. The Pirates were now struggling for life. Earl Smith kept hope alive with a double to right center. It was Ray Kremer's turn to bat, but this was no time to pin a team's chances on a weak-hitting pitcher. Little "Skeeter" Bigbee came off the bench to bat for Kremer. Carson Bigbee had been a Pirate his whole career, going back to 1916. As a regular in 1921 and 1922 he batted over .300 but had fallen into rough waters in his later years. The 1925 season had been particularly hard on Skeeter, as he hit only .238 in limited action. Conditions at Forbes Field worsened and Carson Bigbee must have been having a tough time seeing the ball coming out of Walter Johnson's mighty right hand. Yet somehow, some way, Bigbee scorched a double over Goose Goslin's head, scoring pinch runner Emil Yde with the tying run.

Eddie Moore walked. Max Carey, who had already touched Johnson for four hits, came to bat. When Johnson got Carey to ground to short, it looked as if the teams were going into the ninth inning tied. Next came the unthinkable: Roger Peckinpaugh fielded the ball cleanly but threw wildly to second base. From goat to hero and back to goat. Two runs came home and for the first time all day, the Pirates had the lead. Clyde Barnhart popped out to second and the inning was over. So were the dreams of the Washington Senators. Unless . . .

The Pirates needed a pitcher to save the game and put the icing on the cake of their improbable comeback. Not much was left in the Pittsburgh bullpen so manager Bill McKechnie swallowed hard and called on John Cyrus "Red" Oldham to hold the Senators in check. Red Oldham had come up with the Tigers and in five seasons with Detroit made almost no impression on the league except for his inability to get batters out. After a two-year absence, he signed on with Pittsburgh in 1925 but pitched in only 11 games.

The Senators could not have asked for a better opportunity. Ray Kremer was finally out of the game and Red Oldham was facing the top of the Washington order. Sam Rice, who led all players in the Series with 12 hits, was the first to face the overmatched Oldham and struck out. Red was not exactly a strikeout kind of pitcher. He had fanned only ten batters all season and there he was, striking out the great Sam Rice to start the ninth inning. The second batter was Bucky Harris, hero of the 1924 Seventh Game. It had been a poor Series for Harris, who had only two hits in his first 22 at-bats. Bucky found a pitch to his liking and lined it hard—into the glove of Pirates second baseman Eddie Moore. One more out to go. It would have to be Goose Goslin.

Goose Goslin is in the Hall of Fame and he's not there for striking out in clutch situations. Goose is there because he had a lifetime batting average of .316, and because he hit three home runs in the 1924 World Series and three more in the 1925 World Series. In seven seasons, Red Oldham had a losing record and an earned run average over 4.00. But Red cooked the Goose that day. He struck out Goose Goslin to end the game.

The Pirates had mounted not one but two great comebacks. They were down three games to one in the Series and down by four runs early in Game Seven. For Roger Peckinpaugh, it was a sadder story. He was a magnificent shortstop in his day but will be remembered by so many for his poor fielding in the 1925 World Series, especially those two costly errors in the Seventh Game. How ironic that he would end his playing career in a Chicago White Sox uniform, part of a trade for a pitcher named . . . Sloppy Thurston.

October 15, 1925

	1	2	3	4	5	6	7	8	9	R	H	E
WASHINGTON (AL)	4	0	0	2	0	0	0	1	0	7	7	2
PITTSBURGH (NL)	0	0	3	0	1	0	2	3	X	9	15	2

PITCHERS: WAS: Johnson (L); PGH: Aldridge, Morrison, Kremer (W), Oldham (SV)

DOUBLES: Bigbee, Carey (3), Cuyler (2), J. Harris, Moore, Smith

TRIPLES: Traynor

HOME RUNS: Peckinpaugh

ATTENDANCE: 42,856

TIME OF GAME: 2:31

1926

Alexander the Great

St. Louis Cardinals   3
New York Yankees   2

Oklahoma's Norma Smallwood was Miss America, and the NBC radio network started up. It was 1926, when life was so very good. Americans flocked to read Ernest Hemingway's *The Sun Also Rises* and A. A. Milne's *Winnie the Pooh*. Dr. Robert Goddard performed his liquid-fueled rocket experiments near Worcester, Massachusetts, and Erik Rotheim invented the aerosol spray can. They say that someone invented television in 1926, but there wasn't a whole lot to watch. Two "magicians" passed each other in the night: Harry Houdini died and Chuck Berry was born.

There was a lot to see and do in 1926. *Gentlemen Prefer Blondes* was the toast of Broadway. Benny Goodman and Duke Ellington were recording some special sounds that would live forever. Jelly Roll Morton, Sophie Tucker, and Fred Waring's Pennsylvanians kept everyone tapping their toes. Gene Tunney defeated Jack Dempsey in one of the greatest boxing matches of the century. And there was baseball, bigger and better than ever.

After two consecutive thrilling Game Sevens in 1924 and 1925, baseball fans surely had taken in their fill of postseason excitement. Or did they? One thing was missing from the drama of a full-package World Series: Babe Ruth had yet to play in a Seventh Game. If the Roaring Twenties were to

Around the Horn in 1926

- ☉ The pennant-winning Yankees were last in the American League in shutouts with four.
- ☉ Despite playing in cozy Fenway Park, the Boston Red Sox were last in all of baseball in extra-base hits.
- ☉ Dutch Levsen pitched two complete-game victories on the same day, August 28, for Cleveland. Although it had been done forty-four times before, no pitcher has done it since.

live up to their name, the Babe had to take the Yankees to the limit and show his stuff.

George Herman Ruth was an uncommon blend of myth and muscle that made baseball fans shiver at the very thought of the Babe in a World Series Seventh Game. The Yankees did their part to get into the Series, winning the American League by three games over a stubborn Cleveland club. They needed a worthy National League opponent.

The St. Louis Cardinals had never been to a World Series in the modern era. From 1901 to 1919, they finished either last or next-to-last in the National League ten times; only once did they finish as high as third place. Make no mistake about it: the early Cardinals were a bad team. They improved in the 1920s, led by Rogers Hornsby, who batted over .400 three times between 1922 and 1925, and finally won a pennant in 1926. At last, the Cardinals were a bona fide good team. But in the World Series of 1926 they had to play a great team. The prospect of a Seventh Game was remote, as oddsmakers made the Yankees 3–1 pre-Series favorites.

But who were these Cardinals, these sudden pretenders to the National League throne? They had some hitting, but nothing to match the likes of Babe Ruth and Lou Gehrig. Player-manager Rogers Hornsby had his worst season of the decade, hitting "only" .317. Sunny Jim Bottomley, Les Bell, and Taylor Douthit put up some fair numbers but they were no match for the mighty Yankees.

St. Louis had a few decent pitchers. Flint Rhem, Bill Sherdel, and Jesse Haines were the mainstays of the pitching staff, but few thought they could compete with the Yankees' marvelous trio of Herb Pennock, Urban

Shocker, and Waite Hoyt. The Cardinals also picked up an old veteran in the twilight of his career but they certainly couldn't count on him for too much. His name was Pete Alexander and he was thirty-nine years old.

Herb Pennock held the Cardinals to three hits in Game One and Lou Gehrig drove in both Yankee runs to give New York the opener, 2–1. St. Louis woke up in Game Two with a 12-hit barrage and won easily, 6–2, behind Pete Alexander's complete-game win.

The Series moved to Sportsman's Park in St. Louis, where Jesse Haines shut out the Yankees in Game Three, 4–0, before New York came back to knot the Series at two games each on the strength of Babe Ruth's three home runs in Game Four. The Yanks pulled out a miracle finish in Game Five, tying it in the ninth and winning it in the tenth, 3–2. The Cardinals were going back to Yankee Stadium in need of two miracles of their own. Pete Alexander gave them the first, pitching another complete-game victory to force Game Seven.

It was a matchup between two pitchers who had each already won a game earlier in the Series. Jesse Haines and Waite Hoyt were both poised big-game pitchers. Neither hurler blew away the opposition in the early going, even though the game was scoreless after two innings. Babe Ruth broke the deadlock with a solo home run into the right-center-field seats. You knew the Babe would come through in Game Seven. You just knew it.

For all that was written about the great Yankee hitting of the Ruth-Gehrig era, not much was said about New York's defense. Nothing needed to be said because it was rarely a factor during those years. It was usually adequate and that was enough. But it was not adequate in the fourth inning of Game Seven of the 1926 World Series. It was downright awful.

After Rogers Hornsby bounced out to start the fourth inning, Jim Bottomley singled. Les Bell grounded to shortstop Mark Koenig, who booted the ball for error number one. Chick Hafey blooped a single to load the bases. Bob O'Farrell lifted an easy fly ball to Bob Meusel but Meusel dropped the ball for error number two of the inning and the game was tied, as Jim Bottomley trotted home. The inning should have been over but the Cardinals had the bases loaded with only one out. Tommy Thevenow put the hurt on the Yankees with a clean single to right, scoring two runs. Waite Hoyt finished the inning with no more runs coming across but he had been victimized by his mates' sloppy play. Meanwhile, Jesse Haines scattered hits but refused to let in any more Yankee runs until the sixth inning, when

Hank Severeid doubled home Joe Dugan to cut the Cardinals' lead to a single run.

Herb Pennock replaced Waite Hoyt for New York and the Cardinals could not find a way to increase their lead. Jesse Haines had been brilliant, getting in and getting out of trouble every inning. The seventh inning would be different.

Earle Combs singled to start the inning and took second on a sacrifice bunt. That brought Babe Ruth to bat. Say whatever you will about manager Rogers Hornsby, he was not stupid and was not about to pitch to the Babe. He walked him intentionally. Bob Meusel was a mere .315 hitter and certainly a better risk than the mighty Bambino. Meusel obliged by grounding to third, not hard enough for a double play but hard enough to erase Ruth on the force-out. There were now two outs, with runners on first and third, and the batter was Lou Gehrig.

Jesse Haines knew that he had to pitch carefully to the talented Yankees first baseman. Gehrig had been having a terrific Series, with eight hits in 22 at-bats. Haines pitched carefully, too carefully, walking Gehrig to load the bases. That brought up Tony Lazzeri, second only to Ruth during the regular season in home runs and runs batted in for New York. Haines was obviously struggling and manager Hornsby could not afford to stay with him any longer.

Some say that Pete Alexander was so hung over from celebrating his Game Six win that he could barely move from his seat in the bullpen during the Seventh Game. He had pitched a complete game only twenty-four hours earlier. His old arm had to be falling off. There was no way he could be expected to pitch in Game Seven. But Rogers Hornsby wanted Alexander to face Lazzeri. Maybe Hornsby remembered that Lazzeri had faced Alexander four times in Game Six and failed to get a hit. Whatever the reason, Pete Alexander limped to the pitcher's mound, took the ball, warmed up as best he could, and tried to focus on the Yankees' slugging second baseman.

The crowd called out Tony's nickname: "Poosh-em-up-Tony, Poosh-em-up-Tony!" A hit would mean two runs and the lead. Alexander's first pitch was low, for ball one. The second pitch came straight over the plate and Lazzeri did not even offer. The count was a ball and a strike. The next pitch was a pitch that Poosh-em-up-Tony liked and he drilled it hard and far to left field, hard and far but foul by only a few feet. Alexander wasted no time with the next pitch, striking out Lazzeri and bringing the entire Cardinals team onto the field to congratulate old Pete for his heroic task. There were six outs to go.

The Cardinals could not add to their lead. Alexander then pitched the eighth inning and retired the Yankees in order. Curiously, Yankee manager Miller Huggins let pitcher Herb Pennock bat for himself with two out in the eighth. Pennock was never known for his hitting (his lifetime batting average of .191 proves that), although, to be fair to Huggins, there was little else left on the Yankee bench. The Cardinals went down in order in the top of the ninth and Pete Alexander needed three more outs for the save.

Mixing his pitches well, Alexander got Earle Combs and Jumpin' Joe Dugan to ground out to Les Bell at third. Only one more out to go, but now batting was the man who had reached base safely every time so far in the game. Babe Ruth had homered and walked three times. Hornsby walked over to his pitcher to discuss the delicate situation. Should they walk him again? Alexander was no coward, he wanted to pitch to the Babe.

Alexander's first pitch was a strike, so there was no mistaking the pitcher's intentions. The next pitch was just outside. The Babe fouled one off and fell behind, a ball and two strikes. Then came balls two and three. Alexander would not let the Babe beat him. He delivered the full-count pitch and it was inches off the plate. Ruth refused to swing at the pitch and walked to first base. The crowd booed, because they wanted to see Babe Ruth take his mighty swing against an honest strike. No matter, because Ruth represented the tying run and Bob Meusel was up with Lou Gehrig on deck.

What followed was what can be fairly described as the most shocking moment of any Seventh Game, maybe even in the history of the World Series. With Meusel at the plate, Babe Ruth took off toward second base, *an attempted steal*. Catcher Bob O'Farrell, known for his strong and accurate arm, gunned the ball down to Rogers Hornsby in plenty of time to apply the tag to the sliding Ruth. What was the Bambino thinking?

So it was that Babe Ruth became the answer to one of the great baseball trick questions: How can a batter be perfect in his only five trips to the plate and still make the final out of the game? The answer is by hitting a home run, walking four times, and being caught stealing, just as the Babe did in 1926.

History will remember Pete Alexander's dramatic entry into the game and the strikeout that ended the Yankee threat in the seventh inning. What is often forgotten is how the Yankees let the Cardinals take the lead in the first place, with sloppy fielding that gave St. Louis all of its runs.

John B. Foster, writing in the *Spalding's Official Base Ball Guide* for the 1926 World Series, observed: "The New York Americans were as children under the thumb of Alexander, whose remarkable success against this team of slashing batters was one of the great triumphs of these world series contests."

October 10, 1926

	1	2	3	4	5	6	7	8	9	R	H	E
ST. LOUIS (NL)	0	0	0	3	0	0	0	0	0	3	8	0
NEW YORK (AL)	0	0	1	0	0	1	0	0	0	2	8	3

PITCHERS: STL: Haines (W), Alexander (SV); NYY: Hoyt (L), Pennock

DOUBLES: Severeid

TRIPLES: None

HOME RUNS: Ruth

ATTENDANCE: 38,093

TIME OF GAME: 2:15

1931

Spit and Polish

Philadelphia Athletics   2
St. Louis Cardinals   4

The Great Depression was hard upon the land. You could buy a genuine Stetson hat for seven dollars but you probably didn't have seven dollars. If you could buy a ticket to a movie, you might have gone to see Charlie Chaplin in *City Lights* or Boris Karloff in the original *Frankenstein*. You could gaze at the new Empire State Building, the tallest building in the world, and that didn't cost a penny.

Salvador Dali painted his droopy watch picture, *The Persistence of Memory*. Jacob Schick invented the electric razor and legendary aviatrix Amelia Earhart climbed to a record 18,415 feet in her Pitcairn Autogyro. Irma Rombauer wrote *The Joy of Cooking* and Mickey Mantle was born in Spavinaw, Oklahoma. Baseball was the furthest thing from the Mantle family in 1931 because times were especially hard in Oklahoma. But if you did go to a baseball game, you would have seen grown men playing a child's game and it was a sight to behold.

Baseball was changing. Power was replacing speed. For the first time in history, the players hit more home runs than triples and it would be that way for the rest of time. Even though Babe Ruth had been revolutionizing baseball with his mighty and many home runs since becoming a Yankee in 1920, the rest of baseball was only gradually learning how to hit the long

Around the Horn in 1931

- The New York Yankees set the modern mark for runs scored in a season—1,067. That works out to nearly 7 runs a game.
- There were three pitchers named "Lefty" in the American League—Lefty Grove, Lefty Gomez, and Lefty Stewart.
- In the second game of a July doubleheader in St. Louis, the Cardinals beat the Cubs, 17–13, and the two teams set the all-time record for most doubles in a game—23. It was a good year for doubles all around, as Earl Webb of the Red Sox set the major-league record for most doubles in a season with 67.

ball. They finally learned how to swat the ball out of the park in 1931 and the triple was rapidly becoming a rarity of the diamond.

Speaking of Babe Ruth, the Bambino remained the most feared hitter of his day. He was thirty-six years old but "managed" to hit .373 with 46 home runs and 163 runs batted in. His teammate Lou Gehrig hit .341, also with 46 home runs, with a league-leading 184 RBIs. Despite the best one-two punch in all of baseball, and despite .300 seasons from Joe Sewell, Earle Combs, and Ben Chapman, the New York Yankees were only the second best team in the American League. Rookie pitcher Lefty Gomez won 21 games but they did not win the pennant. Hard to believe.

From 1929 to 1931, there was no argument on the subject of baseball supremacy: the Philadelphia Athletics were tops. In 1929, they captured the American League pennant by 18 games over the Yankees and beat the Chicago Cubs in a five-game World Series. They expended only a little more effort in 1930 but the result was the same—a six-game Series win over the St. Louis Cardinals.

The Athletics seemed to get only better in 1931. Al Simmons led the league in batting with a .390 average (his third consecutive year batting at least .365), catcher Mickey Cochrane batted .349, and Jimmie Foxx tallied 30 home runs and 120 runs batted in.

Philadelphia's pitching was even more impressive. The years 1929 to 1931 were banner years for hitters but the A's Lefty Grove and George Earnshaw amassed 146 wins between them against only 43 losses in that three-year period. Grove was totally dominating in 1931, winning 31 and losing 4, with an ERA of 2.05.

The only obstacle between the Philadelphia Athletics and a third straight championship was the team from St. Louis. The Cardinals were a good team, but few believed they would put up much of a fight in the World Series.

Future Hall of Fame second baseman Frankie Frisch had a decent year, batting .311 and leading the National League in stolen bases. Chick Hafey led the National League in batting at .349, but when it came to offense the Cardinals paled in comparison to the American League champions.

The comparison was no better when it came to pitching. Wild Bill Hallahan led the team with 19 victories but his name told all: he led all National League pitchers in walks surrendered. A young Paul Derringer won 18 games and the veteran spitballer Burleigh Grimes, near the end of his career, managed 17 wins. It was a creditable staff but no match for the likes of Grove, Earnshaw, and the A's third starter, 20-game winner Rube Walberg.

America called on baseball to give her a full World Series, to take her mind off the national despair. America needed to see the unappreciated and unheralded underdog rise to the occasion. The problem was that Connie Mack's Athletics were in no mood to see any underdog spoil their streak of World Series victories.

Behind ace Lefty Grove, the A's easily won the first game of the World Series, 6–2. But things did not go according to Connie Mack's plan when Wild Bill Hallahan allowed seven walks but outpitched George Earnshaw in Game Two, 2–0. No matter, the A's were going back home for Game Three and Lefty Grove would be on the mound.

One can only wonder what the sportswriters of the day were thinking after the first two games. Did any of them seriously believe that St. Louis had a chance? The Baseball Writers Association of America had its own "World Series Special Train" and its members were treated to a "Special Luncheon" to make the trip even more memorable. The Philadelphia writers did not ask for humble pie, but Game Three gave them a generous helping, as Burleigh Grimes pitched no-hit ball into the eighth inning and beat Lefty Grove and the A's on a two-hit masterpiece, 5–2. The outcome of the World Series was suddenly in doubt.

George Earnshaw evened the Series in Game Four with a two-hitter, winning 3–0. When St. Louis took the pivotal Game Five, 5–1, behind Wild Bill Hallahan, the underdog Cardinals returned home needing only one victory for the championship. Not against Robert Moses Grove! Lefty stopped the Cardinals cold in Game Six, 8–1.

It was the first Seventh Game since 1926, and what a pitching matchup it was—Earnshaw against Grimes, pitchers who had each tossed two-hitters in earlier games. There was one element that favored the home-town Cardinals, the emergence of its scrappy left fielder, John "Pepper" Martin. Martin had become the primary offensive weapon of the Cardinals, setting a World Series record with 12 hits (including four doubles and a home run, to go with five stolen bases) through the first five games.

Philadelphia caught an early break when Chick Hafey, the Cardinals' best hitter, was scratched from the lineup. The strategy for Connie Mack's A's was simple: keep Pepper Martin and MVP Frankie Frisch off the bases. Holding Sunny Jim Bottomley in check, too (he had hit .348 in the regular season)—would that be asking too much?

George Earnshaw gave Mr. Mack exactly what he wanted. The heart of the St. Louis order, from number-three batter Frisch to cleanup hitter Martin to Ernie Orsatti to Bottomley and all the way down to the pitcher's spot, went hitless. The only hits allowed by Earnshaw over seven innings went to two of the lesser players—the light-hitting leadoff hitter, Andy High, and the number-two hitter, right fielder George Watkins. Quite a pitching performance! *But not good enough.*

Andy High, who had appeared in only 63 games for the Cardinals in 1931, led off the bottom of the first inning with a bloop single into short left field. George Watkins followed with another bloop single to left. Earnshaw had made good pitches but two Cardinals stood on the bases. Frankie Frisch laid down a perfect sacrifice bunt and the Cardinals had runners on second and third.

Andy High came home on a wild pitch that also sent Watkins to third base. After Pepper Martin walked and stole second base, Earnshaw struck out Ernie Orsatti on a low pitch that bounced off Mickey Cochrane's glove. With first base empty, Cochrane had to throw to first to retire Orsatti. As Cochrane threw to Jimmie Foxx, George Watkins dashed toward home and scored as Foxx made a poor throw back to the plate. The Cardinals had a 2–0 lead, without the benefit of a hard-hit ball.

Andy High singled for the second time in the third inning. George Watkins then delivered the most important hit of his seven-year career, a two-run homer into the right-field stands. It was now 4–0. Could Burleigh Grimes, the old spitballer from Clear Lake, Wisconsin, hold the lead?

The A's outhit the Cardinals, seven to five, but Burleigh Grimes found the "out" pitch when he needed it. He gave everything he had with every pitch. When he reached the ninth inning, he had no more to give. Two walks and a single loaded the bases for the A's. With two outs, pinch hitter Doc Cramer drove in two runs with a single and the score was 4–2, with the tying runs on base. Burleigh Grimes was spent.

St. Louis manager Gabby Street brought in his ace, Wild Bill Hallahan, to face the sharp-eyed Max Bishop. Wild Bill got Bishop to line softly to Pepper Martin to end the game and the Series.

Those who remember 1931 probably remember only the sadness and the poverty of the Great Depression. For a few days, at least, there was baseball to remind us of the possibilities that lay ahead. It was good that an underdog could win the World Series, going all the way to the seventh and deciding game. A great fight was what it would take to bring America out of its woes. Eventually, like the Cardinals of 1931, America won the battle.

October 7, 1931

	1	2	3	4	5	6	7	8	9	R	H	E
PHILADELPHIA (AL)	0	0	0	0	0	0	0	0	2	2	7	1
ST. LOUIS (NL)	2	0	2	0	0	0	0	0	X	4	5	0

PITCHERS: PHI: Earnshaw (L), Walberg; STL: Grimes (W), Hallahan (SV)

DOUBLES: None

TRIPLES: None

HOME RUNS: Watkins

ATTENDANCE: 20,805

TIME OF GAME: 1:57

1934

Garbage Time

St. Louis Cardinals   11
Detroit Tigers   0

There was not a lot of subtlety to 1934. Jobs were scarce and money was even scarcer. Franklin Roosevelt's New Deal was in high gear but for millions of Americans prosperity was a long way off. You could get the new flavor of Life Savers, wild cherry, and that probably was enough to bring a big smile to your face. If that didn't do the trick, you might have found a friend to help you sneak into the movie theater to watch the screen debut of Donald Duck. Or you might have seen Clark Gable and Claudette Colbert in *It Happened One Night*. Everyone loved the movies, with the possible exception of gangster John Dillinger, who was shot down in front of the Biograph Theater in Chicago in July 1934.

TWA began flying the new Douglas DC-2 and America's first Laundromat opened in Fort Worth, Texas. The popular songs of the day were "Anything Goes," "Blue Moon," and "Smoke Gets in Your Eyes." And there was baseball because as hard as life was, this was America.

It was Babe Ruth's last year in Yankee pinstripes. The Bambino was aging badly, at least by the standards that New York had for Ruth. By today's standards, hitting .288 and swatting 22 homers in 125 games is enough for a multiyear multimillion-dollar contract. Lou Gehrig was now the big star, winning the Triple Crown with the best season of his career. Even with a good year from their ace, Lefty Gomez, the Yankees could not catch the

Around the Horn in 1934

- Casey Stengel led the Brooklyn Dodgers to a sixth-place finish in his first hitch as a big-league manager. He would manage on and off for ten more seasons, producing a winning record only once and never finishing higher than fifth place, before taking over at the helm of the New York Yankees in 1949.

- Only three years after leading the 1931 Philadelphia A's to the pennant, Al Simmons, Mule Haas, and George Earnshaw found themselves with the last-place Chicago White Sox.

- Brooklyn's hot-tempered Van Lingle Mungo led all National League pitchers in walks; he never reached the potential most baseball writers saw in him but eventually achieved fame and glory for the 1970 bossa nova song bearing his name (written by David Frishberg).

high-flying Detroit Tigers, who got to the World Series for the first time since 1909.

There was no mystery to the success of the Detroit Tigers. They hit better than any other team in all of baseball, a lot better. As a team, they hit a sizzling .300. Up and down the lineup there was great hitting—Charlie Gehringer, Marv Owen, Jo-Jo White, and Hank Greenberg, to name a few who did well in 1934. Detroit also picked up two classy veterans who had played in previous World Series. Mickey Cochrane came over from the Philadelphia A's to catch and to manage; it was the move that made the difference. Veteran Goose Goslin, picked up from the Senators, hit over .300 and was one of four Tigers to knock in 100 or more runs.

It was not a year of great pitching in the American League but Schoolboy Rowe and Tommy Bridges were as good a starting duo as any. They won 46 games between them and provided enough stability to keep player-manager Mickey Cochrane happy.

Player-manager Frankie Frisch hit .305 for the Cardinals and led the famous "Gas House Gang" past the New York Giants by a skinny pair of games to return to the World Series after a three-year absence. Pepper Martin led the league in stolen bases and dirty uniforms because that was how the Cardinals played. In only his second full season in the bigs, Ducky Medwick led the league in doubles and triples and knocked in over a hundred runs. But the big noise came from the bat of Ripper Collins, who decided to have the best year of his career, hitting .333 with 35 homers and 128 RBIs.

The Cardinals had some very good pitching, coming off the arms of Bill Walker, Tex Carleton, and Paul Dean. But they also had Dizzy Dean. Diz won 30 games for St. Louis in 1934, and until Denny McLain won 31 for the Tigers in 1968 it seemed a safe bet that no one would ever win 30 again.

Most baseball fans have distinct images of these two teams. They think of the St. Louis Cardinals as a bunch of hustling underachievers, more apt to score runs with speed and hustle than with the long ball. And they think of the 1934 Detroit Tigers as a more patient, potent offense content to score its runs on homers from the likes of Hank Greenberg, but not a team to manufacture runs with stolen bases and such baseball subtleties. The truth is totally the opposite: the Cardinals outhomered the Tigers, 104 to 74, while the Tigers stole more bases than the Cardinals, 124 to 69.

There was some excellent baseball played in the first six games of the 1934 World Series, which was fortunate because—and there is no use putting a lid on the ultimate truth here—Game Seven was a one-sided blowout that was over too early to even try to make it sound exciting. That is a fact. The Seventh Game was a stinker, made even more odious by the fact that the home team got walloped.

Game One was a decisive 8–3 Cardinals win behind Dizzy Dean's complete-game pitching. Game Two was probably the best of the Series. Schoolboy Rowe gave up single runs in the second and third innings and pitched nine shutout innings to give Detroit a thrilling 3–2 win in 12 innings; Goose Goslin won it with an RBI single.

Dizzy's brother Paul won Game Three, 4–1, and the Tigers jumped all over the Cardinals with a 10–4 thrashing in Game Four. The biggest surprise of the 1934 World Series came when Detroit beat Dizzy Dean, 3–1, in Game Five, to bring the Tigers back to Detroit needing only one victory to capture its first world championship.

Facing elimination on enemy soil, the Cardinals forced a Game Seven behind Paul Dean's complete-game win. Home-field advantage? Not in 1934, where the visitors won four of the first six games. And the visiting team won Game Seven, big time.

Dizzy Dean was not about to let his brother take all the glory for the Dean family. He pitched a six-hit shutout, but the story of Game Seven is not a story of masterful pitching. It is a tale of relentless hitting. The Cardinals pounded out 17 hits, the most ever by a team in a Seventh Game. Everybody for the Cardinals picked up at least one hit, even the pitcher and even the substitute who came in to save Ducky Medwick's life. Save Ducky Medwick's life? More on that later.

Eldon Auker started for Detroit and pitched two decent innings. He gave up three hits in the first two innings but no one scored. The third inning was something else, the biggest outburst of runs in any Seventh Game. It started with one out and Dizzy Dean at the plate. Diz doubled to left and barely beat Goose Goslin's throw at second base. Then came the deluge. An infield single, a walk, and a double sent Eldon Auker to the showers. Schoolboy Rowe retired the first batter he faced but gave up a single and double before giving way to Chief Hogsett. Chief gave up a walk and a single before facing Dizzy Dean, coming up for the second time in the inning. Diz singled to drive in a run and become the only player to collect two hits in one inning in a Game Seven. After a walk to Pepper Martin, Chief Hogsett was gone and Tommy Bridges, the fourth pitcher of the inning, came in to end the nightmare. Seven runs had crossed the plate. It was over.

As Dizzy Dean might have said (but he didn't), it was even "more over" when the Cardinals pushed across two more runs in the sixth inning and gave the crowd something to "cheer" about. Pepper Martin opened with a single and took second when Goose Goslin fumbled the ball. With two out, Ducky Medwick rammed a triple to right center and slid hard into Detroit third baseman Marv Owen. Owen took exception to Medwick's aggressive slide and the two began to fight. That was all the crowd needed. Medwick scored on a Ripper Collins single (his fourth hit of the day) and the inning ended. When Medwick took the field, the Tigers' partisans pelted him with bottles, fruits, and every kind of trash imaginable. If only the Tigers' pitchers could have thrown the ball like their angry fans had thrown their garbage.

The crowd would not stop their persistent barrage of little Joe Medwick. Commissioner Landis was facing a riot and "ordered" Medwick to leave the game, for his own safety. With the game comfortably in their pockets, the Cardinals agreed to take Ducky out. The crowd finally had something to cheer about.

The Cardinals added more injury to the insult by tacking on two more runs in the seventh inning. That made the score 11–0 and St. Louis was happy to let it stay that way. Ducky Medwick's replacement, Chuck

Fullis, singled to lead off the eighth inning. He didn't score but he made his point.

The Tigers put two men on in the bottom of the ninth inning, but they stayed there when Hank Greenberg struck out and Marv Owen grounded out to end the debacle at old Navin Field. Tigers fans who endured the massacre could take comfort in the removal of Joe Medwick from the game and from the merciful brevity of the game—only two hours and nineteen minutes. When the reporters looked up they realized that this was the third Seventh Game in nine years and that the Cardinals had won them all.

There was nothing subtle about 1934, especially Game Seven of baseball's World Series.

October 9, 1934

	1	2	3	4	5	6	7	8	9	R	H	E
ST. LOUIS (NL)	0	0	7	0	0	2	2	0	0	11	17	1
DETROIT (AL)	0	0	0	0	0	0	0	0	0	0	6	3

PITCHERS: STL: D. Dean (W); DET: Auker (L), Rowe, Hogsett, Bridges, Marberry, Crowder

DOUBLES: D. Dean, DeLancey, Fox (2), Frisch, Rothrock (2)

TRIPLES: Durocher, Medwick

HOME RUNS: None

ATTENDANCE: 40,902

TIME OF GAME: 2:19

1940

Heartache for Bobo

Detroit Tigers   1
Cincinnati Reds   2

America was climbing its way out of the Depression and a war in Europe was on the horizon. The movies were a good diversion and in 1940 you might have seen Alfred Hitchcock's first American film, *Rebecca*, John Ford's *The Grapes of Wrath*, or George Cukor's *The Philadelphia Story*. If you were hungry in Pasadena, California, you might have visited a curious drive-in hamburger restaurant that the brothers Richard and Maurice McDonald opened that year. If you were craving something cold and sweet near Joliet, Illinois, you might have stopped at the brand-new Dairy Queen.

Richard Starkey was born in 1940 but everyone would get to know him later as Ringo Starr. Music greats Smokey Robinson and Ricky Nelson were also born, along with future Yankee first baseman Joe Pepitone. General Motors invented the automatic transmission to make it easier for everyone to get to the baseball game. Ah, baseball.

The news from the American League was that after four years of Yankees dominance, someone else won the pennant. The Detroit Tigers returned to the top spot with much of the same talent that brought them there in 1934 and 1935. On offense, Charlie Gehringer, Pete Fox, and Hank Greenberg were joined by new stars Rudy York and Barney McCoskey. Schoolboy Rowe and Tommy Bridges, aces of the '34 and '35 squads, were

Around the Horn in 1940

- ⊃ Bob Feller pitched a no-hitter on Opening Day.
- ⊃ For the first time, an American League team blasted four home runs in the same inning. Boston's Ted Williams, Jimmie Foxx, Joe Cronin, and Jim Tabor turned the trick in the sixth inning in a game late in September.
- ⊃ Johnny Mize of the St. Louis Cardinals won the National League slugging crown by more than a hundred points, .636 to .534, over Chicago's Bill Nicholson.

back but the pitching star of the 1940 staff was a burly journeyman pitcher by the name of Lewis Norman Newsom. But everybody called him "Bobo."

Bobo was already with his sixth different team in ten years. He was big and strong so whoever owned him could always count on a lot of innings from Bobo. He finally had some success with the Tigers in 1938 and 1939 but put it all together in 1940 when he won 21 games. He would pitch another ten years, with some new teams and teams he'd been with before, but there was never anything like the 1940 season for Bobo Newsom. When he retired from the game after the 1953 season, he had won 211 games for ten different clubs. He also lost 222 games, but you always got your money's worth from Bobo. Especially in 1940.

The Cincinnati Reds had won the pennant in 1939 but got swept by the New York Yankees in the World Series. They were back again in 1940 with a balanced team led by a pair of veteran 20-game winners. Bucky Walters led the National League in wins and earned run average while his teammate Paul Derringer gave the Reds a slice of history when he started and won the first night game in baseball history. The unrelated McCormicks—Frank and Mike—each hit over .300 and the Cincinnati manager was no stranger to World Series success. Bill McKechnie had led the 1925 Pirates to their miraculous Seventh Game win over the Senators.

Although the Reds won the pennant by a comfortable dozen games over the Brooklyn Dodgers, by no means was the 1940 season an easy one for Cincinnati. When their all-star catcher, Ernie Lombardi, went down with an injury during the summer, Will Hershberger took over behind the plate. Even though Hershberger was hitting over .300, he was so despondent over what he thought was poor pitch calling in a game the Reds lost that he committed suicide in a Boston hotel on August 2. Without a catcher, the Reds were in deep trouble until coach Jimmie Wilson put on the gear and guided the team to the finish line. The Reds had overcome a terrible tragedy to make it to the Series.

Few people think of the 1940 World Series as one of the great Fall Classics, and for good reason. Not one of the first six games was close. But Game Seven was a different story and the drama that came about through one more tragedy off the field, this time only hours after Game One, made the Seventh Game all the more memorable.

The Tigers erupted for five runs in the first inning of Game One and Bobo Newsom coasted to an easy 7–2 win. It was even more special for Bobo because his proud father watched him pitch that game. The next morning, the elder Mr. Newsom died of a heart attack. After Cincinnati won the second game behind Bucky Walters and the teams split the next two, Bobo Newsom took the mound in Game Five. He dedicated that day to his father and pitched a three-hit shutout to bring the Tigers to the edge of the championship.

The Series returned to Cincinnati, where Bucky Walters shut out the Tigers to force a Seventh Game. Paul Derringer, winner of Game Four, was on the mound for Bill McKechnie's Reds. For Del Baker's Tigers, it was Bobo Newsom.

It was a cold day in Cincinnati but that didn't stop Bing Crosby from showing up at the park. Nattily attired in a bright yellow shirt with a navy blue collar, Bing saw quite the game.

Newsom and Derringer were perfect in the first inning. Though each team had a base runner in the second, the game was scoreless after two innings. In the third, Detroit eked out a run when Charlie Gehringer's infield single brought home catcher Billy Sullivan. For a while, it looked as if that lone run might hold up for Bobo Newsom. He scattered hits but refused to let a Reds player cross home plate. Until the seventh inning.

Frank McCormick led off with a double to left field. Up stepped Jimmy Ripple, who had come over to Cincinnati from Brooklyn during the season and hit over .300 in his 32 games with the Reds. Ripple ripped a double to right, scoring McCormick with the tying run. Jimmie Wilson bunted Ripple to third with the go-ahead run. Out of the dugout to bat for Eddie Joost came Ernie Lombardi, one of the best hitters to play the game. If Ernie had a flaw in his game, it was his speed, or total lack thereof. But no one could stroke the ball like Ernie Lombardi, and this was the perfect situation for him after being scratched from the starting lineup and most of the games in the Series because the cold weather aggravated his bad ankle.

Newsom pitched carefully to Lombardi and walked him. To everyone's relief and no one's surprise, Lonnie Frey came in to run for the lumbering future Hall of Famer. The number-eight hitter, shortstop Billy Myers, was next to bat. Myers was the glaring weakness in the Reds' lineup. He was a fine fielder but during the regular season had hit only .202 and had struggled through the World Series with just three singles. The Reds didn't need a hit from Billy Myers, just a long fly ball. And Billy gave them what they needed, a fly ball to center field hit far enough to allow Jimmy Ripple to dance home. Paul Derringer made the last out of the inning but the Reds had taken the lead, 2–1.

Charlie Gehringer singled to start the Detroit eighth inning but never moved from first base. Paul Derringer sliced through the meat of the Tigers' order, retiring Hank Greenberg, Rudy York, and Bruce Campbell to end the inning. In the ninth inning, Derringer put the Tigers down in order. The aging veteran Earl Averill, who would one day be enshrined in the Hall of Fame, made the final out, grounding out weakly to second base. And it was over.

It was the first Seventh Game to see both starting pitchers toss complete games, a feat that has been duplicated only once more, in 1968. There is a sense that the game ended with a whimper and not a bang. Winning runs that score on sacrifice flies can give that feeling. So do games that take only one hour and forty-seven minutes, the shortest Seventh Game in history.

The Detroit Tigers wanted to win so badly, for themselves and for Bobo. But Cincinnati, too, wanted to experience the taste of a real World Series victory. Their only "success" in a World Series had been the tainted 1919 Series against the White Sox, and no one ever counted that as a legitimate win. Curiously, the Reds lost Game Seven in 1919, 5–4, in 10 innings (does that sound like a fixed game?). But Cincinnati had another driving force behind them in 1940, the memory of Will Hershberger. When the Series was over, the Reds' players voted a full player's share, $6,099.06, to Will's mother, Mrs. Maude Hershberger.

For reasons unknown, the Reds' players were not so generous with the man who delivered the Seventh Game's key hit. Jimmy Ripple, who doubled to tie the game and scored what proved to be the winning run, received only half a share. Sure, he had only been with the Reds since August 23, but his was the clutch hit that brought the championship to Cincinnati. When the word got out, a fan sent Jimmy Ripple a note: "I see where the Reds voted you in for only a half share in the Series. You surely have earned more, so I am enclosing my $10 to help make it up."

October 8, 1940

	1	2	3	4	5	6	7	8	9	R	H	E
DETROIT (AL)	0	0	1	0	0	0	0	0	0	1	7	0
CINCINNATI (NL)	0	0	0	0	0	0	2	0	X	2	7	1

PITCHERS: DET: Newsom (L); CIN: Derringer (W)

DOUBLES: Higgins, M. McCormick, F. McCormick, Ripple

TRIPLES: None

HOME RUNS: None

ATTENDANCE: 26,854

TIME OF GAME: 1:47

1945

The Sorrow at Wrigley

Detroit Tigers   9
Chicago Cubs   3

The war ended and the boys came home. For millions of Americans, that pretty well sums up the year 1945. Tens of thousands of soldiers remained overseas to clean up both the European and Japanese theaters of operations but the world was finally a safer place. World War II had exacted a heavy toll on America and it was time to rebuild. Earl W. Tupper did his part, inventing Tupperware to hold all those wonderful foods that would soon be in our iceboxes (refrigerators, if you were lucky). Franklin Delano Roosevelt died and the country went into mourning, but Harry Truman gave America the no-nonsense leadership it needed. If you needed to feel good, you might have gone to see Bing Crosby and Ingrid Bergman in *The Bells of St. Mary's*. Or you might have gone to a baseball game, because that always made you feel good.

Baseball had not been the same during the war. Its talent had been diluted when many of its brightest stars enlisted or were drafted. Ted Williams, Bob Feller, and Joe DiMaggio were only three of the hundreds of major leaguers who sacrificed the best parts of their careers to military service.

Baseball did its best to continue its beloved traditions. The World Series continued to be played but it never went to the limit of seven games. Maybe baseball knew that a seven-game Series while its best talent was

Around the Horn in 1945

- ↻ Steve Gerkin went 0–12 for Connie Mack's last-place A's but still had a respectable 3.62 ERA.
- ↻ Yankees second baseman Snuffy Stirnweiss led the American League in batting average, stolen bases, and triples. The last person to do that was Ty Cobb, who did it three times.
- ↻ It was slugger Jimmie Foxx's last year in baseball. He hit .268 with seven homers for the last-place Philadelphia Phillies but pitched in nine games, hurling 22⅔ innings with a microscopic 1.59 ERA. If only they had known!

overseas just would not be right. When the war was finally over, baseball participated in the celebration by giving its fans a full seven-game Series with the promise that more would follow in the years to come. Maybe the talent wasn't top-notch, but the enthusiasm was boundless.

Hank Greenberg came back from his four-year hitch in the army to spark the Tigers to their fourth American League pennant in twelve years. The rest of the Detroit offense was weak, as only one Tigers regular, second baseman Eddie Mayo, hit higher than .277. They didn't hit home runs and they didn't steal bases but they scored enough runs to support a decent pitching staff led by future Hall of Famer Hal Newhouser. "Prince Hal" won 25 games and led the American League in every important pitching category on his way to being named the league's MVP.

The Chicago Cubs nosed out the St. Louis Cardinals by three games to win the National League pennant. The Cubbies had the best hitting and the best pitching in the National League, a distinction that no future Cubs team has ever boasted. Like their counterparts in the American League, the Cubs did not hit a lot of home runs or steal many bases, but they practiced the art of timely hitting. First baseman Phil Cavaretta led the team and the league in hitting with a robust .355 average. Don Johnson and Stan Hack also logged in .300 seasons and outfielder Andy Pafko knocked in 110 runs while hitting .298. Good hitting is nothing unusual for Cubs teams, but pitching? Yes, pitching! Theirs was the best in the National League, led by Hank Wyse's 22 wins and the midyear acquisition of Hank Borowy from the Yankees.

You had to favor the Cubs in the 1945 World Series. Pitching was about even but hitting was by far in favor of the Cubs. Their team batting average was twenty-one points higher than Detroit's. So much for the teams "on paper."

Wartime travel restrictions remained in effect for the 1945 World Series so the first three games were played in Detroit, with all remaining games, as needed, to be played in Chicago. The Cubs jumped all over Hal Newhouser for seven runs in the first two innings of the opener on their way to a 9–0 rout behind the six-hit pitching of Hank Borowy. The Tigers roared back to win three of the next four games. Chicago's only win was Claude Passeau's one-hit shutout in Game Three.

On the verge of elimination, the Cubs jumped in front of the Tigers, 5–1, after the first six innings of Game Six. The Tigers chipped away with a pair in the seventh but the Cubs matched them with two in the bottom of the seventh and were only six outs away from their first Seventh Game in the long and legendary history of the franchise. The Tigers erupted for four runs in the eighth inning, tying the game and forcing the Cubs to bring in Hank Borowy to hold Detroit in check. Borowy had started the day before but was brilliant in keeping Detroit off the board until the Cubs won, 8–7, on Stan Hack's double in the twelfth inning. The Cubs had forced a Seventh Game, but not the way they had intended it. They had not planned on using Borowy in relief and the move, as necessary as it was, would cost them dearly in Game Seven.

With only one day of rest between the sixth and seventh games, Chicago manager Charlie Grimm could not resist going back to the pitching hero of Game Six. Hank Borowy had the whole winter for rest and he was certainly Chicago's best pitcher. Besides, he had pitched so well in Game Six on zero days of rest. The emotional lift that Borowy would give the team was certainly a factor that played into Grimm's decision. But it was the wrong move.

By the time most of the fans had settled into their seats, the Seventh Game was over. Borowy gave up three quick hits without recording a single out before Grimm realized that Hank had nothing to give. Paul Derringer, winner of Game Seven in 1940 for Cincinnati, came in to quash the Tigers' uprising but was totally ineffective. Detroit's five-spot was the biggest torrent of runs in the first inning of any Seventh Game. There would be no coming back at the "Friendly Confines" of Wrigley Field on October 10, 1945.

The Cubs scored one run in the bottom of the first but there was no getting to Hal Newhouser that day. The Tigers answered with a run in the top of the second and Derringer, who had allowed only one unearned run in his complete-game 1940 finale, was a disaster, surrendering five walks and two hits in his meager one and two-thirds innings of work.

The Cubs came back with one inconsequential run in the fourth to cut the Tigers' lead to 6–2. When the Tigers put up a run in the seventh and two more in the eighth, the 41,590 fans who had somehow crammed into Wrigley Field could not wait for the carnage to end. The Cubs gave their fans the final run of the game on Bill "Swish" Nicholson's double in the eighth, and the end was near. When Don Johnson grounded into a force-out to end the game, Cubs fans around the world probably had no idea they would never see their beloved team in another World Series game, let alone another Seventh Game, for at least the next fifty-eight years. (The bitter loss to the Florida Marlins in the seventh game of the 2003 National League Championship Series doesn't count, although the pain for Cubs fans is just as bad.)

The irony of the 1945 Seventh Game is that the Cubs, by far the better hitting team, outhit the Tigers, 10–9, while losing the game, 9–3. They were the better hitting team, just not the better scoring team.

October 10, 1945

	1	2	3	4	5	6	7	8	9	R	H	E
DETROIT (AL)	5	1	0	0	0	0	1	2	0	9	9	1
CHICAGO (NL)	1	0	0	1	0	0	0	1	0	3	10	0

PITCHERS: DET: Newhouser (W); CHI: Borowy (L), Derringer, Vandenberg, Erickson, Passeau, Wyse

DOUBLES: Johnson, Mayo, Nicholson, Richards (2)

TRIPLES: Pafko

HOME RUNS: None

ATTENDANCE: 41,590

TIME OF GAME: 2:31

1946

He Who Hesitates Is . . .
Pesky?

| Boston Red Sox | 3 |
| St. Louis Cardinals | 4 |

The baby boom officially started, as Linda Ronstadt, Dolly Parton, Barry Manilow, Donald Trump, Pat Sajak (you know, the host of "Wheel of Fortune"), and millions of others entered the world with Dr. Benjamin Spock's *Common Sense Book of Baby and Child Care* as its unofficial guidebook. Dirty diapers were no problem because Tide laundry detergent made its debut. The year 1946 also marked the initial appearance of the bikini bathing suit.

"Zip-A-Dee-Doo-Dah" and "Shoofly Pie and Apple Pan Dowdy" were hit songs and someone came up with artificial snow. You could buy an electric blanket for $39.50 and the first computer, ENIAC (Electronic Numerical Integrator and Calculator), made its appearance, but you couldn't buy one. A ticket to the movies cost about forty cents, and everyone agreed with the title of James Stewart's new hit movie: *It's a Wonderful Life*.

Baseball was back at full throttle in 1946. The boys who had marched off to serve their country with rifle and bayonet were now honoring America with bat and ball. Ted Williams, Phil Rizzuto, Warren Spahn, Gil Hodges, and other stars came back to play the game they loved. The World Series of 1945 had been only a promise of better things to come.

In the National League, the St. Louis Cardinals and Brooklyn Dodgers battled down to the wire, and when the season ended the two

Around the Horn in 1946

- Cool Papa Bell finished his career with the Washington Homestead Greys of the Negro League. He hit .430 in his last year and finished with a life-time batting average of .337. Bell was inducted into Baseball's Hall of Fame in 1974.

- The entire Philadelphia Phillies bullpen notched a grand total of five saves. No team since has recorded so few.
- Pete Reiser of the Brooklyn Dodgers stole home seven times, a record that still stands today.

teams had identical records. It was a baseball first, a tie for the pennant, and the teams decided the issue in a best-of-three playoff series. The Cardinals took care of matters in a decisive two-game sweep and were ready to make their ninth World Series appearance a memorable one.

St. Louis had the best pitching in baseball. Howie Pollett led the National League in wins and earned run average and had plenty of help from Murray Dickson and Harry Brecheen. The Cardinals had good players on offense as well. Red Schoendienst, Whitey Kurowski, and Enos Slaughter (remember that name!) came through with solid performances. But the cornerstone of the St. Louis attack was one man, the National League's Most Valuable Player. He wasn't just *any* man. He was "Stan the Man" Musial. With a sweet and compact swing, Musial hit .365, nearly thirty points higher than his closest rival for the batting crown. He also led the league in hits, runs, doubles, and triples. And if they were keeping track of class, he would have cleaned up in that category as well. The Cardinals were a very good team but came into the World Series as extreme underdogs. They had to play the Boston Red Sox.

It had been twenty-eight years since the Boston Red Sox had been in a World Series. After selling Babe Ruth to the Yankees in 1920, the Sox experienced a string of fourteen consecutive losing seasons and finished in last place nine times. They began to climb out of the American League cellar when they acquired stars like Joe Cronin, Lefty Grove, and Jimmie Foxx. But the league started to take Boston seriously when they brought up a skinny kid from San Diego, California, by the name of Ted Williams. Ted was a star in his very first year, 1939, when the Red Sox finished a distant second to the Yankees. Two years later, he became the last man to bat .400 but there was still no pennant in Boston. During World War II Williams gave three prime years of his baseball career to the country he loved, and when he came back the Red Sox were ready.

As if he never left the batting cage, Ted Williams dominated the American League with his keen eye and effortless power. He hit .342, with 38 home runs and 123 runs batted in. He was the league's MVP and, if bases on balls are a measure of fear, the most terrifying batter in baseball, as evidenced by the 156 walks he drew in 1946. Only Babe Ruth had ever walked more in a single season.

As good as Ted Williams was, the Red Sox knew that he alone could not deliver a pennant to the hungry fans of New England. He needed his teammates to perform up to their maximum abilities, and they did. Rudy York, Bobby Doerr, and Dom DiMaggio (Joltin' Joe's little brother) had outstanding years, as did their talented shortstop, Johnny Pesky. Whatever conclusions one may draw from the 1946 season and its perplexing finish, one fact remains: Johnny Pesky, with his .335 average, 43 doubles, and league-leading 208 hits, had a spectacular season. He was far and away the best shortstop in baseball. Keep that in mind as you continue your journey into the 1946 World Series.

The Red Sox had solid pitching to back up their stellar offense. Boo Ferriss and Tex Hughson were 20-game winners, while Mickey Harris and Joe Dobson rounded out the dependable starting rotation. The veteran Bob Klinger led the league in saves and the Boston Red Sox were heavy favorites to win the World Series.

While the Cardinals were busy beating the Dodgers in their two-game playoff series, the Red Sox were trying to stay sharp by playing an informal all-star team that the American League put together. During the game, a Mickey Haefner knuckleball nailed Ted Williams on the right elbow. Even though the pitch may have been only a knuckleball, Ted was definitely injured. Both Williams and the Red Sox insisted the injury was not serious.

Not since Ty Cobb faced off against Honus Wagner in the 1909 World Series, a Series that went to the limit of seven games, had the premier hitter in each league squared off in the Fall Classic. This time it would be Musial against Williams. It would be a Series to savor, the type of Series that baseball had promised to America in return for its patience during the terrible war.

The teams split the first two games at Sportsman's Park in St. Louis. Rudy York's tenth-inning home run gave the Red Sox a dramatic win to start the Series and Harry Brecheen evened the affair with a four-hit shutout in Game Two. They came back to Boston and split the first two games at Fenway Park. Boo Ferriss shut out the Cardinals in Game Three and the Redbirds exploded for 20 hits in a Game Four laugher. The largest World Series crowd in Boston history, 35,982 adoring fans, saw the Red Sox take the pivotal Game Five, 6–3. The hitting star, if anyone is paying attention, was Johnny Pesky, who banged out three hits. The Red Sox headed back to St. Louis needing only one victory for the championship.

But Harry "The Cat" Brecheen, the little lefty from Broken Bow, Oklahoma, stopped the Red Sox cold in Game Six, winning 4–1 to force a Seventh Game.

St. Louis went with Murray Dickson to pitch Game Seven and Boston countered with Boo Ferriss. The Red Sox struck early. Wally Moses singled to lead off the game, went to third on Johnny Pesky's single, and scored on Dom DiMaggio's sacrifice fly.

Bobby Doerr singled to open the second inning and took second on Whitey Kurowski's bad throw. But Pinky Higgins, Hal Wagner, and Boo Ferriss could not bring Bobby home and the Red Sox lost an opportunity to increase their lead. The Cardinals came back to tie the game in the bottom of the second when Kurowski doubled, took third on Joe Garagiola's groundout, and scored on Harry Walker's sacrifice fly.

The third and fourth innings were pitchers' dreams, as no one could reach against either Dickson or Ferriss. Dickson's good fortunes continued into the fifth but Boo weakened in the bottom of the inning. Marty Marion opened with a single. With the pitcher on deck, Cardinals manager Eddie Dyer had the sportswriters scratching their heads when he called on Harry Walker to bunt. Dyer turned out to be a genius, as Dickson doubled to left, scoring Marion. Red Schoendienst followed with a single to drive home Dickson and the Cardinals were suddenly up by two. After Terry Moore singled, Boston manager Joe Cronin removed Ferriss. Joe Dobson relieved and got the Cardinals out without further damage.

Murray Dickson seemed untouchable. By the time he retired the side in order in the sixth and seventh innings, he had set down eighteen Red Sox in a row. He needed only six more outs. He would not get them. In the top of the eighth, Rip Russell pinch-hit for Hal Wagner and broke the string with a single. Catfish Metkovich pinch-hit for Dobson and doubled to left, sending Russell to third and Dickson to the showers. Murray was furious but Eddie Dyer wanted his little lefty, Harry Brecheen, even though Brecheen had pitched a complete game only two days before.

Brecheen fanned Wally Moses and got Johnny Pesky to line to right. Then came Dominic DiMaggio, already in the shadow of his famous and more successful older brother Joe. Dom leaned into Brecheen's best and cracked a long double to right center, tying the game for the Red Sox. That was the good news for Boston. The bad news was that DiMaggio twisted his ankle sliding into second base and had to leave the game. The Cardinals, though, were not out of the proverbial woods. Ted Williams was the next batter. It had been a rough series for Teddy Ballgame, only five singles in twenty-four official trips to the plate, but everyone knew that he was the best hitter in the American League and maybe even the best in all of baseball, no disrespect to Stan Musial intended. More than anything, Williams wanted to make up for his poor October performance with a hit all of Boston would forever remember. Would Eddie Dyer even let Brecheen pitch to "The Kid"? He did and the great Ted Williams popped to second base to end Boston's chance to take the lead. At least they had tied the game.

Boston made three defensive changes to start the bottom of the eighth inning and one, for which manager Joe Cronin had no other choice, turned out to be critical to the outcome of the game. Bob Klinger was the new pitcher, Roy Partee was the new catcher, and Leon Culberson came in to replace the injured Dom DiMaggio. DiMaggio was a superb defensive center fielder, fleet afoot with a strong, accurate arm. Leon Culberson was certainly an adequate major-league outfielder but was not of DiMaggio's caliber. That is no slight against Leon. Few outfielders could match Dom DiMaggio's skills.

Enos Slaughter singled to start the St. Louis eighth. Whitey Kurowski tried to sacrifice Slaughter to third but failed, popping out to the pitcher. Del Rice, who had taken over at catcher for Joe Garagiola in the top of the inning when Joe split a finger on a foul tip, flied out for out number two. Next came Harry "the Hat" Walker, so named because of all the fidgeting he did to his cap when he stood in the batter's box. After a few last-minute adjustments to his hat, Harry scorched a line drive over Johnny Pesky's head. Leon Culberson shagged the ball in left-center field and threw it back to Pesky, who threw it home to Roy Partee, but not in time to nail the streaking Enos Slaughter sliding into home with the fourth Cardinals run.

The Boston writers blamed Johnny Pesky for hesitating before throwing home, but John has always denied any hesitation on his part. Of course, what was critical to the entire play was the absence of Dom DiMaggio in center field. It is only conjecture, but it seems likely that if Dom were out there, he would have retrieved the ball quicker and fired it into Pesky faster. In that case, it is doubtful that Slaughter would have even tried to score.

Hesitation or not, the Cardinals took a one-run lead into the ninth. The Red Sox did not go down easily. Rudy York and Bobby Doerr singled to start the inning and Harry Brecheen was on the ropes. Eddie Dyer stayed with Brecheen and the Red Sox threatened no more. Pinky Higgins, Roy Partee, and pinch hitter Tom McBride could do nothing with Brecheen's offerings and the Cardinals claimed their fourth Seventh Game victory in as many tries.

Even to this day they talk about it in Boston. Howard Hawks directed the 1946 hit movie *The Big Sleep*, and Red Sox fans wondered if he had Johnny Pesky, their great second baseman, in mind when he made that film. No fair!

October 15, 1946

	1	2	3	4	5	6	7	8	9	R	H	E
BOSTON (AL)	1	0	0	0	0	0	0	2	0	3	8	0
ST. LOUIS (NL)	0	1	0	0	2	0	0	1	X	4	9	1

PITCHERS: BOS: Ferriss, Dobson, Klinger (L), Johnson; STL: Dickson, Brecheen (W)

DOUBLES: Dickson, DiMaggio, Kurowski, Metkovich, Musial, Walker

TRIPLES: None

HOME RUNS: None

ATTENDANCE: 36,143

TIME OF GAME: 2:17

CHAPTER 11

1947

Turning to the Right Page

Brooklyn Dodgers   2
New York Yankees   5

In 1947, Chuck Yeager broke the sound barrier flying a Bell X-1 and the world would never be the same. Someone discovered the Dead Sea Scrolls. The House Un-American Activities Committee created the infamous Hollywood blacklist. It was quite a year for history but quite a year for other things as well.

"Peg o' My Heart," "I Wonder Who's Kissing Her Now," and "How Are Things in Glocca Morra?" were the hit songs of 1947 but the world of entertainment was dominated by a new Tennessee Williams play, *A Streetcar Named Desire*, starring Marlon Brando as Stanley Kowalski and Jessica Tandy as Blanche DuBois. Elton John and Hillary Rodham Clinton were born. Robert Penn Warren won the Pulitzer Prize for fiction for *All the King's Men* and Gregory Peck starred in *Gentlemen's Agreement*. Yes, a lot was happening, especially in baseball.

A World Series matching the New York Yankees and the Brooklyn Dodgers became almost a rite of fall during the ten years between 1947 and 1956. Much to the chagrin of the other fourteen major-league clubs, those two teams met in October more often than not, in six of those ten seasons. Much to the delight of baseball fans in search of high drama, four

Around the Horn in 1947

- ☉ The average attendance at St. Louis Browns games was 4,162; average attendance at Cardinals games was nearly four times that number— 16,207. The days of two-team baseball in St. Louis were numbered.

- ☉ The New York Giants finished fourth despite setting a new major-league record for most home runs in a season (221). The Giants' Johnny Mize hit 51 round-trippers, tying him for the National League lead with Ralph Kiner of the last-place Pirates. The next three top home run hitters in the league were also Giants—Willard Marshall, Walker Cooper, and Bobby Thomson.

- ☉ Although the phrase "Spahn and Sain and pray for rain" was the buzz slogan of the 1948 Boston Braves (reflecting their great one-two pitching punch), 1947 was the only season in which Warren Spahn and Johnny Sain each won 20 games for the Braves. Sain won 24 in 1948 but Spahn won only 15.

of those six conflicts required all seven games before a champion could be declared. It was a postwar ritual that seemed to define the nation and its game.

The Yankees and the Dodgers had played in the 1941 World Series, won by the Yankees in five games, but that Series had served as only a taste—mostly a bitter taste for Dodgers fans—of the ongoing saga that would dominate baseball for a full decade.

History may remember the year 1947 as the year of the Marshall Plan, the great rebuilding of war-torn Europe. But for many historians, the defining moment of 1947 was a baseball moment; it was the day that Jackie Robinson broke the color barrier of major-league baseball and began his career with the Brooklyn Dodgers. Baseball would surely reward its fans with a full seven-game World Series and Jackie would have to be a part of it. It would be the poetic and just thing to do. Whether the Dodgers could win was another matter.

The Brooklyn Dodgers had come so close to winning the pennant in 1946, losing to the Cardinals in a playoff. Brooklyn fans can only speculate as to the difference Jackie Robinson would have made at first base in 1946, supplanting the ordinary and forgettable platoon of the left-handed Ed

Stevens (a .242 hitter) and the right-handed Howie Schultz (.253). Robinson, who earned his Rookie of the Year honors in 1947 by hitting .297 and leading the National League in stolen bases, was a crucial addition to the team. The Dodgers won the National League pennant by five games over the Cardinals.

Those who remember the "Boys of Summer," as the Dodgers of the 1950s came to be known, may not recognize this 1947 team at all. Absent were the legendary bigger-than-life figures of Duke Snider, Gil Hodges, and Roy Campanella and with them their long and many home runs. The Dodgers of 1947 hit only 83 home runs, while Dodgers teams from 1949 through 1956 averaged more than double that puny amount (182 home runs per year, if you must know).

The rest of the National League had more talent than the Dodgers. Harry Walker, who started the season with the Cardinals and was soon traded to the Philadelphia Phillies for one Ron Northey (talk about a bad trade!), won the NL batting crown with a .363 average, more than fifty points higher than the leading Dodgers hitter. The Giants' Johnny Mize and the Pirates' Ralph Kiner tied for the league's home run title with 51, 39 more than the leading Dodgers slugger. It is hard to fathom, but the Brooklyn Dodgers won the 1947 pennant despite the fact that twenty other National Leaguers hit more home runs than the top Dodgers home run hitters—Jackie Robinson and Pee Wee Reese led the team with 12 homers each.

The 1947 Brooklyn Dodgers had decent pitching, to be sure. Ralph Branca won 21 games in his first full season and Hugh Casey led all relief pitchers with 18 saves, but the Dodgers won the 1947 pennant because they wanted it more than any other team. No other explanation seems possible, save one: spite. At the beginning of the season, an ugly feud between the Dodgers and the Yankees led to the suspension of Dodgers manager Leo Durocher for the entire season. Durocher had overreacted to New York's clumsy attempt to lure away a Dodgers coach by accusing a Yankees executive of having ties to gamblers. Of course, there was that other compelling reason that explains the Dodgers' pennant: Jackie Robinson.

The New York Yankees had no trouble winning the American League flag, beating out the Detroit Tigers by 12 games. The Yankees were the best team in the league, leading in team home runs, batting average, and earned run average. Although Ted Williams won his second Triple Crown (leading the league in batting average, home runs, and runs batted in) and shortstop Johnny Pesky showed no hesitation in finishing third in batting with a .324 average, the rest of the Boston squad, especially the pitching, fell apart.

Joe DiMaggio was the league's Most Valuable Player, despite statistics that were not even close to the spectacular numbers put up by Williams. Of course there was nothing shabby about a .315 average, 20 home runs, and 97 runs batted in. Yankees pitching, led by Allie Reynolds, Spec Shea, and reliever Joe Page, kept the opposition at bay when it counted.

The Yankees encountered little resistance in the first two games of the Series, beating the Dodgers in Yankee Stadium by scores of 5–3 and 10–3. Brooklyn came back to win Game Three at Ebbets Field, scoring six runs in the second inning and escaping with a 9–8 win. It looked as if the Dodgers were about to fall into a deep abyss in Game Four when they were one pitch away from being down three games to one.

The Dodgers were not only one pitch way from losing the game, they were one pitch away from being the victims of the first no-hitter in World Series history. Bill Bevens, who had compiled a woeful 7–13 record for New York during the regular season, did not allow a single Dodgers hit through the first eight innings of that magical fourth game. His control was another story—he had walked eight batters and his wildness had given the Dodgers a fifth-inning run without the benefit of a hit. No matter—the Yankees took a 2–1 lead into the bottom of the ninth, and Bill Bevens was staring into the face of baseball immortality.

After Bevens retired the first Dodger in the bottom of the ninth inning, Carl Furillo walked. Spider Jorgensen fouled out to Yankees first baseman George McQuinn and Bill Bevens was one out away from his no-hitter. After pinch runner Al Gionfriddo stole second base, the Yankees intentionally walked the dangerous Pete Reiser to bring up Eddie Stanky, who sported a .252 average during the season. Brooklyn manager Burt Shotten called on the diminutive Cookie Lavagetto to pinch-hit for Stanky. Cookie doubled off the right-field wall—the only Dodgers hit of the day—to score the tying and winning runs for Brooklyn. The Series was tied.

The Yankees bounced back to win Game Five, 2–1, behind the four-hit effort of pitcher Spec Shea. The Series returned to Yankee Stadium and the Dodgers now needed not one but two miracles if they were to win their first world championship. Brooklyn jumped to an early 4–0 lead in Game Six, only to see the Yankees tie the score with four runs in the third inning and take the lead on a Yogi Berra single. Brooklyn needed a comeback and got what they needed in the sixth inning, scoring four runs on the strength of five hits off Yankees star reliever Joe Page. The Dodgers took a three-run lead into the ninth inning and narrowly survived the day, as the Yankees loaded the bases but scored only a single run. The first Seventh Game between the New York Yankees and the Brooklyn Dodgers was set for October 6, 1947, at Yankee Stadium.

The Brooklyn pitching staff suffered from obvious fatigue. Because the first six games had all been played in the city of New York, in the boroughs of Brooklyn and the Bronx, there was no need for days off to travel. Perfect weather had given no excuse for any days of rest either. Although six different Yankees pitched in Game Six, three complete games by Allie Reynolds, Bill Bevens, and Spec Shea in Games Two, Four, and Five gave the Yankees staff the edge in the weariness department. Brooklyn had used at least three pitchers in each of the first six games.

The Yankees called on the "Naugatuck Nugget," Spec Shea, to start the Seventh Game. Shea had an outstanding rookie year in 1947, going 14–5 with a 3.07 ERA during the regular season. He had allowed only two runs in winning Series Games One and Five. Spec Shea pitching on only one day of rest was not exactly what the Yankees wanted, but it was far better than what the Dodgers had to offer.

Game Six had taken its toll on the Dodgers' best pitchers, as they had to use their top three starters, Ralph Branca, Joe Hatten, and Vic Lombardi. So Brooklyn called on righty Hal Gregg, who had started only 16 games during the season and posted a sorry 4–5 record with an ERA of 5.88. Although he had been impressive in his previous two outings in the Series (two runs in nine innings of work), he holds the distinction of being the only pitcher to start a World Series Seventh Game with so few regular-season wins and so high an earned run average.

Though the numbers favored Yankees starter Shea, Spec was anything but spectacular. He gave up a single to Eddie Stanky and a walk to Pee Wee Reese in the first inning. Catcher Aaron Robinson bailed out Shea by gunning down both Dodgers trying to steal second base. The Dodgers jumped on Shea for two runs in the second inning. With one out, Gene Hermanski tripled and scored on a single by Bruce Edwards. After Carl Furillo singled Edwards to second, New York manager Bucky Harris went to his bullpen and brought in Bill Bevens. It did not take the Dodgers eight and two-thirds innings to figure out Bevens this time, as Spider Jorgensen immediately doubled to right, scoring Edwards. Brooklyn led, 2–0, and with runners on second and third and only one out, threatened to break the game open and coast to their first-ever world championship.

Up to the plate came pitcher Hal Gregg. It was only the second inning and he had retired the only three Yankees batters to appear in the first inning. With the Dodgers' pitching staff so decimated, there was no reason to bat for the weak-hitting pitcher so early in the game. Gregg made contact but the ball rolled to Yankees shortstop Phil Rizzuto, who threw out Carl Furillo at home. Eddie Stanky popped to short and the inning was over. The score was 2–0 in favor of Brooklyn, but it was an opportunity, an excellent opportunity for more runs, squandered.

Hal Gregg's first-inning success did not continue. In the Yankees' second, he walked George McQuinn and Aaron Robinson. With two outs, Phil Rizzuto rapped the first of his three singles, scoring McQuinn and cutting the Brooklyn lead to 2–1. Bill Bevens struck out to end the inning.

Neither team could score in the third inning. Bill Bevens struck out two and allowed only a harmless walk, while Hal Gregg regained his earlier form by retiring three formidable hitters—Tommy Henrich, Yogi Berra, and Joe DiMaggio—after a leadoff walk to Snuffy Stirnweiss. It was now a matter of time. But time for whom?

Bruce Edwards tallied his second single of the game to open the Dodgers' fourth but Bill Bevens retired the next three Dodgers, including the final out of the inning, pitcher Hal Gregg. Did manager Burt Shotten really believe he had enough runs and that Hal Gregg could hold the Yankees in check? Or was the Brooklyn bullpen so weak that Shotten had no choice but to go with Gregg for as long as he possibly could?

Hal Gregg fell apart minutes later. After striking out George McQuinn to begin the Yankees' fourth, he walked Billy Johnson. Gregg struck out Aaron Robinson but gave up another single to Phil Rizzuto; the tying run was at second base and Bill Bevens was up. Although Bevens was pitching well for New York and it was early in the game, manager Bucky Harris recognized the urgency of the moment and sent his masterful pinch hitter, Bobby Brown, to bat. It was Brown's fourth pinch-hit appearance of the Series and the Dodgers had yet to retire him (a single, a double, and a walk, so far). Brown responded with his second pinch double of the Series, tying the game and sending Rizzuto to third. That was all for Hal Gregg, who would never face another batter in a big-league uniform.

The Dodgers were desperate for a pitcher. Their two-run lead had evaporated and the Yankees were now the threatening team. Hank Behrman had already appeared four times in the Series, three times with great success (no runs in four and one-third innings). The other outing, in the second game, was a catastrophe, as Behrman allowed four runs in only one-third of an inning. Which Hank Behrman would take the mound? Sadly for the Dodgers, it was the latter.

Stirnweiss drew a walk to load the bases. Tommy Henrich singled to right, giving New York a 3–2 lead. Yogi Berra grounded out to end the inning but the damage had been done.

The Yankees brought in their relief ace, Joe Page, even though he had not exactly baffled Brooklyn in his three previous appearances. Page got the save in Game One, although he gave up two runs and four hits in four innings. In Game Three he was the Joe Page that had earned him the reputation as the American League's best reliever, pitching three scoreless innings. But in Game Six, it was a very different and ineffective Joe Page who gave up four runs in only one inning and absorbed the loss. Which Joe Page would take the mound for the Yankees? Unfortunately for Brooklyn, it was *not* the Joe Page of Game One or Game Six.

Joe Page was almost perfect and that is the story of the Seventh Game of the 1947 World Series. The Dodgers could not reach Page for a hit, a walk, or a single base runner until one man was out in the ninth inning. By then it was too late, as New York had added single runs in the sixth and seventh innings to take a 5–2 lead.

Joe Page retired the first thirteen Dodgers to face him, beginning with Eddie Stanky's harmless ground ball to second base in the fifth inning. With one gone in the ninth inning, Eddie Miksis finally solved the riddle of Joe Page with a single to center field. Bruce Edwards, who had singled twice earlier in the game, ended it as no other player before or since has ended a Seventh Game, by grounding into a double play.

Joe Page gave the most dominating relief appearance in Seventh Game history. He would record 23 more wins and another 56 saves for the Yankees over the next three seasons but nothing in those years would come close to that day in October when everything went right for the big lefty from Cherry Valley, Pennsylvania, Joseph Francis Page.

What of the two superstars who also played in that first Game Seven between the Yankees and the Dodgers? Neither Joe DiMaggio nor Jackie Robinson produced a hit. In fact, history records that the 1947 World Series was not productive for either player; Robinson batted .259 with a pair of doubles and DiMaggio batted only .231 with a pair of home runs in games that the Yankees lost. For Joltin' Joe it was his first and only Seventh Game appearance. At least Jackie would have a few more chances.

October 6, 1947

	1	2	3	4	5	6	7	8	9	R	H	E
BROOKLYN (NL)	0	2	0	0	0	0	0	0	0	2	7	0
NEW YORK (AL)	0	1	0	2	0	1	1	0	X	5	7	0

PITCHERS: BKN: Gregg (L), Behrman, Hatten, Barney, Casey; NYY: Shea, Bevens, Page (W)

DOUBLES: Brown, Jorgensen

TRIPLES: Hermanski, Johnson

HOME RUNS: None

ATTENDANCE: 71,548

TIME OF GAME: 2:19

1952

Wait 'til Next Year—Again

New York Yankees 4
Brooklyn Dodgers 2

In 1952, the first Holiday Inn rose up along Route 70 near Memphis, Tennessee. Kellogg's introduced Sugar Frosted Flakes and Mr. Potato Head was born. Televison shows were suddenly popping up and all you needed was a television set to see them. And what shows they were! "The Adventures of Ozzie & Harriet," "I Love Lucy," "The Red Buttons Show," "The Range Rider" (starring Jock Mahoney and Dick Jones), and "The Jackie Gleason Show" all made their debut. *The King and I* was the toast of Broadway, but New Yorkers were more interested in talking about the game they loved and the teams in their own neighborhoods.

The Dodgers earned another shot at the hated Yankees, this time getting a measure of revenge against the New York Giants team that had beat them in the historic playoff game at the Polo Grounds the year before. Nothing could ever erase the pain of Bobby Thomson's ninth-inning home run off Ralph Branca in 1951 but a pennant in 1952 made the fans of Brooklyn ever hopeful once again.

The Dodgers of 1952 were a far different team from the one that had lost to the Yankees in the seven-game Series of 1947. True, it was almost the same squad that had lost in five games in 1949, but this 1952 crop seemed wiser, hungrier, and suddenly a lot tougher, thanks to the addition of a twenty-eight-year-old rookie relief pitcher by the name of Joe Black.

Around the Horn in 1952

- ☉ Boston Red Sox slugger Ted Williams went off to fly combat missions in Korea.
- ☉ Hank Sauer was the National League's MVP, despite playing for the .500 Cubs.
- ☉ Philadelphia Athletics pitcher Harry Byrd won American League Rookie of the Year honors, narrowly beating out Clint Courtney (St. Louis Browns) and Sammy White (Boston Red Sox).

Black came out of the Negro Leagues to post a 15–4 record with 15 saves and a sparkling 2.15 earned run average.

The rest of the Dodgers' pitching staff pitched well enough to take advantage of the powerful offense. The team fielded four quality starters in Carl Erskine, Billy Loes, Preacher Roe, and Ben Wade (for a combined win-loss record of 49–25) but Brooklyn's strength was their balanced offense. For the fourth year in a row, the Dodgers led the National League in both home runs and stolen bases. Jackie Robinson epitomized the Dodgers' game, hitting .308 with 19 homers and 24 stolen bases. His mates have become equally and rightfully as legendary: Gil Hodges (32 homers, 105 RBIs), Pee Wee Reese (a league-leading 30 stolen bases), Roy Campanella (22 homers, 97 RBIs), and Duke Snider (.303 average and 21 homers). These were the famed "Boys of Summer," eager to become the men of fall.

The American League pennant went to the New York Yankees for the fourth consecutive year. Most experts predicted that the Cleveland Indians, on the strength of their great pitching (Early Wynn, Mike Garcia, and Bob Feller), would finally supplant the Yankees but Casey Stengel, in his fourth season as manager of the Yankees, did it with smoke, mirrors, and the first full season of a young Mickey Mantle. It was by no means easy for Casey, as his team clinched the pennant in the final week of the season and edged out the Indians by just two games.

The Yankees surprised the American League with solid pitching, led by Allie Reynolds and his 20–8 record and league-leading 2.07 ERA. The rest of the team performed well enough to win more games than the rest of the league, even though other teams boasted of players with far more impressive statistics. That seemed to be the modus operandi of most of Casey's teams.

When the World Series opened at Ebbets Field on the first day of October, Dodgers fans believed that this was their year. Dodgers fans always believed it was their year, but 1952 was different. Of course, 1947 and 1949 were supposed to have been different (please, no talking about 1951). And when Joe Black pitched a complete-game win to start the Series, backed by the home run power of Reese, Robinson, and Snider, there was good reason for optimism in the borough of Brooklyn.

The Yankees struck back in Game Two behind Vic Raschi's three-hitter and a mighty assault led by Billy Martin's four RBIs. The teams split the next two games at Yankee Stadium, where they would also play a memorable fifth game, won by the Dodgers in 11 innings, 6–5. The World Series returned to Brooklyn, where the Dodgers needed only one victory to claim the championship. How close "next year" must have seemed!

Game Six. So close. So tantalizingly close. For five innings the teams went scoreless, as New York's Vic Raschi and Brooklyn's Billy Loes matched each other, pitch for pitch. In the bottom of the sixth, Duke Snider lifted the spirits of the hometown fans with his third home run of the Series, a solo shot to right field. Yogi Berra tied it with a homer in the seventh and New York took the lead when Vic Raschi singled home Gene Woodling. Mickey Mantle's eighth-inning homer proved to be the margin of victory, as the Duke poled another solo homer but the Dodgers fell one run short.

Brooklyn had to be pleased with Game Seven's pitching matchup. The Yankees were pitching Ed Lopat, whom the Dodgers had reached for 10 hits and five runs in their Game Three victory. Manager Chuck Dressen called upon his ace, Joe Black, who had pitched brilliantly in his two previous starts, winning Game One and losing a heartbreaker, 2–0, in Game Four.

Through the first three innings, neither team could muster even a threat of a run. Leading off the Yankees' fourth inning, Phil Rizzuto doubled down the left-field line. After Mickey Mantle's grounder to second moved Rizzuto to third base, Yankees first baseman and future Hall of Famer Johnny Mize stepped into the batter's box. Think of the irony of the appearance of "the Big Cat" in this situation. For eleven seasons with the Cardinals and then the Giants, Mize had tormented the Dodgers with his timely and powerful hitting; he hit over .300 in his first nine seasons and slammed more than 300 home runs in the National League. Now, in the twilight of his career—he would play only one more season and retire—he had one more chance to inflict pain upon the Brooklyn Dodgers, this time as a Yankee. Of course, he had already inflicted substantial pain in the first six games of the Series, hitting three home runs, one less than his total during the regular season for the Yankees. Joe Black versus Johnny Mize. And Mize won the battle, slapping a single to left field to put the Yankees on top.

In the home half of the fourth inning, the Dodgers loaded the bases with none out. This is the opportunity that champions relish, the opportunity that champions convert. Casey Stengel quickly removed Lopat and brought in his ace, Allie Reynolds. Gil Hodges greeted Reynolds with a slicing line drive to left, caught by Gene Woodling but deep enough to allow Duke Snider to score the tying run. Woodling's errant throw allowed Jackie Robinson to move to third base and the Dodgers had an excellent chance to take the lead.

It had been the story of the Dodgers in the Seventh Game of the 1947 World Series and it became the story again in 1952: opportunities presented, opportunities squandered. George Shuba struck out and Carl Furillo grounded out to end the inning. Brooklyn had knotted the score at 1–1 but everyone at Ebbets Field knew that the home team had wasted a precious chance. Gene Woodling led off the Yankees' fifth inning with a home run and the magnitude of the waste became even more obvious.

The Brooklyn Dodgers refused to fold, tying the game in the bottom of the fifth on Pee Wee Reese's single, scoring Billy Cox. A pattern had emerged: Yankees score a run, Dodgers respond with one of their own. Would that pattern continue? For Dodgers fans there was a more serious question: could Joe Black find his earlier form?

The first half of the pattern continued in the sixth inning, as Mickey Mantle put the Yankees into the lead again with a solo home run. When Johnny Mize followed with a single, the Joe Black question had been answered: he didn't have it that day. Preacher Roe relieved and loaded the bases but the Yankees could not score. Now the Dodgers could only hope to continue their part of the pattern by quickly tying the game. Things looked promising when Roy Campanella opened the bottom of the sixth inning with a single. Gil Hodges, who had gone hitless in the Series—no hits in 19 at-bats—came to the plate against Reynolds. Hodges was "due," thought the fans. It had not been the best season of his career in terms of batting average (.254) but he had led the Dodgers in home runs and runs batted in. Gil Hodges had to come through. He didn't, rapping into a double play to end the pattern of the previous two innings. The Yankees held a 3–2 lead at the end of six.

The Dodgers may have ended their pattern of scoring but the Yankees were not through with theirs, scoring another run in the top of the seventh inning when Gil McDougald crossed the plate on Mickey Mantle's two-out single. The bad news for Brooklyn was that they now had to overcome a two-run deficit; the good news was that Allie Reynolds was through for the Series, having been lifted for a pinch hitter in the top of the seventh inning. Into the fray came Vic Raschi, the Yankees' starter from the previous day. More good news for Brooklyn: Raschi was tired and ineffective.

Carl Furillo opened the Brooklyn seventh with a walk. After pinch hitter Rocky Nelson popped out to Rizzuto (attention, fans of Rocky Nelson—he will have a far better Seventh Game in 1960), Billy Cox singled to right and Pee Wee Reese walked to load the bases. It was another opportunity for Brooklyn and they dared not blow it, for it was unlikely that another chance like this, the bases loaded and less than two outs, would present itself. Casey Stengel recognized that Vic Raschi was not the man of the hour for New York and brought in the lefty Bob Kuzava, the fourth Yankees pitcher of the day. *Bob who?*

Robert Leroy Kuzava began his major-league career with the Cleveland Indians in 1946. He was what the writers called a "journeyman" ballplayer, meaning that he rarely stayed on one team long enough to figure out who served the best hamburgers near the stadium. He moved about in the big leagues, pitching for the Indians, White Sox, and Senators before finding a three-year home with the Yankees, and then moving on with the Orioles, Phillies, and Cardinals before retiring from baseball with a career mark of 49 wins against 44 losses, an earned run average of 4.05, and a total of 13 saves over ten years. He had his moments of glory, but unless he happens to be visiting Cooperstown, New York, as you are reading this paragraph, he is most definitely not in the Hall of Fame. In 1952, he won 8 games and lost 8 games with the New York Yankees; he recorded 3 saves. He was the obstacle that stood before the Brooklyn Dodgers in Game Seven of the 1952 World Series.

Kuzava's first challenge was the Dodgers' all-star center fielder, Duke Snider, who had already collected 10 hits in the Series and tied a World Series record with four home runs in the first six games. The Duke is in Cooperstown now and forever. Despite the fact that it was lefty against lefty, the Dodgers faithful must have identified the favorable matchup before them. A fly-ball out would have cut the Brooklyn deficit to a single run but Kuzava overpowered the Duke and made him pop up to third base. The bases remained loaded and there were two outs. This was certainly the last hopeful prospect for the Dodgers. The next batter was Jackie Robinson. There was no way that Bob Kuzava, a mere mortal from Wyandotte, Michigan, could retire two future Hall of Fame superstars. Was there?

In a twisted turn of events lasting no more than ten seconds, the dreams of the Brooklyn Dodgers fell, soared, and then collapsed into a heap of stranded base runners. Kuzava bore down hard on Robinson and Jackie lifted a routine pop fly to the right side of the infield. First baseman Joe Collins, whom Casey Stengel had brought in as a defensive replacement for Johnny Mize at the start of the inning, had only to move a few feet to his right and wait patiently for the ball to nestle gently in his glove. But the sun was shining brightly on Ebbets Field and its inhabitants, and Collins lost the ball in the bright sunlight. Because there were two outs and all three Dodgers runners were off with contact, the ball dropping to the infield grass would have easily tied the game. But the ball never touched the ground. Yankees second baseman Billy Martin realized that Collins could not make the play and ran in to make a knee-high grab of the ball.

Billy Martin's catch of Jackie Robinson's sun-drenched pop fly was by no means a great defensive play. Martin did not have to jump to his left, lunge to his left, leap high in the air, or dive to the ground. It was not all that difficult but it was an alert, hustling, and intelligent play that saved the game for New York. The Yankees stopped their scoring and the Dodgers stopped their threats, getting only one more base runner before going down in order in the ninth inning. Casey Stengel's brilliant manipulation of his bullpen, coupled with the Dodgers' inability to take advantage of numerous scoring opportunities, including four Yankees errors, made for the difference. When it was all over, Bob Kuzava had bested Duke Snider, Jackie Robinson, and the rest of the Brooklyn Dodgers to earn a save and etch his name into World Series history.

Four days later, a smiling President Dwight Eisenhower appeared on the cover of the *Saturday Evening Post*. Dodgers fans wondered why anyone could be smiling. They "waited 'til next year," and it, too, came with heartache as the Yankees beat the Dodgers in six games in the 1953 Series. Neither team made it to the World Series in 1954 but the Dodgers would have another chance at "next year" in 1955.

October 7, 1952

	1	2	3	4	5	6	7	8	9	R	H	E
NEW YORK (AL)	0	0	0	1	1	1	1	0	0	4	10	4
BROOKLYN (NL)	0	0	0	1	1	0	0	0	0	2	8	1

PITCHERS: NYY: Lopat, Reynolds (W), Raschi, Kuzava (SV);
BKN: Black (L), Roe, Erskine

DOUBLES: Cox, Rizzuto

TRIPLES: None

HOME RUNS: Mantle, Woodling

ATTENDANCE: 33,195

TIME OF GAME: 2:54

1955

Believe It!

Brooklyn Dodgers	2
New York Yankees	0

It was good to be alive in 1955. You could turn on the radio and hear Bill Haley and the Comets singing "Rock Around the Clock." If the newfangled music wasn't to your liking, there was the more traditional fuddy-duddy favorite "Cherry Pink and Apple Blossom White" by Perez Prado. Fast food was in its infancy but for the first time you could find Colonel Harland Sanders selling his special-recipe ("eleven herbs and spices") fried chicken. Ray Kroc made sure you could buy a McDonald's hamburger for only fifteen cents with a side order of crispy fries for twelve cents. You could go to the movies and watch Nicholas Ray's *Rebel Without a Cause*.

There was so much going on in 1955 it's a wonder anyone found time to work. Everyone knew all the words to "The Ballad of Davy Crockett." Annette Funicello became a Mouseketeer and Disneyland opened in California. America was hooked on the new TV shows—"Gunsmoke," "The Life and Legend of Wyatt Earp," "Highway Patrol," and "The Millionaire." "The Phil Silvers Show" made its debut, a riotous comedy about an army sergeant named Ernest Bilko; creator Nat Hentoff is said to have came up with the lead character's name as a tribute to a lesser-known baseball player, Steve Bilko.

If you lived in Brooklyn, you could dream of what it would be like to celebrate a World Series victory. Of course, as a Dodgers fan it had been

Around the Horn in 1955

- No one seemed to notice when a rookie outfielder hit .255 with five home runs for the last-place Pittsburgh Pirates. All of baseball would soon know this talented right fielder. His name was Roberto Clemente.

- The Baltimore Orioles had a combined 88 home runs and stolen bases. They were the last team to have a combined total of home runs and stolen bases under 100.

- "Marvelous Marv" Throneberry, who became a symbol of the ineptitude of the early New York Mets, made his major-league debut in a Yankees uniform. He went two for two in pinstripes. At the same time, his brother Faye was tearing up Fenway Park with a .257 average. Marv would end his career with more home runs and a higher batting average than his brother but somehow got the reputation as the bungling and incompetent player.

more hallucination than dream over the past seven years. There was no way a Dodgers fan could fathom that ecstasy unless he called his cousin in the Bronx and begged for a blow-by-blow narrative of the emotions—by now commonplace—of five of the past seven seasons.

It was a familiar scene in baseball: Yankees versus Dodgers in the World Series. Brooklyn had lost to their cross-city rivals in their five previous October outings, twice going to a Seventh Game, in 1947 and 1952. Yankees manager Casey Stengel was perfect in his World Series efforts, five championships without a defeat. The success of the Yankees had transformed the team into a legend and that legend was every bit as powerful a force as was their talent on the field.

The Dodgers were back on top of the National League. They beat out their nearest rivals, the Milwaukee Braves, by a comfortable 13½ games. There would be no playoff nightmares for the Dodgers this year, just plenty of time to ready themselves for one more chance to win their first championship in franchise history.

The Dodgers' squad of 1955 was a great team, perhaps their best of the era. Brooklyn fans knew that the quality of their team was no guarantee of success in the World Series; they were arguably better than the Yankees in 1947, 1949, 1952, and 1953, but had nothing to show for their claimed superiority. But what a team it was! Duke Snider had put together another remarkable season, slugging 42 home runs and delivering 136 RBIs to go with a .309 batting average. MVP Roy Campanella, Gil Hodges, Pee Wee Reese, and Carl Furillo all put up great numbers, too. Only Jackie Robinson experienced a subpar year, batting .256 in only 105 games. On balance, though, this was a powerful and productive team.

The Dodgers also had superb pitching, led by Don Newcombe's 20–5 season. Starters Carl Erskine and Billy Loes combined for a 24–13 mark, while the relief corps was a major part of the Dodgers' success. Clem Labine, Don Bessent, and Ed Roebuck appeared in relief 121 times, chalking up 26 saves and more than 20 wins. If the Dodgers had a weak spot in their pitching, it was probably their fourth starter, Johnny Podres, who posted a mediocre 9–10 record with an equally mediocre 3.96 earned run average.

While National League fans quarreled deep into the night over who was the league's premier center fielder (Duke Snider or Willie Mays), no such argument came up in American League circles. Mickey Mantle led the junior circuit in home runs, triples, and slugging percentage; he was the undisputed mainstay of the Yankees' offense. Teammate Yogi Berra was the league's Most Valuable Player, driving in 108 runs while slugging 27 home runs and batting .272. Solid performances from Bill Skowron, Gil McDougald, and Hank Bauer helped the Yankees overtake the defending league champion Indians by three games.

The Yankees' pitching staff posted the league's lowest earned run average. The leader of the mound corps was Whitey Ford (18–7, 2.62 ERA), who had already established himself as the most reliable hurler of the Stengel era. But Casey had a way of finding some no-name pitcher, often through a one-sided trade with one of the league's basement teams, to have one or two good seasons. In 1955, that pitcher was the veteran Tommy Byrne, whom Casey had resurrected in 1954 after a four-year exile to the St. Louis Browns, Chicago White Sox, and Washington Senators, the composite equivalent of the most depressing gulag in Siberia. Byrne had been with New York from 1943 through the beginning of the 1951 season and responded to his return to grace with a spectacular 16–5 season.

The Yankees also took a chance on a right-handed pitcher from Michigan City, Indiana. He had come up with the St. Louis Browns in 1953 and moved with the franchise to Baltimore in 1954, where he raised a few eyebrows and a bevy of batting averages when he went 3–21 with the seventh-place Orioles. The Yankees must have known something because Don Larsen went 9–2 with a neat little 3.06 earned run average for Stengel's 1955 squad. New York also obtained "Bullet" Bob Turley from the Orioles' bargain table and Turley won 17 games for the Yanks. How did they do it? How did the Yankees always seem to get these productive players from the bottom feeders of the American League in exchange for little more than a cheese sandwich and a dessert to be named later? That was all part of the Yankees' mystique of the Stengel era.

For most fans of the game—at least those with a grip on reality—the only question in 1955 was whether the Yankees would dispatch the Dodgers quickly or toy with them and break their hearts in six, maybe seven games. After the Yankees won the first two games in New York, the answer seemed to be the first, a quick and merciful end to another crop of Dodgers dreams. The Series then moved to Brooklyn, where strange things began to happen: the Dodgers won a few games.

Johnny Podres won Game Three on his twenty-third birthday as his mates gifted him with eight runs and the little lefty from Witherbee, New York, pitched well enough to earn the victory. Home runs by Campanella, Hodges, and Snider in Game Four propelled the home team to an 8–5 win and the Series was suddenly and unexpectedly tied. The long ball proved to be the difference in Game Five, too, as Sandy Amoros and Duke Snider (who hit a pair!) gave Brooklyn a 5–3 win and put them one victory away from taking it all. Of course, they were also only two losses away from another calamity of autumn.

Whatever drama might have existed before the Sixth Game at Yankee Stadium died early and emphatically when the Yankees scored five runs in the first inning—Bill Skowron's three-run homer was the big blow—and coasted to an easy 5–1 win behind Whitey Ford's second Series win. The stage was set: another Seventh Game and another chance for Dodgers woe.

Who would start the Seventh Game? The logical choice for Dodgers manager Walter Alston, in only his second year at the helm in Brooklyn, was Don Newcombe. "Newk" had been the ace of the staff during the regular season and was well rested, having pitched in only the Series opener. And the Dodgers could use Newcombe's bat; during the regular season, he hit .359 with seven home runs. But Newcombe had been shelled by the Yankees' bats in Game One, allowing eight hits and six runs in less than six innings. So it was not really a difficult decision for Alston, who had made up his mind even before the beginning of Game Six: Johnny Podres would be his starter for Game Seven.

Only once before in the history of the World Series had a pitcher with a losing record during the regular season started a Seventh Game. That peculiar distinction belonged to Dodgers pitcher Hal Gregg, who went 3–4 for Brooklyn in 1947. Dodgers fans remembered the unhappy fate of Gregg and the Dodgers that year.

The Yankees countered with the veteran Tommy Byrne, who had pitched brilliantly in the Yankees' win in Game Two. Byrne had allowed the Dodgers only five hits in his complete-game triumph and his right arm was well rested for the task. One factor benefited the Dodgers' cause: a nagging leg injury kept Yankees star Mickey Mantle from the starting lineup.

The Gillette Company, manufacturers of razors and blades for the stubbly beards of American men, paid $1 million to sponsor the World Series on NBC. It was money well spent when an estimated 60 million viewers tuned in to watch the historic Seventh Game. Vermont Supreme Court Justice Olin M. Jeffords (father of U.S. Senator Jim Jeffords) had scheduled an oral argument for 1:30 but rescheduled it when his colleagues pointed out that the World Series finale would be under way by then. But as exciting as the event was, there were a few unsold bleacher seats remaining at Yankee Stadium at game time, at only $2.10 each. How could anyone not want to be at Yankee Stadium on the afternoon of October 4, 1955?

Photographs of the crowd show multitudes of men in white shirts and proper ties. Was it the old-time respect for the game or did a lot of guys play hooky from work that day? It was not that big a deal; an ad in the *New York Times* pitched custom-tailored white broadcloth shirts for only $5.95, with no extra charge for French cuffs. The sun was bright, the air was crisp, and baseball filled the day. Boxing legend Rocky Marciano and racing legend Eddie Arcaro were among the 62,465 who witnessed the miracle.

Both teams went out in order in the first inning; there would be no early rout for either side. The first to reach base was Gil Hodges, who coaxed a two-out walk in the second inning but stayed there when Don Hoak grounded out. In the bottom of the inning, Bill Skowron lashed a two-out double off Podres but could not score when Bob Cerv, playing center field in place of the injured Mantle, grounded out to Pee Wee Reese. No score after two innings.

Tommy Byrne remained unhittable through three innings, surrendering only another harmless walk in the top of the third inning. In the bottom of the third, the Yankees got serious and the Dodgers got lucky. With two out, Phil Rizzuto walked and Billy Martin singled, Rizzuto stopping at second base. Gil McDougald connected with a Podres offering and bounced the ball to the left side of the infield, into the path and body of Yankees runner Phil Rizzuto. According to the rules of baseball (currently rule 7.08(f)), a runner who is hit by a batted ball in fair territory is automatically out. So it was that Phil Rizzuto, by running into the ball hit by Gil McDougald, made the final out of the Yankees' third inning and thwarted any chance of a Yankees run. Gil McDougald was credited with a hit, by a most unusual custom of professional baseball, but the Yankees scoring chance was done. Would the Dodgers' infield have caught the McDougald ground ball and turned it into an out anyway? Probably. But this was a Seventh Game and stranger things have happened in those circumstances. No matter, the game remained scoreless after three innings and high drama was unfolding in the Bronx.

In the Dodgers' fourth inning, after Duke Snider struck out, Roy Campanella doubled into the left-field corner. Carl Furillo followed with a ground ball to the right of Phil Rizzuto. The Yankees' shortstop moved gracefully to the ball and threw it smartly to first base in time to retire Furillo, but Campanella alertly moved to third base. Two were out and Gil Hodges came to bat. Hodges had had a respectable Series to that point, gathering five hits, including a home run, and driving in three runs in the first six games. But which Gil Hodges was really coming to the plate? Was it the Gil Hodges who went 0 for 21 in the seven-game Series of 1952? Or was it the Gil Hodges who led the Dodgers in hitting in the six-game 1953 Series, batting .364, albeit in a losing cause?

Hodges answered the prayers of the Brooklyn faithful, slicing a single to left field and scoring the slow-footed Campanella with ease. How important it was for Campy to advance to third on the Furillo ground ball. Don Hoak grounded out to end the inning but the Dodgers were leading, 1–0, and needed "only" eighteen more outs for the title.

Yogi Berra, who holds the record for most career World Series hits (71), led off the Yankees' fourth with a double. One could hear the groans all the way from Brooklyn in the Yankee Stadium grandstand. Podres bore down and got Hank Bauer to fly out harmlessly to right field. Bill Skowron followed with a ground ball to second. Berra moved to third and Bob Cerv came to bat in the same circumstance that faced Gil Hodges only moments before. But Bob Cerv could not deliver, popping out to Reese. Johnny Podres had frustrated another Yankees threat.

Neither team could produce a base runner in the fifth inning, although the Yankees' Elston Howard gave a scare with a deep fly to left field. The score was still 1–0, now with "only" twelve outs to go. The Dodgers came to bat in the sixth inning, hungry for another run, an "insurance run" as baseball buffs like to call it. Reese opened the inning with a single. Manager Alston called on Duke Snider to bunt; although Snider's reputation was that of a powerful slugger, he was a capable bunter, with more than 50 sacrifice bunts in his career, and he laid down an excellent bunt. Byrne fielded it cleanly and threw to Skowron, who dropped the throw for an error. Alston would not let his boys end the inning without scoring at least one run. He asked slugger Roy Campanella to bunt and Campy obliged, moving the runners to second and third.

Casey Stengel ordered an intentional walk for Carl Furillo to load the bases and set up a possible double play. He also brought in Bob Grim to pitch. Grim had not been particularly effective in the regular season but recorded a save in the first game of the Series. Of course, it was hard to argue with Stengel's tactics, given his perfect World Series record with New York. The first batter to face Grim was Gil Hodges, who had already driven home the only Dodgers run. Hodges sent a deep fly ball to right center field, not deep enough for a hit but deep enough to bring in Pee Wee Reese with the second Dodgers run. When Grim intentionally walked Don Hoak to reload the bases, the Dodgers knew that they had a supreme opportunity to bust the game wide open. Manager Alston went to his bench and called on George "Shotgun" Shuba to bat for Don Zimmer. Shuba failed. The Yankees knew it could have been a lot worse.

Up by two runs, manager Walter Alston had to replace second baseman Don Zimmer, who was now out of the game by virtue of the pinch-hit strategy in the top of the inning. His defensive options were limited because Jackie Robinson was unable to play in the Seventh Game due to a strained Achilles tendon. In truth, Walter had only one choice, to move Jim Gilliam from left field to second base and bring in Sandy Amoros to play left. From a purely technical perspective, he could have let pinch hitter George Shuba stay in the game and play left field but Shuba was nowhere near the defensive player that Amoros was. Amoros was known for his glove but had also distinguished himself in the Series with his bat, hitting a home run in Game Five and batting .333 in limited action. At the time, there was one other factor that probably seemed insignificant to everyone in the park: Sandy Amoros threw with his left hand. This meant that unlike either Jim Gilliam, who started in left field that day, or George Shuba, Sandy Amoros was the only left fielder who could catch the ball with his right hand. The significance of that trivial detail would manifest itself in resplendent fashion within minutes.

Billy Martin walked to lead off the bottom of the sixth inning. Gil McDougald then beat out a bunt down the third-base line. The Yankees had the tying runs on base and the American League's Most Valuable Player was again at the plate. Yogi Berra had already collected 10 hits in the Series, more than any other player on either club. He was New York's hottest hitter and he was exactly where Yankees fans wanted him, in the batter's box staring down the young Johnny Podres. Berra, a left-handed hitter who usually pulled the ball to right field, jumped on a Podres pitch and sliced it to left field. If it stayed fair, it had a chance of clearing the short fence near the left-field foul pole, only 301 feet from home plate. Even if it did not have the necessary distance, it was an almost certain base-clearing double. *Almost* certain. Gil McDougald thought so; he was determined to score from first base on the Berra hit. But with fleetness of foot that had never been seen in any previous World Series game, Sandy Amoros broke toward the left-field corner. As he approached the foul pole, just before the ball was preparing to crash against the fence, he thrust out his gloved right hand and snared it. There was no way a left fielder who caught the ball with his left hand would have had a chance at that slicing line drive. No way!

The Amoros catch was the greatest catch of any Seventh Game, arguably the best defensive play of any World Series game. Some may cast their vote for the famous Willie Mays over-the-shoulder running catch of the long drive off the bat of Vic Wertz in the opening game of the 1954 World Series, but the Amoros catch, coming when it did, probably meant the difference between winning and losing the Series. Let the purists debate, because Dodgers fans are unanimous. But the greatness of the play only began with the lunging catch, for Amoros then turned and threw the ball to Pee Wee Reese, who fired it to Gil Hodges in time to double up the stunned McDougald, who was already smelling the jubilation of the game-tying run. It was a double play and in an instant the Dodgers' defense had extinguished the Yankees' threat. When Hank Bauer made the third out on a ground ball to Reese, the Dodgers were only nine outs away.

The Dodgers went quietly in the seventh inning. In the Yankees' half of the inning, Elston Howard singled with two out, and one more moment of high drama emerged at Yankee Stadium. The injured Mickey Mantle came off the bench to bat for Bob Grim. Mantle's legs were hurting but everyone knew that his powerful arms were capable of one last heroic swing that could tie the game. Only the bravest of Dodgers fans could bear to watch. Johnny Podres won the battle, inducing a meek pop fly to the short-stop. Six outs to go.

Bullet Bob Turley came in to pitch the eighth inning and retired the Dodgers in order. It was time for another Yankees threat. Phil Rizzuto opened the bottom of the inning with a single, New York's seventh hit of the afternoon. Would Alston stay with Podres? After Billy Martin flied out to right, Gil McDougald rapped his third single of the afternoon, sending Rizzuto to third base. Would Alston *still* stay with the young lefty? Clem Labine, the Dodgers' relief ace, was a logical choice and many Dodgers fans would have welcomed a pitching change. Alston let Podres pitch to Yogi Berra; after all, it was the lefty-to-lefty confrontation that conventional base-ball wisdom said favored the pitcher. But everyone in the stands and on the field remembered Berra's last at-bat, the slicing drive that Sandy Amoros rescued at the foul pole. Johnny Podres was up to the task. Yogi Berra flied to short right field, where it made no difference which hand Carl Furillo used to catch the ball. Rizzuto stayed put at third.

Johnny Podres had scattered eight hits over the course of seven and two-thirds innings. No one knew how much arm was left in the young man but Walter Alston knew how much heart was there, so Podres stayed in to face the dangerous right-handed Yankees right fielder, Hank Bauer. The tying runs were on base and Bauer, hitter of 20 home runs during the regu-lar season, represented the go-ahead and potential winning run for the Yan-kees. Podres bore down and struck out Bauer. It was only his fourth strikeout of the day but he never had a bigger one in his life. Three more outs. Three more chances for the Yankees' legend, from Ruth to DiMaggio to Casey and his boys, to shatter the Dodgers' dream.

One more run, maybe two, and the Dodgers Nation could rest a lit-tle easier. With one out in the top of the ninth inning, Don Hoak singled and Sandy Amoros walked. It was time to cement the victory with a flock of runs. Manager Alston could have pinch-hit for Podres but let the young pitcher hit. It was John's game to win or lose. He flied out for out number two and Jim Gilliam made the third out. The bottom of the ninth inning fell upon the Bronx, a familiar time for Yankees rallies.

In six of the first eight innings, the Yankees had managed at least one base runner against Podres. One lone base runner was all it took to bring the tying run to the plate. Bill Skowron, who had homered the previous day, led off and tapped harmlessly back to Podres. One down, two to go. Bob Cerv followed with a routine fly to Sandy Amoros and the Dodgers were one out away from erasing all the bad memories of the past. No one knows how many nails of Dodgers fans were bitten to the shank when Elston Howard stepped in and sent a ground ball to shortstop. Reese gobbled up the ball—and threw it low and wide to first base. In a flash, as the ball headed toward the dirt around first base, millions of Dodgers fans were engulfed with cold dread. But Gil Hodges, who had driven in both Dodgers runs that day and possessed one of the best gloves at the first-base position, stretched out and scooped the ball into his mitt only inches above the ground, and an unfamiliar joy swept across Brooklyn. It was finally "next year."

The telephone company in Brooklyn reported the greatest system overload since the day World War II ended. Arthur Daley, writing in the *New York Times*, summed up the spent emotions of the city:

> This was a game that was as fragile as the most delicate bit of Dresden china and the Brooks never had a firm hold on it. Those rude Yankees kept threatening to jar it loose from their grasp. . . .
>
> The Brooks squeezed out this victory like a thrifty housewife forcing the last drop out of an orange juice squeezer. . . .
>
> So enduring had been the impression that Brooklyn never could win a world series that the folks from Canarsie to Greenpoint undoubtedly will be checking their newspapers today just to be sure.

Johnny Podres went on to record impressive statistics in several more seasons with the Dodgers. He posted the lowest earned run average in the National League in 1957 and his won-loss percentage of .783 (18–5) led the senior circuit in 1961. He even won two more World Series games, in

1959 and 1963. But his shutout of the Yankees on October 4, 1955, meant more to the Dodgers' spirit than anything anybody else has ever done.

Millions have told the story of Johnny Podres to their children and to their children's children. As long as there is baseball, as long as there is America, the story will remain part of the national legacy.

October 4, 1955

	1	2	3	4	5	6	7	8	9	R	H	E
BROOKLYN (NL)	0	0	0	1	0	1	0	0	0	2	5	0
NEW YORK (AL)	0	0	0	0	0	0	0	0	0	0	8	1

PITCHERS: BKN: Podres (W); NYY: Byrne (L), Grim, Turley

DOUBLES: Berra, Campanella, Skowron

TRIPLES: None

HOME RUNS: None

ATTENDANCE: 62,465

TIME OF GAME: 2:44

1956

Back to Reality

New York Yankees 9
Brooklyn Dodgers 0

There was plenty of excitement for everybody in 1956. The movies were bigger than ever before. *The Ten Commandments*, *Around the World in 80 Days*, and *The King and I* dazzled our senses with Cinemascope and Technicolor. Soviet fat boy Nikita Khrushchev boasted, "We will bury you," but we knew they wouldn't. The DeSoto Firedome convertible was not something you saw every day, because they made only 646 of them.

Life was imitating art and vice versa. After all, the Tony Award for best musical went to *Damn Yankees*.

Something that had never before happened in the history of the world occurred at the start of the 1956 baseball season: the Brooklyn Dodgers came onto the field as defending world champions. To defend their crown they first would have to win the National League pennant with almost the same group of star players who brought them the title. In 1955 they won by more than a dozen games, but the 1956 season would present a formidable obstacle in the Milwaukee Braves. The Braves, led by Warren Spahn, Eddie Mathews, and a young Henry Aaron, gave the baseball world a glimpse of things soon to come but wound up a single game short of the Dodgers in 1956.

The fortunes of the Brooklyn Dodgers were down from 1955. Jackie Robinson was thirty-seven years old and played only part-time with the

Around the Horn in 1956

- Kansas City's Art Ditmar led the American League in losses with 22 but in 1960 he would lead the New York Yankees in wins and start the first game of the World Series. His teammate Troy Herriage went 1–13 for the Athletics but never made his way out of Kansas City.
- Tommy Lasorda ended his big-league playing career with the Kansas City Athletics. Tommy was a pitcher with a career record of 0–4 and ERA of 6.48. In 1997, he was elected to the Hall of Fame for his managerial skills, not his pitching skills.
- For the second time in his career, New York Giants catcher Wes Westrum caught three foul pop-ups in the same inning. No one has done it since and only two catchers had done it before.

Dodgers, hitting .275. His 12 stolen bases that year were good enough to tie him for sixth in the league but everyone could see that this was not the Jackie Robinson of old. No matter, because most of his mates performed well. *Most*. Duke Snider led the league in home runs with 43 round-trippers, Gil Hodges slugged 32 homers, and Jim Gilliam surprised everyone by hitting .300 as a full-time player. But one part of the Dodgers' attack was weakened. An early-season injury to Roy Campanella left Campy hobbled and a far howl from his MVP season the year before. His average slipped almost a hundred points from .318 to .219 and his power suffered a corresponding drop, going from 32 home runs and 107 RBIs to 20 dingers and 73 ribbies.

The Dodgers' offense by itself could not win the pennant. Of course, how often does offense alone win a championship? So the Dodgers' pitching was up to the task, led by Don Newcombe's dominating 27–7 season. Clem Labine led the league in saves with 19 and appeared in 62 games, all but three in relief. The late-season acquisition of veteran Sal Maglie gave the Dodgers the pitching edge they needed to nudge past the Braves by a single game and the Reds by two. It also helped make up for the U.S. Navy taking Johnny Podres for the season. To no one's surprise, Brooklyn's opponent in the World Series was the New York Yankees.

New York's Mickey Mantle did it all, winning the American League's MVP honors and the Triple Crown with his .353 batting average, 52 home runs, and 130 runs batted in. As if the Yankees needed anyone else on offense, Bill Skowron chimed in with a .308 average and 23 home runs of his own and Yogi Berra had another great year, hitting .298 and 30 homers while driving in 105 runs. There seemed to be few flaws in the Yankees' offense.

As for pitching, Whitey Ford was there when manager Casey Stengel needed him, posting a 19–6 record and leading the league in earned run average at 2.47. And as the Yankees had done year after year, they found a couple of unknowns to come through when Ford was not pitching. Johnny Kucks had made his major-league debut with the Yanks in 1955, winning 8 games and losing 7—not real impressive when you are pitching for the Yankees. In 1956, at the age of twenty-two, he had the best season of his big-league career, winning 18 games as New York's number-two starter. The Yankees also squeezed a productive year out of unheralded Tom Sturdivant (16–5) and there was no stopping the boys from the Bronx.

Baseball had itself another Dodgers-Yankees World Series, for the sixth time in ten years. If you lived in New York, where a subway token cost only fifteen cents, you loved it. It was good against evil, the powers of light versus the powers of darkness, the common man taking on the aristocracy. Whatever it was, America was getting used to it. And when it started in Brooklyn on October 3, 1956, America had not a hint of the historic drama that would soon unfold. Unfortunately, for fans of great Seventh Games, the high drama took place during some other skirmish between the warring teams.

Little need be said about the first four games. The Dodgers won the first two at home and lost the next two in Yankee Stadium. None of the games were close and they are important only because they set the stage for Game Five, the game that everyone remembers from that year. Yes, that was Don Larsen's perfect game, which put the Yankees ahead three games to two in the Series. This book is about Seventh Games, not fifth games, so all that needs to be told is that Don Larsen retired every Dodger he faced. It sounds so mundane, doesn't it? But only a few pitchers had ever performed such a feat in the history of the game, and no one else had ever done so in a World Series. It was historic and amazing and much has been written about it (including this paragraph) but it meant only that the

Dodgers would have to win Game Six in order to force a Game Seven—and that is what this book is about.

In case Don Larsen's perfect game has blinded you to the fact that the 1956 World Series went the distance, think of what the Dodgers must have been thinking. They had just been the unwilling victims of a master-piece by a pitcher whose career numbers to that point were barely note-worthy (30 wins against 44 losses) and whose final career statistics would be similarly unimpressive—he lost 10 more games than he won in fourteen seasons. The bad news for Brooklyn was that they had just been humili-ated *and* they needed to win the two remaining games of the Series; the good news was that being on the short end of a perfect game counted as only one defeat *and* they were going back to Ebbets Field.

In case anyone is interested, there was a Seventh Game that year. The way Brooklyn got to that Seventh Game was every bit as dramatic as Don Larsen's two-hour and thirty-seven-minute outing. As for the Seventh Game? They can't all be gems. Game Six was too tough of an act to follow.

The Dodgers were facing elimination. Manager Walt Alston was leery about using his ace, Don Newcombe, in Game Six because the Yankees had whacked him pretty hard in Game Two, although the Dodgers had come back to win it. How better to relieve your anxiety than to bring in your premier relief pitcher! Alston called on Clem Labine to start the sixth game. Labine had started just three games all season. What was Walter thinking?

He must have been thinking good thoughts. Even though the Dodgers could not get through to Yankees pitcher Bob Turley, neither could the Yankees do a thing with Labine. For only the second time in World Series history, a game was scoreless after the regulation nine innings of play; someone would be a hero.

With Game Six scoreless in the bottom of the tenth, Jim Gilliam walked and went to second on Reese's sacrifice bunt. Casey Stengel ordered an intentional walk to Duke Snider and Jackie Robinson came to bat. Jackie singled over the head of left fielder Enos Slaughter—the same Enos Slaugh-ter who had scored from first base for the Cardinals in 1946—and the Dodgers had forced a Seventh Game. No one knew that Robbie's dramatic hit in the bottom of the tenth inning on October 9, 1956, would be his last.

It was time for another Game Seven. The Dodgers had scored just one run in their last 18⅔ innings but there they were, facing the New York Yankees in a Seventh Game. As everyone knows, when it comes down to one game, anything can happen.

There was no way to avoid it: Don Newcombe, winner of 27 games during the regular season, would get the start, despite his shaky Game Two performance. The truth is that Newk had never done well in the postseason, sporting an ugly 0–3 record. But you cannot fault Alston's decision to go with the man who got him there.

The Yankees called on their sophomore phenom, Johnny Kucks. Sure, he had a good year, but it was nothing like Newcombe's year. The tension and drama that filled the streets of Brooklyn that brisk October afternoon lasted about six minutes. The Yankees' Hank Bauer led off the game with a single and stole second. After Newcombe fanned Billy Martin and Mickey Mantle, Yogi Berra belted a two-run home run. Ouch.

The Dodgers came up in the bottom of the first eager to do some damage off Yankees pitcher Kucks. With one out, Pee Wee Reese walked and Duke Snider singled. The Dodgers would come back and come back hard. However, the only thing that came back hard was Jackie Robinson's ground ball, right back to the mound. Kucks fired to Martin at second, who threw back to Skowron at first for an inning-ending double play. No one at Ebbets Field would have believed it if someone had said that this was the only time the Dodgers would put two runners on in any one inning that day. That is how good Johnny Kucks was.

Newcombe seemed to recover from his "mistake" to Berra. He got through the Yankees' second without giving up any runs. The Dodgers went in order in the bottom half of the inning. In the top of the third, Billy Martin singled. With two out, Yogi Berra stepped to the plate. It seems that if Newcombe recovered from his first-inning mistake to Yogi, he didn't learn from it. Yogi swatted another two-run homer and the score was 4–0. At least Newcombe had struck out the Yankees' best hitter, Mickey Mantle, not once but twice. And it had been only two bad pitches that put the Yankees on the board. It soon became three bad pitches. Elston Howard led off the Yankees' fourth with a solo home run and Walter Alston dismissed Don Newcombe from the game. A succession of Dodgers pitchers followed, but the celebrated Yankees power had made its mark.

If anyone at Ebbets Field entertained thoughts of a late-inning rally, Bill Skowron took care of those thoughts with a grand-slam home run in the seventh inning. Although other players have hit grand slams in the World Series, Skowron's was the only one in a Seventh Game. That was the end of the scoring. It was a crushing and sorrowful performance by the Dodgers in their last World Series game in Brooklyn. They would play one more season in the borough of Brooklyn before becoming the Los Angeles Dodgers in 1958.

Someone had to make the final out. Nobody concedes a match in baseball. With two out in the ninth inning Duke Snider picked up his bat and approached home plate. The Duke would not give Casey Stengel the satisfaction of being the last out that day; he singled to center. No one likes to be the last out in a game, but when defeat is certain—as it was that day in Brooklyn—you need a man of courage to sacrifice himself and end the suffering. Jackie Robinson struck out to end the massacre. There was no way that Jackie Robinson *tried* to make that last out. But if any man could shoulder the pain of making the last out in the Seventh Game of a World Series, it was Jackie Robinson. Considering the scorn and abuse he had endured in his major-league career, it was just one more heroic act in a lifetime of nobility. It was also his last at-bat in a Dodgers uniform; Jackie retired before the 1957 season began.

There have been nine shutouts in Seventh Game history and Johnny Kucks can boast that he is the only pitcher to hurl one and claim a losing record over the course of his big-league career. No matter what you want to say about Johnny Kucks, on October 10, 1956, he was the best pitcher in baseball and no one can take away from him that last moment of glory. In the remaining four years of his career he pitched with the Yankees and finally with the Kansas City A's, winning 28 games and losing 40, for a career mark of 54–56.

Don Newcombe stayed with the Dodgers long enough to see Los Angeles and finished his career in Cleveland on nearly the same day that Johnny Kucks made his last appearance in a big-league uniform. Newk deserved better than what he got in the World Series, especially in his only Seventh Game appearance.

Elvis Presley had two big hits in 1956: "Don't Be Cruel" and "Heartbreak Hotel." Was he thinking of a particular team in Brooklyn when he sang them?

October 10, 1956

	1	2	3	4	5	6	7	8	9	R	H	E
NEW YORK (AL)	2	0	2	1	0	0	4	0	0	9	10	0
BROOKLYN (NL)	0	0	0	0	0	0	0	0	0	0	3	1

PITCHERS: NYY: Kucks (W); BKN: Newcombe (L), Bessent, Craig, Roebuck, Erskine

DOUBLES: Howard, Mantle

TRIPLES: None

HOME RUNS: Berra (2), Howard, Skowron

ATTENDANCE: 33,782

TIME OF GAME: 2:19

1957

Sweet Lew

Milwaukee Braves 5
New York Yankees 0

Life was heaven in '57. The Everly Brothers scored big with "Bye Bye Love." Buddy Holly and the Crickets recorded "That'll Be the Day" and "Peggy Sue." Americans were glued to the tube by new shows like "Have Gun Will Travel," "Maverick," and "Leave It to Beaver." *The Bridge on the River Kwai* won the Oscar for best picture by if you were really cool, you drove around in a red '57 Chevy. Even today, that defines the essence of cool.

The world entered the space age during the World Series of 1957. On October 4, between the second and third games, the Soviet Union launched *Sputnik I*, the first unmanned satellite placed into orbit. You had to figure that the World Series would take on some kind of "otherworldly" character.

Someone finally took the National League pennant out of New York and off the East Coast. From 1951 through 1956 either the Dodgers or the Giants won it, and except for one year they played the Yankees for the world championship. What about October baseball for the rest of the country? The new kids on the block took care of things.

These new kids were not all that new but they were playing in a new city. The Braves had moved from Boston to Milwaukee after the 1952 season. Owner Lou Perini figured that Boston was not big enough for two

Around the Horn in 1957

- The lead-footed Washington Senators set the all-time record for fewest stolen bases by a team in a single season: 13.
- Willie Mays became the second and last player to date to join the exclusive 20-20-20-20 club—at least 20 doubles, triples, home runs, and stolen bases in the same season. The only other member of the club is Wildfire Schulte of the 1911 Chicago Cubs. (Schulte was the first major leaguer to hit 20 home runs in a season.)
- Washington's Roy Sievers led the American League in home runs and RBIs. It was the only time in major-league history a player on a last-place team could boast that dual achievement.

teams and was the first National League owner to hear the voice that beckoned, "Go west!" The Braves did not want to venture too far west so they settled on the western shore of Lake Michigan, in a city known more for beer than baseball. In their first season at Milwaukee's County Stadium, the Braves broke all National League attendance records and were duly rewarded by gracing the cover of the first issue of *Sports Illustrated* in 1954. In turn, they rewarded their new fans with winning teams from the very beginning of their stay in Wisconsin. In 1957, in only their fifth season in Milwaukee, they won the pennant.

The 1957 Milwaukee Braves were a powerful team, led by a young slugger by the name of Hank Aaron. Aaron's 44 home runs and 132 RBIs were tops in all of baseball. At the end of the season, he had amassed a total of 110 home runs in his four-year career. As good as Aaron was at the age of twenty-three, no one saw him as a serious threat to break Babe Ruth's magical record of 714 lifetime homers. Not then anyway.

Aaron did not do it alone. Future Hall of Famer Eddie Mathews, playing in his fifth season, put up impressive power numbers of his own and the rest of the team chipped in with timely hitting to beat out the Cardinals by eight games. Bob "Hurricane" Hazle gave the Braves an end-of-season boost by hitting .403 in 41 games. As for pitching, everyone knew that the ace of the Braves was the lefty with the high leg kick, Warren Spahn. Spahn led the team and all of baseball with 21 victories and did it at the age of thirty-six. Spahn's age was no big deal in 1957. Stan Musial led the National League in hitting at the age of thirty-six and Ted Williams led the American League in batting at the age of thirty-eight.

Milwaukee had two other capable starting pitchers, Bob Buhl and Lew Burdette. Buhl won 18 games, lost only 7, and was always tough to hit, even though he walked a lot of enemy batters. Lew Burdette, winner of 17 games in 1957, had broken in with the 1950 Yankees but never got a chance to show his stuff in New York, as the Yankees sent him off to the Boston Braves after seeing him in only two games. The Yankees made very few personnel mistakes in the 1950s but letting Lew go was one of them.

The Yankees won the American League pennant again. There were things you could count on in the fifties and Yankees supremacy in the American League was one of them. Mickey Mantle led the team with 34 homers and a .365 average and the rest of the offense was adequate. The real strength of the team was pitching, and it came from unexpected players. Tom Sturdivant and Bob Turley gave Casey Stengel solid performances and relief pitcher Bob Grim was the league leader in saves. But the Yankees' magic was most evident when they picked up little Bobby Shantz from the Kansas City Athletics' rummage sale. Shantz, all five feet six inches of him, led the league in ERA and gave Casey the versatile starter/reliever he needed to plug up the holes created by Whitey Ford's injury and Johnny Kucks's terrible season.

Whitey Ford recovered from his injuries in time to open the World Series with a win over Warren Spahn in New York. Lew Burdette won Game Two, allowing single runs in the second and third innings but nothing after that. The Yankees should have savored that second run, coming in as it did on a cheap infield single, because that was all Burdette would give them through the remainder of the Series. After splitting the next two games in Milwaukee, Burdette got the call for Game Five and shut out the Yankees and Whitey Ford, 1–0. The Milwaukee Braves were a victory away but would have to claim it in New York.

In the Sixth Game, the Yankees' Hank Bauer broke a 2–2 tie with a seventh-inning home run and Bob Turley bested Bob Buhl to set up the third Seventh Game in as many years. It was Warren Spahn's turn to pitch but Spahnie had come down with the flu so Milwaukee manager Fred Haney called on Lew Burdette for one more game. Stengel countered with Don Larsen, and not because he had pitched a perfect game the year before. Larsen had already pitched well in the Series, earning the win in Game Three with seven and a third innings of solid relief.

Larsen was sharp to start the game, retiring the Braves in order in the opening frame and striking out Bill Bruton and Bob Hazle. When Hank Bauer led off the Yankees' first with a double, Stengel again looked like a genius. But the Yankees could not bring Bauer home and the game moved into the second inning, then into the third, scoreless. That was when the Braves erupted for four runs and their dream of a world championship moved closer to reality.

The Milwaukee third started harmlessly when Lew Burdette fouled out. Bob Hazle followed with a single. Johnny Logan grounded to Tony Kubek, playing third base for only the second game of the Series, who fielded the ball cleanly but threw wildly to second base. Third base was not Tony's best position and it showed on that play. He made two errors in the 1957 Series, both at the third-base position. Would a better throw have meant an inning-ending double play? The official rules of scoring do not allow the assumption of a double play but simple addition, as in "two outs plus one equals three," makes everything abundantly clear: but for Kubek's bad throw, the game might have stayed scoreless for some time.

Eddie Mathews took advantage of the situation with a two-run double to the corner in right field. Never one to leave pitchers in too long, Stengel brought in Bobby Shantz to face Aaron. Hammerin' Hank responded with a single up the middle, scoring Mathews. Wes Covington singled and Aaron took third. Frank Torre grounded to second base, but not hard enough to let the Yankees turn the double play. Aaron came home on the force play and the Braves led, 4–0. Lew Burdette had all the runs he would need.

Burdette did not overpower the Yankees. He struck out only three. But the Yankees could not find a way to score. They had two runners on in the sixth inning when Gil McDougald ended the threat with an easy grounder to Mathews. Tony Kubek led off the seventh with a single, only the second time the Yankees could get their leadoff hitter on base, but New York could do nothing to draw closer to the Braves and their four-run bulge. In the Milwaukee eighth, catcher Del Crandall hit a solo home run to finish the scoring for the day.

The Yankees were surely finished. They could not solve the puzzle of Selva Lewis Burdette Jr. They went down in order in the eighth. The only question seemed to be whether they could score at least a run and avert the embarrassment of a shutout. After Yogi Berra popped to first to open the bottom of the ninth inning, Yankees fans began to lose hope. But they were not just any team, they were the New York Yankees. If any team could mount a comeback, it was this group of hard-nosed ballplayers led by the master of postseason success, Casey Stengel. And sure enough, Gil McDougald singled. Facing a five-run deficit, a one-out single in the bottom of the ninth can hardly be deemed a rally but it was a start. Tony Kubek followed with a routine fly ball to Hank Aaron for the second out and the Yankees were down to their final out. All but the heartiest and most optimistic Yankees fans began making their way to the exits.

Jerry Coleman teased a single to right, sending McDougald to second. The fifth Yankees pitcher of the day had been the veteran Tommy Byrne and it was his turn to bat. Casey let him hit, not because it was the end of Byrne's career but because Byrne was always a good hitter, at least as good as anyone Casey could bring off the bench. Byrne singled and the bases were loaded. The batter was Bill Skowron. Everyone remembered that Skowron, only one year before, had hit the only grand-slam home run in Seventh Game history. A second grand slammer, of which Moose Skowron was perfectly capable, would take the Yankees to within a run and bring up the top of the batting order. The shutout was now in jeopardy and a Braves victory was no longer assured.

Bill Skowron found the pitch he wanted and pulled it sharply down the third-base line. Eddie Mathews, feared mostly for his bat but always respected for his glove, made a diving stop and stepped on third base to end the game. Lew Burdette had shut out the Yankees twice in the Series and became the first pitcher since 1920 to record three complete-game wins in a World Series.

Lew Burdette's pitching success did not end with his heroics in the 1957 World Series. He won 78 games over the next four years with Milwaukee and ended his career in 1967 with more than 200 victories. Some have accused Lew of "loading 'em up," of throwing illegal spitballs. At one time during the Series, Yankees first baseman Joe Collins asked the home plate umpire to examine the ball because, in Collins's own words, "Something didn't look kosher to me." Whatever the reason for Burdette's success, the fans of Milwaukee will never forget him.

A crowd of 400,000 showed up to greet the Braves when they arrived in Milwaukee. A band played "On Wisconsin," the fight song of the University of Wisconsin at Madison, because the Braves never had a song of their own. The beer flowed freely that night. Oh well, it was Milwaukee, and the beer always flowed. On this night there was a good reason for it.

October 10, 1957

	1	2	3	4	5	6	7	8	9	R	H	E
MILWAUKEE (NL)	0	0	4	0	0	0	0	1	0	5	9	1
NEW YORK (AL)	0	0	0	0	0	0	0	0	0	0	7	3

PITCHERS: MIL: Burdette (W); NYY: Larsen (L), Shantz, Ditmar, Sturdivant, Byrne

DOUBLES: Bauer, Mathews

TRIPLES: None

HOME RUNS: Crandall

ATTENDANCE: 61,207

TIME OF GAME: 2:34

1958

Turnabout Is Fair Play

New York Yankees 6
Milwaukee Braves 2

Everyone remembers 1958, because that was when Americans first gyrated with a hula hoop. We had our first tastes of JIF brand peanut butter, Cocoa Puffs, and Rice-a-Roni ("The San Francisco Treat"). Men's all-wool flannel suits were only $28.88 at Robert Hall, including alterations. The U.S. Army's newest private was Elvis Presley and back home Ross Bagdassarian had two giant hits, silly as they were, with "Witch Doctor" and "The Chipmunk Song." If you wanted real music, though, there was Duane Eddy's "Rebel Rouser," Bobby Darin's "Splish Splash," and "Tears on My Pillow" by Little Anthony and the Imperials.

Things were hot in 1958, but the hottest thing going was Elizabeth Taylor in *Cat on a Hot Tin Roof*. Michael Jackson was born and so was Madonna Louise Ciccone (did she donate the last two names to charity?). The coolest new TV shows were "77 Sunset Strip" and "Bat Masterson." Boris Pasternak won the Nobel Prize for literature but he politely declined. The New York Yankees had no intention of declining another World Series title, especially at the expense of the upstart Milwaukee Braves.

The Yankees won the American League pennant for the fourth year in a row and ninth time in ten years. But they were facing an unfamiliar and totally unnatural situation. They were not the defending champions of baseball. That honor belonged to the Braves of Milwaukee, Wisconsin, and

Around the Horn in 1958

- ☽ The Cleveland Indians traded Roger Maris to the Kansas City Athletics.
- ☽ Cleveland's Vic Power became the last player to steal home twice in the same game (August 14).
- ☽ Even though Warren Spahn, Lew Burdette, and Bob Rush were the big-name starters for the Milwaukee Braves and their only pitchers with 10 or more wins, Carl Willey led the team and the league in shutouts with four. Willey started only 19 games and went 9–7, but with a 2.70 ERA, lower than the ERA of any of the big three Braves pitchers.

the two teams would meet again in 1958 to retest each other's mettle. The World Series had gone to seven games in each of the last three years, matching the string that baseball saw in 1924, 1925, and 1926. Could it be four in a row with the 1958 Series?

Was there ever a doubt that the Yankees would win the American League in 1958? The Red Sox may have had the batting champ in Ted Williams, the RBI leader in Jackie Jensen, and the league's all-star third baseman in Frank Malzone, but they had terrible pitching and finished third. The White Sox may have had a strong pitching staff, led by Billy Pierce and Dick Donovan, and the league's premier shortstop and base stealer in Luis Aparicio, but could fare no better than second, a distant 10 games behind New York.

As expected, Yankees hurler Whitey Ford had another great season, winning 14 games and posting the league's lowest earned run average. But it was Bob Turley, giving his best season with 21 wins, who made the difference for New York. Mickey Mantle led the offense with his league-leading 42 home runs and the Yankees were ready to take back what the Braves had wrestled from them in 1957.

The Braves won the National League pennant with much the same squad that had given them the championsip in 1957. Hank Aaron and Eddie Mathews provided the offensive punch, while Warren Spahn and Lew Burdette each won 20 games to anchor the pitching staff. They knew that history was against them. The New York Yankees were in their twenty-fourth World Series since first making it into the Fall Classic in 1921. While the Yankees did not win all of their World Series appearances, they had never lost two in a row since losing in their very first trips in 1921 and 1922. The Braves thought it would finally happen in 1958.

The Series opened with a matchup of sylish lefties, Whitey Ford against Warren Spahn. Billy Bruton's single in the bottom of the tenth off reliever Ryne Duren won it for Milwaukee. The Braves exploded for seven runs in the first inning of Game Two, capped by pitcher Lew Burdette's three-run homer, coasting to a 13–5 win. They went to New York up by two games.

The Yankees bounced back in Game Three behind Don Larsen's six-hit shutout. Warren Spahn turned around to blank the Yankees on five hits in Game Four to put Milwaukee ahead, three games to one. Only one team in history, the 1925 Pittsburgh Pirates, had overcome such a deficit. If the Yankees were to become the second team, they would have to win Game Five at home and the final two games on the road. At least the 1925 Pirates had the luxury of playing their final two games at home.

So the Yankees went to work. The first order of business was Game Five and they had to face their old October nemesis, Lew Burdette. Lew had beat them three times in the 1957 Series and again in the second game of the 1958 Series. If anyone had the Yankees' number, it was Lew. But not that day. Bob Turley came back from the whipping that the Braves gave him in Game Two to shut out Milwaukee and send the Series back to the Beer City.

The Yankees were facing elimination on enemy ground in Game Six but forced a Seventh Game with a tough 4–3 win in ten innings. New York scored two in the top of the tenth, gave up a run in the bottom of the inning, and narrowly escaped when Frank Torre lined out with runners on base to end the game. Ryne Duren took the Game Six win with four and two-thirds strong innings of relief but needed last-out help from Bullet Bob Turley.

So it was that for the first and last time in the history of the World Series (so far), there would be a Seventh Game in four consecutive years. The Yankees had crawled back to even the Series, but the Milwaukee Braves must have felt good about their chances. They were at home and had Lew Burdette on the mound, the same Lew Burdette who had shut out the Yankees in the Seventh Game of the 1957 World Series. The Yankees countered with Don Larsen, known not just for his 1956 perfect game but also for his more recent shutout performance in Game Three. Two World Series star pitchers were about to treat the fans to a ball game.

The Braves struck first but could have, should have, scored more. After Red Schoendienst singled and Billy Bruton walked to open the bottom of the first inning, Frank Torre bunted the runners to second and third. Hank Aaron walked to load the bases and Don Larsen was in trouble. Wes Covington grounded out to first, scoring Schoendienst and moving Bruton and Aaron along. Yankees manager Casey Stengel made the move he had to make, ordering an intentional walk to the dangerous left-handed slugger Eddie Mathews to load the bases. To the plate came the Braves' sturdy catcher, Del Crandall, to face a struggling Don Larsen.

Delmar Wesley Crandall had come off a fine season. He was an all-star catcher with one other significant accomplishment on his résumé: he was then one of only ten players to hit a home run in a World Series Seventh Game. He would inscribe his name in the history books a few innings later but in the first inning of Game Seven in 1958, with the bases loaded for his Braves, Del Crandall watched as strike three darted across home plate. For all the fuss and fury, the Milwaukee Braves led by only one run, 1–0.

Poor defense reared its ugly head in the top of the second. Yogi Berra walked to start the inning. Casey Stengel took the conservative approach and ordered Elston Howard to bunt. Frank Torre fielded the bunt cleanly but threw wildly to first. Jerry Lumpe, a decent if unexciting line-drive hitter in only his third year with the Yankees, then hit a ground ball to Frank Torre. Torre's only play was at first base and he threw to Lew Burdette, who hustled over to the bag. But again it was a bad throw and the bases were loaded. Bill Skowron grounded into a force play for the first out of the inning, but it allowed the Yankees to tie the game. The run was, of course, unearned, as the Braves should have been on their way to the dugout except for Frank Torre's two errant throws. Tony Kubek followed with a sacrifice fly and the Yankees were in the lead. When Don Larsen made the third out of the inning, the Yankees realized they had been the beneficiaries of some very good luck, for they had taken the lead with two runs without benefit of a hit. It was only the second time a team had been so fortunate in a Seventh Game; the 1909 Pittsburgh Pirates also turned the trick.

In his seven-year career in the big leagues, Frank Torre committed only 28 regular-season errors and was known as one of the National

League's best-fielding first basemen. He is now better known as the big brother of Joe Torre, who hit nearly .300 in his eighteen seasons in the bigs and went on to a successful managerial career with the Mets, Braves, Cardinals, and Yankees. Brother Frank's fielding prowess has been long forgotten by most, although his two lapses in Game Seven in 1958 remain unforgiven by some.

Don Larsen settled down after his difficult first inning and retired the Braves in order in the bottom of the second. In the home half of the third, Billy Bruton singled to start an uprising. Frank Torre tried so hard, probably too hard, to make up for his two costly errors and popped out. But Hank Aaron poked a single to left. Old Casey had no more patience with Don Larsen and brought in Bob Turley. Turley, a 21-game winner during the season, had pitched the Game Five shutout in New York and saved Game Six. He was Casey's hot pitcher and there was no need to mess around with anyone else.

If Yogi Berra really did coin the phrase "It's déjà vu all over again," he might have had the first and third innings of the 1958 Seventh Game in mind when he said it. Just as in the first inning, Wes Covington came to bat with one out and runners aboard, this time on first and second. And just as in the first inning, Covington bounced out, advancing the runners to second and third. And just as in the first inning, Casey Stengel ordered his pitcher to walk Eddie Mathews to load the bases. And just as in the first inning, Del Crandall came to bat.

Del Crandall had another chance to deliver. He was in no mood for "déjà vu," recalling how he took a called strike three to end the first inning. This time he made contact, sending the ball back at a stunned Bob Turley. The Yankees' pitcher could not field it and it deflected off him in the direction of second baseman Gil McDougald. McDougald calmly picked up the ball and flipped it to first base to end the inning. In two at-bats, Del Crandall had left six of his teammates on base. Burdette and Turley battled on, with neither pitcher giving way to opposing batters for anything of substance. Then came the bottom of the sixth inning.

Bob Turley had not yet allowed a hit in his relief outing. Wes Covington flied out and Eddie Mathews grounded out to open the bottom of the sixth. It was Del Crandall's turn to hit. Can anyone imagine the feelings of disappointment that Del must have felt at that moment? He had twice made the last out with the bases loaded, letting down not only his fellow Braves but the city of Milwaukee and its surrounding towns as well.

The eager little boys from Wauwatosa, Racine, and Kenosha begged for one good hit and Del Crandall came through for them. He caught a fat one and drove it deep to left field, deep, deep, and deep enough. Crandall had made history. He became the only player to ever hit home runs in successive Seventh Games. The game was tied and it was a brand-new day in Milwaukee. If only his power had come alive a few innings earlier.

Johnny Logan lined out to end the inning but Del Crandall's home run had breathed new hope into the hometown fans, who now prepared themselves for a nail-biting finish. No one scored in the seventh inning and the tie was unbroken, until two were out in the eighth inning.

Lew Burdette had looked sharp for seven and two-thirds innings. Then it all fell apart. Yogi Berra doubled and Elston Howard singled to break the tie. But it was only one run and the Braves were as capable of making up a one-run shortfall as any team in baseball. Andy Carey then singled and Bill Skowron brought his bat to the plate. And he used it to destroy the dreams of another world championship in Milwaukee. His three-run home run was more than the Braves could overcome.

Bob Turley continued his strong pitching. Milwaukee went down in order in the eighth inning. In the bottom of the ninth, Eddie Mathews walked to open the frame but Crandall and Logan made outs to bring the team to the edge. Joe Adcock's pinch single teased the crowd for an instant but Red Schoendienst ended the game with a line drive to Mickey Mantle. The Yankees had wrestled the last three games of the Series from the Braves to exact their revenge for 1957.

It was Bob Turley's finest hour, and he would never again win more than nine games in any of his remaining five seasons in baseball. The Braves would return to the World Series many years later, but only long after leaving Milwaukee for Atlanta. No one knew it at the time, but the 1958 Seventh Game victory was Casey Stengel's last championship. Coming back from so far down must have been the sweetest of all for the Old Professor.

October 9, 1958

	1	2	3	4	5	6	7	8	9	R	H	E
NEW YORK (AL)	0	2	0	0	0	0	0	4	0	6	8	0
MILWAUKEE (NL)	1	0	0	0	0	1	0	0	0	2	5	2

PITCHERS: NYY: Larsen, Turley (W); MIL: Burdette (L), McMahon

DOUBLES: Berra, McDougald

TRIPLES: None

HOME RUNS: Crandall, Skowron

ATTENDANCE: 46,367

TIME OF GAME: 2:31

1960

Maz the Magnificent

New York Yankees   9
Pittsburgh Pirates   10

Two days before the 1960 World Series opened, America caught its first glimpse at the town of Mayberry when "The Andy Griffith Show" made its national debut. And it was shortly before that when Fred Flintstone made his first appearance on national television. If you were not a TV fan, or just did not have a television set, you could go the movies and see *Psycho* or *Inherit the Wind*. Or you could stay home and play with your new Etch-A-Sketch.

There was great music, too, in 1960. Mark Dinning recorded one of the all-time great teenage death songs, "Teen Angel." Connie Francis was singing "Everybody's Somebody's Fool" and Roy Orbison belted out "Only the Lonely." Brian Hyland had a tongue-twisting hit with "Itsy Bitsy Teenie Weenie Yellow Polka Dot Bikini," but the real twisting hit belonged to Ernest Evans—aka Chubby Checker—who scored with the new dance sensation and song "The Twist."

There was also serious news in 1960. The Russians shot down an American U-2 spy plane and captured its pilot, Francis Gary Powers. America saw the first televised presidential debate and politicians learned from Richard Nixon that a little makeup can go a long way when John Kennedy was declared the winner and went on to the presidency. Of course, there was baseball because America still loved to play.

Around the Horn in 1960

- ◔ Don Larsen, author of baseball's only World Series perfect game in 1956, was suddenly at the bottom of the league, going 1–10 with the last-place Kansas City A's. Don was no stranger to horrible won-loss records, as he had posted a 3–21 mark with the Orioles in 1954.
- ◔ In the most controversial trade of the year, the Cleveland Indians sent their popular slugger Rocky Colavito to Detroit in exchange for high-average singles hitter Harvey Kuenn.
- ◔ Baltimore's Brooks Robinson won the first of his sixteen consecutive Gold Glove Awards. He replaced Boston's Frank Malzone as the American League's perennial Gold Glover at third base.

The Yankees bounced back from a third-place finish in 1959 to take the American League by eight games over the Baltimore Orioles. Casey Stengel had pulled another rabbit out of his cap and found a previously unheralded pitcher to lead his staff to the pennant. Art Ditmar had been a so-so pitcher for New York since 1957 but blossomed into Stengel's top starter in 1960 by winning 15 games. Ditmar's record in 1960 is probably more an indication of the overall weakness of the Yankees' pitching staff than a glowing tribute to Art's pitching skills. It was a difficult year for pitching all around the American League. No one won 20 games and only three pitchers were able to win more than 15. The Yankees had mediocre pitching in 1960, a year when mediocrity was at a premium.

The New York Yankees won the 1960 pennant with raw and unrelenting power. They set an American League record for home runs with 193 round-trippers, led, as usual, by Mickey Mantle and his league-leading 40. Close behind at 39 was the Yankees' newest steal from the Kansas City A's, a young left-handed batter with a swing made for the short right-field porch of Yankee Stadium, Roger Eugene Maris. Naturally, Bill Skowron and Yogi Berra contributed too.

As good as the Yankees were—and they were very, very good—the National League provided a formidable foe for them in the World Series.

For the first time since 1927, the Pittsburgh Pirates were in the World Series. Most Pirates fans did their best to forget the 1927 Series, when the Yankees swept away the Bucs with a team also built on home run power, led by Babe Ruth and Lou Gehrig. The 1960 Pirates may not have hit home runs to match the Yankees but they hit for higher average and featured two solid starters, Vern Law and Bob Friend, and a classy reliever, Roy Face.

Die-hard Pirate fans still talk about the 1960 World Series, often and with tones of reverence. If you were a baseball fan in 1960, you remember it well. The theme of the first six games was clear: when the Yankees won, they won by a lot. When the Pirates won, they won by a little. It was that simple.

The Pirates tagged Yankees starter Art Ditmar for three runs in the first inning of the opener and held on to win, 6–4. The Yankees went ahead in the Series by winning Games Two and Three by a combined score of 26 to 3. Mickey Mantle led the assault on the hapless Pirate pitchers with three home runs in the two games and Pittsburgh had to be wondering what hit them. No other team in the history of the World Series had ever scored so many runs in back-to-back games. But they counted for only two wins.

Undaunted by the Yankees' excessive display of fireworks, the Pirates nipped them in Game Four, 3–2. Pittsburgh took the lead in the Series by winning Game Five, 5–2, in the only game of the Series that saw the Pirates outhit the Yankees. The teams returned to Pittsburgh, where the Pirates needed only one game to win it all. The Yankees gave the ball to their veteran southpaw, Whitey Ford. Even though 1960 was an off year by Whitey's standards (he won only 12 games, but with a team-best earned run average of 3.08), Whitey had already shut out the Pirates in the Game Three blowout, 10–0. Whitey did it again in Game Six, shutting out Pittsburgh and sending the Series to a Seventh Game. The damage was even greater this time: 12–0.

Perhaps it was the ethic of the day. If you started the game and your team was winning, you finished the game, unless something was seriously wrong with you. Casey Stengel could have removed Ford after six, maybe seven innings, because the outcome of Game Six was already assured. Why didn't Casey save a little bit of Whitey, "just in case"?

The story of Games One through Six is a story of contrasts and extremes. The Yankees had outscored the Pirates, 46 to 17. The Yankees had outhit the Pirates, 78 to 42. The Yankees had outhomered the Pirates, eight to one. But the games were tied, three apiece. No one could have foreseen what happened in Game Seven. If ever there were a case for requiring the use of seat belts at a baseball game, it was Game Seven of the 1960 World Series.

The Pirates wanted to keep the scoring down, to make sure the supercharged Yankees offense did not get into high gear. The Yankees wanted to do what they did best, score lots of runs and leave the Pirates gasping for air. Bob Turley, hero of the 1958 Seventh Game and winner of the Game Two Yankees blowout, started for Casey Stengel. Vern Law, winner of Games One and Four, started for Pittsburgh manager Danny Murtaugh.

Vern Law retired the Yankees in order in both the first and second innings. Meanwhile, the Pirates jumped all over Bob Turley. Rocky Nelson, getting only his second start of the Series, hit a two-run homer in the first to give the Pirates a quick 2–0 lead. They doubled that lead in the second when Vern Law grounded into a bases-loaded double play for one run and Bill Virdon singled home another. Bob Turley was gone but Vern Law was sharp, giving up only a pair of singles through the first four innings. The Yankees were on their third pitcher, Bobby Shantz, and were holding the Pirates in check after the second inning.

Bill Skowron led off the Yankees' fifth with a solo home run. It was Skowron's third Seventh Game homer, and no one before or since has hit more. (Teammate Yogi Berra also has three.) There was no reason for Pirates fans to panic. After all, a 4–1 game was exactly the kind of game the Pirates had been winning and the kind they wanted.

After surrendering the home run to Skowron, Law retired the next three Yankees batters and the Pirates were now nursing a 4–1 lead, hoping to add to it in the bottom of the inning. But they could not get through to Bobby Shantz and the three-run Pirate lead was their margin going into the sixth inning. Vern Law had made only one bad pitch, to Skowron, and the hometown fans were counting on him to continue his masterful performance. He never retired another Yankee.

Bobby Richardson led off the sixth with a single. When Tony Kubek walked, manager Danny Murtaugh decided that it was time for his ace reliever, Elroy Face. Roy Face had become a legend in 1959 as he won 18 games and lost only once, all in relief. In 1960 he was still effective, though not as spectacular, with a 10–8 record and 24 saves. Of greater significance to Danny Murtaugh was what Roy Face had already done in the 1960 World Series—he had saved all three Pirates wins. He was a master of the forkball, a pitch that, when it was working, dipped sharply as it approached home plate. It was a thing of beauty, when it was working. But when it failed to dip . . .

First to face Mr. Face was Mr. Maris and Mr. Maris fouled out. Next came Mickey Mantle and Mickey rapped a single to center to bring home Bobby Richardson. The score was now 4–2 and the confidence that had filled Forbes Field only moments earlier changed to concern. Not panic, just concern. Yogi Berra changed that feeling into dread when he jerked a forkball that forgot to fork deep down the right-field line for a three-run home run. Yogi waddled and danced as he saw the ball arch into the stands. The Yankees had come back to take the lead, 5–4, and Forbes Field was in shock. It would get worse.

The Pirates could not mount any kind of threat in the bottom of the sixth inning but at least they kept the Yankees from further scoring in the seventh inning. In the bottom of the seventh, Smokey Burgess, the portly left-handed Pirates catcher who showed the world that you don't have to be slender and handsome to hit big-league pitching, singled. Joe Christopher ran for Smokey because running was not Smokey's forte. Don Hoak lined to left field and up came Bill Mazeroski. Maz was the best defensive second baseman of his era, a smooth-fielding, hustling kind of player who every manager dreamed of putting in his infield. He was not known for his hitting prowess and that was why Danny Murtaugh batted him eighth in the lineup. But it had been an unusually productive Series for Maz. His Game One homer was the only Pirates home run in the first six games, and he had also banged out a couple of doubles. This, though, was not Bill Mazeroski's time. He grounded into a double play and the inning was over.

There were two innings left in regulation play but it was as if the teams had decided to begin playing a whole new game. Pittsburgh needed a new catcher because Smokey Burgess was no longer available. Hal Smith put on the shin guards, chest protector, and mask and took the warm-up throws from Elroy Face. The Pirates had the time and the talent to come back from a one-run deficit and looked ahead to the bottom of the eighth inning, when the top of their order would get a chance to hit. Roy Face would first have to get by Roger Maris and Mickey Mantle. Neither got the ball to leave the infield and the first two Yankees, the most dangerous two Yankees, were out. Yogi Berra, already a Yankees hero for his sixth-inning home run, drew a walk. Bill Skowron, who had also homered that day, bounced a single to third base. John Blanchard followed with a single to score Yogi and extend the Yankees' lead. Cletis Boyer followed with a line double to left, scoring Bill Skowron and bringing a cloud of gloom upon Forbes Field. The Pirates had blown a four-run lead and now, with the score 7–4, had a three-run mountain to climb. Bobby Shantz, who had been pitching so brilliantly for New York, hit for himself and made the final Yankees out of the inning.

In the bottom of the eighth, Gino Cimoli batted for Roy Face and singled. It was only one base runner but all rallies in baseball begin with a single runner. Bobby Shantz made a great pitch to Bill Virdon, getting the Pirates' center fielder to ground sharply to Tony Kubek at shortstop. As the ball bounced past the pitcher's mound, everyone—including Tony Kubek—thought, "Double play." But fate moved its hand and the ball struck something, perhaps a pebble or a clump of infield dirt, and at the last second the ball unexpectedly took what ballplayers call "a bad hop." It all depends on perspective. For Bill Virdon and the Pirates it was a good hop. Instead of landing in Tony Kubek's glove, the ball struck Kubek in the throat, sending him to the ground in pain.

The bad hop put Virdon on first base, moved Cimoli to second, and took Kubek out of the game. Joe DeMaestri came in to play shortstop. The Pirates had caught a break but were still down by three runs. Dick Groat singled to score Cimoli and Pittsburgh was down by only two runs with two runners on and nobody out. Bobby Shantz, victimized by the bad hop, came out and Jim Coates, winner of 13 games during the season for New York, came in to stop the rally. Coates had thrown two shutout innings against the Pirates in Game Four, so there was no reason for Casey Stengel to believe he could not hold onto some kind of lead going into the ninth inning. With no outs, Danny Murtaugh called on Bob Skinner to bunt and he executed the sacrifice. The tying run was at second base and Rocky Nelson was the batter. Nelson had started the Pittsburgh scoring with a two-run homer in the first inning. Now all the Pirates needed was a single and the game could be tied. Nelson flied out, but not deep enough to allow Virdon to score. There were two outs and it was up to the Pirates' young right fielder, Roberto Clemente.

Clemente had broken in with Pittsburgh in 1955 at the age of twenty. He was still learning to play the game in 1960, when he hit .314 with 16 home runs, and was not yet the superstar that he would soon become. And if the truth be told, Jim Coates made Roberto Clemente look bad with a great pitch that Clemente could only hammer into the dirt toward first base. Fate moved its hand again, as Clemente reached first base safely on the well-placed infield chopper. Bill Virdon scored and the Yankees' lead was one run. Hal Smith, who had entered the game to replace Smokey Burgess, was the batter.

The name Hal Smith does not conjure up legendary acts of baseball heroism for most fans. One problem for Hal Smith—Harold Wayne Smith—was that while he was playing for Pittsburgh in 1960, another Hal Smith—Harold Raymond Smith—was playing for the St. Louis Cardinals. The other problem for the Pirate Hal Smith is that he was one of those instant heroes whose heroic act was quickly eclipsed by someone else's even more heroic act. Hal Smith (the Pirate) hit a three-run home run off Jim Coates to catapult the Pirates into a two-run lead with only one inning to go. The Yankees were down but, being the Yankees, they never believed they were out. When Ralph Terry came in to record the final out of the Pirates' eighth inning, the Yankees looked at the scoreboard and saw a two-run deficit. They knew how easy it had been for them to score runs in the Series so it was just a matter of getting down to business. And that is what they did in the top of the ninth inning.

Bobby Richardson and pinch hitter Dale Long greeted the new Pirates pitcher, Bob Friend, with singles to open the Yankees' ninth. Danny Murtaugh quickly lifted Friend in favor of the lefty Harvey Haddix, forever known for the twelve-inning perfect game that he threw against the Braves in 1959, only to lose that game in the thirteenth inning. He retired Roger Maris on a foul pop-up for the first out. Mickey Mantle brought the Yankees to within one run with a single, scoring Bobby Richardson and sending Dale Long to third with the tying run. Yogi Berra was the batter.

Yogi jumped all over an inside pitch and ripped it down the first-base line, but Pirates first baseman Rocky Nelson made a great play to rob Berra of a hit. Nelson had been holding Mantle on first base and was only a few feet off the bag when he caught the sharply hit grounder. Acting out of pure instinct, Nelson stepped on the bag to retire Berra and lunged to tag Mantle with what would have been the Series-ending out. Mickey realized what was happening and dove back to the bag, eluding Nelson's tag by a whisker.

Mantle's lightning-fast reflexes not only avoided the out, it also allowed Dale Long to score the tying run. When Bill Skowron grounded to shortstop to end the inning, Hal Smith's home run was quickly forgotten.

Poor Hal Smith. If only the Pittsburgh bullpen could have prevented the Yankees from tying the game, his home run might have been the most famous in World Series history. But someone else that day would have that distinction.

Bill Mazeroski led off the bottom of the ninth. He had faced Ralph Terry twice in Game Four, striking out and popping out. If either player had an advantage, it was Ralph Terry. As for Game Seven, Mazeroski had a bunt single back in the first inning but popped out in the fourth and grounded into a double play to end the seventh inning. The first pitch from Terry was high for ball one.

Ralph Terry's second pitch came at 3:36 p.m. It, too, was high but right where Bill Mazeroski liked his pitches. He swung and the ball sailed toward the outfield. Left fielder Yogi Berra turned and knew where it was going. The game was over and Bill Mazeroski was the instant and unforgettable hero. He waved his cap as he rounded second base.

If you were a Pirates fan in 1960, you knew exactly where you were and what you were doing when Maz hit the home run. It was and remains the only Seventh Game to end on a home run. It is also the only Seventh Game in which not a single batter struck out. It was almost like the pickup games we played as children—provide your own pitcher and just have fun. Everybody hits!

Millions of boys and girls, of all ages, have fantasized about stepping up to the plate in the last of the ninth inning of the Seventh Game of the World Series and hitting the clutch home run. In our minds, it is the ultimate thrill for a ballplayer. Only one man, Bill Mazeroski, has lived it.

For Casey Stengel, it was his last game as manager of the New York Yankees. For Ralph Terry, it was a heartbreaking setback, but in only two years he would have a chance to redeem himself.

October 13, 1960

	1	2	3	4	5	6	7	8	9	R	H	E
NEW YORK (AL)	0	0	0	0	1	4	0	2	2	9	13	1
PITTSBURGH (NL)	2	2	0	0	0	0	0	5	1	10	11	0

PITCHERS: NYY: Turley, Stafford, Shantz, Coates, Terry (L);
PGH: Law, Face, Friend, Haddix (W)

DOUBLES: Boyer

TRIPLES: None

HOME RUNS: Berra, Skowron, Nelson, Smith, Mazeroski

ATTENDANCE: 36,693

TIME OF GAME: 2:36

1962

Terry to McCovey
to Richardson

New York Yankees	1
San Francisco Giants	0

What do we remember about the year 1962? For some of us, it was the television debut of "The Beverly Hillbillies." For others it was our first glimpse at pop-art guru Andy Warhol's homage to Campbell's Tomato Soup. Many remember the music—Gene Pitney's "The Man Who Shot Liberty Valance," The Four Seasons' "Sherry" and "Big Girls Don't Cry," Booker T. and the MGs' "Green Onions." The folk-music scene hit the pop charts with a rousing hit from Peter, Paul & Mary, "If I Had a Hammer."

Movies were memorable. *Lawrence of Arabia* and *To Kill a Mockingbird* raised American filmmaking to new heights. But there was also a dark side to 1962, especially in the fall. Schoolchildren practiced "Duck and Cover" in preparation for nuclear attack and it suddenly was not so far-fetched when the Cuban Missile Crisis hit. But before those days of anguish, days that resolved themselves into a national sigh of relief, baseball gave us its best.

For fans of the national pastime it was the year they saw the National League join the expansion wagon by adding two new teams; the American League had already bulked up to ten in 1961. Purists groaned as they witnessed Casey Stengel manage, between naps, one of the worst teams to play on grass, mud, or concrete. Stengel's New York Mets lost 120 games and were so bad that they were almost lovable. Correction: for many fans,

Around the Horn in 1962

- The New York Mets' record of 40–120 (for a winning percentage of .250) was not really the worst record in baseball history. They lost the most games ever but that was made possible by the 160-game schedule. The 1916 Philadelphia A's posted a worse winning percentage—.235, with a 36–117 record. Leading that woeful Philadelphia team were pitchers Tom Sheehan and Jack Nabors with a combined record of 2 wins and 34 losses.
- Red Sox pitchers Earl Wilson and Bill Monbouquette each tossed a no-hitter.
- Kansas City's Bill Fischer pitched 84 ⅓ consecutive innings without allowing a base on balls. It is a record that has yet to be broken.

who cared not about winning or losing, the Mets were a supremely lovable group of losers. After only a few games—they lost the first nine of the regular season—they never felt the pressure of having to win, as that other New York team must have felt.

The vexing question for the American League was this: what happens when the defending world champions experience a major power reduction as their top two sluggers hit 52 *fewer* home runs in 1962 compared with their 1961 output? Add to the mix a seventy-nine-point drop in batting average from their one-time all-star catcher. And if that's not bad enough, their Hall of Fame lefty dips from a 25–4 record to a respectable but hardly stellar 17–8 mark. When their top reliever of 1961 (he led the league with 29 saves) goes down with a sore arm and is replaced by the immortal Marshall Bridges, would any student of the game give this team any chance of repeating as league champions? A repeat performance as World Series winners would seem totally out of the question. Unless that team is the New York Yankees.

Roger Maris hit "only" 33 home runs, feeding the throngs of skeptics who refused to acknowledge the undisputable fact that he had broken Babe Ruth's single-season home run record only one year earlier by hitting 61 homers. Never mind that he led the team with 100 runs batted in, he was the great pretender to many Yankees loyalists who refused to forgive the sin of Roger Maris, the sin of daring to breathe the same air as that breathed by the immortal Ruth. Only the astute New York fans would appreciate the true value of the complete Roger Maris when the 1962 World Series came to its exciting conclusion.

Mickey Mantle played through more pain than most players endure in an entire career, appearing in only 117 games. He hit over .300, connecting for 30 home runs and earning the league's Most Valuable Player Award for his courage as well as his production. Although Elston Howard's batting average fell from .346 in 1961 to an ordinary .279, he maintained a steadying influence on the Yankees' pitching staff and knocked in 91 runs. Bobby Richardson had the best year of his career, batting .302, and the rest of the team responded with performances that were good enough to beat out the rest of the American League.

The Yankees had one other stellar performer: Ralph Willard Terry, the pride of Big Cabin, Oklahoma. He led the league with 23 wins and proved to be a reliable workhorse for the Yankees, pitching nearly 300 innings. This was no one-year wonder boy, as Terry had chalked up an impressive 16–3 mark in 1961 and he was the unmistakable ace of the New York Yankees in 1962. He had obviously overcome the trauma of giving up the infamous ninth-inning home run to Bill Mazeroski in the Seventh Game of the 1960 World Series. Or had he?

The National League appeared to belong to the Los Angeles Dodgers from day one. Led by speedster Maury Wills and his record-setting 104 stolen bases, the Dodgers seemed unbeatable. Tommy Davis had the best year of his career, hitting .346 and knocking in 153, while Don Drysdale notched 25 wins to earn his only Cy Young Award. Of course, there was the emerging Sandy Koufax, who finally tamed his wildness and was showing signs that he would become the most dominating left-handed pitcher of his time.

Koufax was on his way to his first great season, winning 14 games by the middle of July, when a bizarre circulatory injury ended his year. It also meant the beginning of a downward spiral for Los Angeles that led to yet one more agonizing chapter in the book of Dodgers heartaches. With Koufax on the disabled list, the Dodgers lost 10 of their last 13 games and the surging San Francisco Giants forced a tie on the last day of the season. Just as in 1951, when the Brooklyn Dodgers and New York Giants met in a three-game playoff, these same franchises—now displaced to the West Coast—would fight to the last inning of the third game for the opportunity of meeting the New York Yankees in the World Series.

After splitting the first two games of the playoff, it appeared as if Los Angeles would salvage the pennant, taking a 4–2 lead into the ninth inning of Game Three at Dodgers Stadium. Tragically, the ghosts of 1951 returned to haunt the woeful Dodgers, as San Francisco scored four times in the top of the ninth inning to win the series. There was no dramatic home run, as Bobby Thomson had stroked at the Polo Grounds in 1951, just a total collapse of the entire Dodgers team: two singles, three walks, a wild pitch, and an error. Hardly dramatic, but certainly effective enough to bring the Yankees to San Francisco.

Although the 1962 National League pennant came to San Francisco through the late-season collapse of the Dodgers, the Giants were a formidable team in their own right and were at least as mighty as the Yankees offensively. Future Hall of Famers Willie Mays, Orlando Cepeda, and Willie McCovey all had stellar seasons, combining for more than 100 home runs and 300 runs batted in. Regulars Felipe Alou and Harvey Kuenn each batted over .300 and third baseman Jim Davenport just missed the .300 mark with the best season of his career (.297 and 14 home runs). On paper, where games are, of course, never played, the Giants were more than an equal match for the mighty Yankees.

Even the pitching staff of the Giants seemed up to the task of taking on the Yankees. Veteran Jack Sanford had the finest year of his twelve-year career, winning 24 games. Billy O'Dell, Billy Pierce, and a young Juan Marichal provided San Francisco with three more strong and healthy starters.

The teams split the first two games in San Francisco, as the Yankees' Whitey Ford won the opener, 6–2, and Jack Sanford shut out New York on three hits, 2–0, in Game Two. The hard-luck loser for the Yankees in the second game was Ralph Terry, who seemed to be jinxed by World Series play. Not only had he given up the home run to Bill Mazeroski in 1960, he had also taken the loss in Game Four of that Series against the Pirates. And if that were not enough to shake a young pitcher's confidence when it counted, he was the losing pitcher in the only game New York failed to win in the 1961 World Series against Cincinnati. To compound the problem for Ralph Terry, he had lasted less than three innings in the 1961 Series finale, ultimately won by New York, 13–5. Was Ralph Terry destined to be the Yankees' version of Don Newcombe, the talented Brooklyn Dodgers pitcher whose World Series record of no wins against four losses and an embarrassing earned run average of 8.59 has forever tainted his otherwise brilliant career? Could Ralph Terry ever win "the big one"?

The Series moved to New York and the teams split Games Three and Four, setting up a rematch of the Game Two Sanford-Terry duel in the crucial Game Five. Although the Giants tagged Ralph Terry for eight hits and three runs, Tom Tresh rescued New York with a three-run homer in the bottom of the eighth inning to snap a 2–2 tie and Ralph Terry held on for his first World Series win, 5–3. It was not easy, as Terry surrendered a run and two hits in the ninth and narrowly escaped when pinch hitter Ed Bailey lined out hard to Roger Maris to end the game. The Yankees were one win away from another championship.

The Series moved back to San Francisco, where three days of pouring rain put everything on hold. When the skies finally cleared, Billy Pierce held the Yankees to three hits to force the first Seventh Game ever played on the West Coast. The three days of rain meant that all pitchers were well rested and it would be one final contest between Ralph Terry and Jack Sanford.

How well did the Game Seven pitchers sleep the night before their final confrontation? Undoubtedly they had their restless moments but none so anxious as those felt by the leaders of the free world in Washington, D.C. It was 8:45 on the morning of Game Seven when the CIA presented President John Kennedy with irrefutable evidence that the Russians had placed nuclear missiles in Cuba. Game Seven of the 1962 World Series would be played in the shadow of the Cuban Missile Crisis and a terrifying threat of global nuclear war. The game went on, and it mirrored the brinksmanship being played by the world's leaders.

Terry and Sanford were brilliant. Through four innings, Sanford allowed only one hit and two walks; Terry allowed nothing. The greatest sluggers of the game—Mays, Cepeda, McCovey, Mantle, and Maris—were silent. Until the fifth inning.

Moose Skowron, the Yankees' lumbering first baseman, had delivered only three hits in the Series through the first six games but he led off the Yankees' fifth with a single to left. The number-eight hitter, Cletis Boyer, followed with a single to left center, sending Skowron to third. To the plate came Ralph Terry, who in his previous five plate appearances in the 1962 World Series had struck out four times and grounded out harmlessly the only time he put the ball in play. During the regular season, Ralph Terry batted .189, with not a single extra-base hit and only two walks. Against the ace of the Giants' staff, Ralph Terry drew a walk to load the bases with no outs.

It was only the fifth inning, and the Giants had scored at least two runs in each of the first six games, so there was no reason for panic. True, the runs did not come easily and the Giants had not shown the explosive power that had been the mark of their regular season, but strategy dictated playing the infield back in hopes of a double play, conceding the run. The strategy worked, as Tony Kubek bounced into a routine double play, short to second to first. Skowron scored but the threat of a big inning was over and Sanford retired the next batter, Bobby Richardson, on a foul fly to Orlando Cepeda. But the Yankees had drawn first blood, as the winner of five of the first six games had also done.

Ralph Terry did not wilt, retiring the three Giants batters he faced in the bottom of the fifth inning. After the Yankees failed to score in their half of the sixth inning and Terry retired the first two Giants he saw in the bottom of the inning, the scoreboard began to tell an eerie and familiar tale: not a single Giant had reached base. Could Ralph Terry do it? He was ten outs away from pitching the second perfect game in World Series history. Opposing pitcher Jack Sanford, a .153 hitter during the regular season, broke the suspense with a single to right-center field but advanced no further when Felipe Alou grounded out to end the inning.

Jack Sanford kept the Yankees from scoring any more runs in his final inning of work. It was now time for the Giants to start hitting and they did exactly that. They just could not score. With one out in the seventh inning, Willie Mays sent a hard line drive to the left-field corner, the first well-hit ball off of Terry in the game. Rookie Tom Tresh took off at the crack of the bat and made a fine running catch near the wall, robbing Mays of a hit. The significance of Tresh's great catch became immediately apparent when Willie McCovey followed with a triple to deep center field. Ralph Terry was now hittable, but no one told Orlando Cepeda, who struck out to strand McCovey at third base.

Sanford loaded the bases to start the eighth inning and he was finished. Reliever Billy O'Dell came in to face Roger Maris. Roger had not had much of a World Series, only four hits in the first six games and three outs already in Game Seven. This was his chance to break it open for the Yankees, with the bases loaded, no outs, and a drawn-in infield. But Roger grounded to second baseman Chuck Hiller, who threw home to nail Bobby Richardson for the first out. Elston Howard grounded into a double play and the score remained 1–0 in favor of New York. San Francisco had six outs left.

Yankees manager Ralph Houk's relief corps had not been effective in the first six games of the Series so he had little choice but to stay with Terry in the late innings. Terry responded with a perfect eighth inning; the Yankees were three outs away from another world championship and Ralph Terry was three outs away from erasing the Mazeroski nightmare.

The Yankees went down in order in the top of the ninth and for the Giants it was now time for heroics, from someone, from anyone.

Matty Alou, batting for O'Dell, dragged a perfect bunt to open the bottom of the ninth with a single. The tying run was on base with no one out. In Terry's Game Five complete-game victory, he had shown signs of weakness at the end, giving up two hits and a run in the ninth and escaping on a line-drive final out.

Terry did not weaken, at least not right away. He struck out both Felipe Alou and Chuck Hiller to bring the Yankees to within one out of victory. To the plate stepped Willie Mays, the major leagues' leading home run hitter in 1962. But Mays had not had a good Series to that point, going homerless and with but a single run batted in. "He was due," the pundits said. Mays had hit Terry hard in his previous at-bat, only to be robbed of a hit by Tresh's brilliant defensive play. Could Willie hit another good one?

Willie Mays lined a double to the right-field corner. Because there were two outs, Matty Alou, a capable base runner, was running on contact. The crowd roared, as they expected to see Alou crossing the plate with the tying run. That is what baseball fans expect from two-out doubles and a good runner on first. But Roger Maris, paying no heed to his miserable offensive performance throughout the Series, made the most important and probably most unheralded defensive play of his career. With all the speed, hustle, and skill he could muster, Maris retrieved the ball in the quickest New York minute ever witnessed—make that a New York nanosecond— and rifled it back to the infield before Alou could even think of scoring.

This was a ninth inning to savor. Two Giants stood in scoring position and a hit would surely win the Series for San Francisco. The batter was the left-handed Willie McCovey, who had tripled to deep center in his last at-bat. On deck was the right-handed Orlando Cepeda, who had managed only three hits in the Series. The conventional wisdom would seem to favor one of two strategies: (1) intentionally walk the left-handed McCovey to face the right-handed and seemingly less threatening Cepeda, or (2) bring in a left-handed reliever to face McCovey.

Manager Ralph Houk eschewed the obvious and let Terry pitch to McCovey. And McCovey hit the ball. He hit it hard. He hit it so hard that Yankees fans around the world felt their collective hearts sink deep into their stomachs. He hit it so hard that for an instant Giants fans began to swell with ecstasy. But he hit it directly to Yankees second baseman Bobby Richardson, who needed only to extend his glove a few inches and tuck it away for the final out.

McCovey's line drive, had it reached the outfield, would have scored both Alou and Mays with the tying and winning runs for San Francisco. There is no doubt as to the effects of such a hit. It was hit so hard that six feet to the left, to the right, or higher, would have made McCovey the hero. Instead, Ralph Terry had redeemed himself from the slider that did not slide in Pittsburgh. Sometimes we do get a second chance.

And to those Yankees fans who refuse to honor the memory of Roger Maris, take special note of that brilliant play in right field that preserved the game in the ninth inning of the Seventh Game in 1962. Baseball credits only pitchers with "saves" but Roger Maris deserves one for his work that day.

Willie McCovey launched a mighty missile on October 16, 1962, but it missed its mark. Fortunately for us all, it was the only missile launched that fateful October. A few days later, the Russians withdrew their missiles, ending the Cuban Missile Crisis. The "Yankees" had won, on both fronts. For the moment, everything was back to normal.

October 16, 1962

	1	2	3	4	5	6	7	8	9	R	H	E
NEW YORK (AL)	0	0	0	0	1	0	0	0	0	1	7	0
SAN FRANCISCO (NL)	0	0	0	0	0	0	0	0	0	0	4	1

PITCHERS: NYY: Terry (W); SFG: Sanford (L), O'Dell

DOUBLES: Mays

TRIPLES: McCovey

HOME RUNS: None

ATTENDANCE: 43,948

TIME OF GAME: 2:29

1964

Singin' the St. Louis Blues

New York Yankees 5
St. Louis Cardinals 7

The year 1964 may best be remembered for the landmark piece of legislation that brought America into the moral world. The Civil Rights Act of 1964 did not instantly change the hearts and minds of those who hated, for reasons that defy all reason, but it was a beginning. So, too, was it a beginning for another struggle, a struggle for the health of a nation, for that was when the surgeon general reported that cigarettes cause cancer. For a lot of people, though, 1964 was first and foremost the year of the Beatles. The four lads from Liverpool made their American TV debut on "The Ed Sullivan Show" and dominated the pop charts with "She Loves You," "I Want to Hold Your Hand," and dozens to follow.

There was more to popular culture than the Beatles. Television gave us the immortal "Gilligan's Island" and "The Man from U.N.C.L.E." Hollywood gave us the bizarre political satire *Dr. Strangelove or; How I Learned to Stop Worrying and Love the Bomb*, as well as the toe-tapping *Zorba the Greek*. Was there even room for baseball? Of course there was!

From 1947 to 1964, the New York Yankees dominated the American League as no team had ever before or has ever since dominated its sport. In those eighteen seasons, the Yankees won fifteen pennants and captured the World Series ten times. They defined the word *dynasty* and no one knew when it would end.

Around the Horn in 1964

- ⊙ Dean Chance tossed 11 shutouts and was the last American League pitcher with 10 or more shutouts in a single season.
- ⊙ Relief pitcher Dick "the Monster" Radatz led the Boston Red Sox staff with 16 wins and a 2.29 ERA.
- ⊙ Boston's Dick Stuart, aka "Dr. Strangeglove," lived up to his name, leading his league in errors by a first baseman for the sixth consecutive year.

Going into the season, the Yankees had won four straight pennants but there were a host of reasons to believe they would *not* repeat in 1964. The Orioles had Brooks Robinson, Boog Powell, and a sensational rookie pitcher by the name of Wally Bunker. The White Sox had the best pitching staff in the league, led by Joe Horlen, Juan Pizarro, and Gary Peters. They challenged the Yankees but finished whiskers behind. Five in a row it was!

So what did these Yankees have? How did they do it? They had Mickey Mantle and Roger Maris but those two were not even close to being the same M & M boys of 1961. The magic number was still 61, as in 61 home runs, but in 1964 that was their *combined* total of round-trippers. Productive but hardly intimidating. Ellie Howard had an outstanding year, batting over .300 for the third and last time in his career. The rest of the offense wasn't much but it was enough.

At the age of thirty-five, Whitey Ford put together another fine year, with a 17–6 record and a 2.13 earned run average. The colorful Jim Bouton won 18 games and Al Downing, best known for giving up Henry Aaron's 715th home run a decade later, chipped in with 13 wins. Impressive? Not very. So what? They were the New York Yankees, coming off a humiliating sweep at the hands of the Dodgers in the 1963 World Series. In the eighteen years in which they won fifteen pennants, the Yankees had never lost two World Series in a row.

As the Yankees were scrambling to beat out the White Sox and Orioles in September, the Phillies were comfortably ahead of the rest of the National League by six and a half games with only two weeks to play. But

Philadelphia crumbled as no other team had ever crumbled in the final days of a pennant race, losing ten straight and watching the St. Louis Cardinals edge by them for the pennant.

"Thank you, Chicago Cubs!" That's what Cardinals fans were saying because after playing 54 games with the Cubs, Louis Clark Brock came over to St. Louis along with Paul Toth and Jack Spring in exchange for Ernie Broglio, Doug Clemens, and Bobby Shantz. Lou Brock made an instant difference, hitting .348 for the Cardinals and stealing 33 bases.

The rest of the Cardinals' offense was more than respectable. MVP Ken Boyer led the league with 119 RBIs, while Bill White and Curt Flood posted .300 seasons. As for pitching, the Cardinals had Bob Gibson, in his sixth season but still learning how to pitch. Gibson won 19 games, the best total of his career to that point (his five 20-win seasons came later). Ray Sadecki, at 20–12, and Curt Simmons, at 18–9, gave the Cardinals two more solid starters. The biggest challenge for the Cards was that they were playing the storied New York Yankees, who always found a way to win even when—and especially when—they were not supposed to win.

The teams swapped lopsided victories in the first two games at St. Louis and swapped one-run games in New York to even the Series at two games each. Game Five turned out to be the most dramatic, as the Yankees' Tom Tresh whacked a two-out, two-run homer in the bottom of the ninth to send the game into extra innings, only to have Tim McCarver win it for the Cards with a three-run blast in the tenth. The Yankees went to St. Louis facing sudden elimination in Game Six.

The Cardinals took an early 1–0 lead in the sixth game but the Yankees tied it, inched ahead, and blew it open on Joe Pepitone's grand-slam home run. It was time for another Seventh Game, the tenth for the Yankees and the fifth for the Cardinals.

Bob Gibson was Cardinals manager Johnny Keane's choice to start Game Seven. Curt Simmons had pitched the day before and 20-game-winner Ray Sadecki had been surprisingly ineffective in his two starts. Although Gibson had been hit hard in the second game, allowing four runs in eight innings, he was brilliant in Game Five, when he pitched 10 innings and struck out thirteen Yankees. But could he perform as well on only two days of rest?

The Yankees were in a more precarious pitching position for Game Seven. Whitey Ford left Game One with an arm injury and was out for the

Series. Their number-two starter, Jim Bouton, had pitched into the ninth inning in Game Six the day before. That left Yankees manager Yogi Berra with few good choices. He called on the rookie Mel Stottlemyre.

Neither team could score in the first three innings. The Cardinals never mounted any kind of serious threat in the early innings but in the bottom of the fourth Ken Boyer singled and Dick Groat walked to start the inning. Tim McCarver hit what should have been a double-play ball to Joe Pepitone but Phil Linz threw wildly to first, allowing Boyer to score the first run. After Mike Shannon singled, McCarver and Shannon pulled off a double steal, with catcher Tim McCarver being credited with the only steal of home in Seventh Game history. The Yankees were coming apart. Dal Maxvill's single brought home the third run of the inning and the Yankees were in a hole. Stottlemyre finished the inning without further damage but he was through for the day.

Gibson continued to blank the Yankees through the fifth inning and New York brought in a new pitcher, Al Downing. It was an outing that Al Downing has tried to erase from memory. The first batter he faced, Lou Brock, homered to deep right-center field. The second batter, Bill White, singled to center. The third batter, Ken Boyer, doubled to right center, sending White to third. There was no fourth batter. Yogi Berra had seen enough. Rollie Sheldon relieved and pitched well, allowing no hits in two innings. But in that fifth inning, White and Boyer scored on an infield out and a sacrifice fly. The score was 6–0. No team had ever come back from six runs down in a Seventh Game. But the Yankees did not give up. Why not be the first?

In the top of the sixth inning, Mickey Mantle sliced the Cardinals' lead in half with a three-run homer into the left-center-field bleachers. It was Mickey's 18th and final World Series home run and came in the last World Series game he would play. Gibson recovered and retired the next three Yankees and also kept them from scoring in the seventh. Things were looking good for St. Louis and looked even better when Ken Boyer hit a solo home run off Steve Hamilton in the bottom of the seventh inning. When the Yankees went down in order in the eighth, a world championship in St. Louis was certain. *Almost* certain.

The Cardinals won the Seventh Game of the 1964 World Series, but not before the Yankees made it interesting in a most improbable way. After Tom Tresh struck out to start the Yankees ninth, Cletis Boyer homered to cut the lead to 7–4. It was the first and last time two brothers on opposing teams had homered in a World Series game. A Ken Boyer home run was understandable; he had hit 24 that year, as he had hit the year before. But Cletis? Clete had hit only 8 homers the whole season. Was Gibson weakening?

Pinch hitter John Blanchard eased the anguish of the St. Louis fans by striking out, bringing the Cardinals to within one out of the championship. Everyone figured that Gibson would have no trouble in making Phil Linz the final out of the Series. Linz had hit .250 for the Yankees during the regular season, mostly as a fill-in for the injured Tony Kubek. He made the national news when Yogi Berra objected to his harmonica playing on the team bus but he rarely made news with his bat. Like his teammate Clete Boyer, Linz had hit only eight home runs during the regular season. Surprise of surprises, he hit one into the left-field bleachers to narrow the score to 7–5. What was wrong with Bob Gibson?

The crowd at Busch Stadium grew restless and with good reason. If Bob Gibson could give up home runs to the likes of Cletis Boyer and Phil Linz, what would happen when he faced the next batter, Bobby Richardson, and the batters after that—Roger Maris and Mickey Mantle? Bobby Richardson was even less of a home run threat than Boyer or Linz but he had already set a World Series record back in the seventh inning when he got his 13th hit of the Series. Bob Gibson had to retire the Yankee's hottest hitter or else he would be facing Roger Maris as the tying run. Gibbie was tired but refused to buckle. He gave his all and got Richardson to pop to second baseman Dal Maxvill to end the game.

The Cardinals had won their fifth Seventh Game without a defeat. As for the Yankees, it was all over. The dynasty had come to an end. In 1965 they would finish in sixth place, their worst finish since 1925. They would not appear in another World Series until 1976. For Yankees fans, a twelve-year span between World Series appearances is a major drought. But it's all relative; for fans of the Houston Astros, twelve years between World Series appearances would be a gift from the gods.

As for Seventh Game appearances, the Yankees were now at .500—five wins, five losses, with nine of those ten appearances coming during that eighteen-year dynasty that started with their 1947 win over the Dodgers. They would not see another Seventh Game until the year 2001.

October 15, 1964

	1	2	3	4	5	6	7	8	9	R	H	E
NEW YORK (AL)	0	0	0	0	0	3	0	0	2	5	9	2
ST. LOUIS (NL)	0	0	0	3	3	0	1	0	X	7	10	1

PITCHERS: NYY: Stottlemyre (L), Downing, Sheldon, Hamilton, Mikkelsen; STL: Gibson (W)

DOUBLES: K. Boyer, White

TRIPLES: None

HOME RUNS: C. Boyer, Mantle, Linz, K. Boyer, Brock

ATTENDANCE: 30,346

TIME OF GAME: 2:40

1965

A Pitcher Named Sandy

Los Angeles Dodgers   2
Minnesota Twins   0

Lyndon Johnson signed Medicare into law in 1965 and riots in the Watts neighborhood of Los Angeles exploded into our living rooms through the magic of television. But we found time to enjoy the good life. Music? Plenty of it. Sam the Sham and the Pharaohs rocked the airwaves with "Wooly Bully." A skinny kid from Minnesota named Robert Zimmerman who had taken the name Bob Dylan scored his first of many hits with "Like a Rolling Stone." So much great music—"Stop in the Name of Love" (The Supremes), "Unchained Melody" (The Righteous Brothers), "I Got You Babe" (Sonny and Cher). Who had time to watch television, go to the movies, or see a play? Who even wanted to?

We all did! Plenty of us watched the tube, the silver screen, and the stage. Don Adams and Barbara Feldon tickled the national funny bone with the spy spoof, "Get Smart." *Doctor Zhivago* and *The Sound of Music* were the movies to see and the toughest ticket on Broadway was the Tony Award–winning musical *Fiddler on the Roof*. So what could baseball possibly add to this richness of culture? Plenty.

The story in the American League was not who won the pennant but who didn't. The New York Yankees finished in sixth place, 25 games out of first place, and were never even in the race. In a complete reversal of for-

---

Around the Horn in 1965

- Al Jackson and Jack Fisher were both 20-game losers for the New York Mets. It's the last time one team has had two 20-game losers in one season.

- In one of baseball's worst trades ever, the Cincinnati Reds sent Frank Robinson to the Baltimore Orioles for Milt Pappas, Jack Baldshun, and Dick Simpson.

- For the first time in his career, Pete Rose hit over .300. He would miss that mark only once in his next fifteen seasons.

---

tunes, the Minnesota Twins jumped from a sixth-place finish in 1964 to the top of the American League behind a stable of power hitters and a few good pitchers. They were the old Washington Senators, in only their fifth season in Minnesota, and there they were, ready for October baseball.

When we recall the Minnesota Twins of the 1960s, we instinctively think of Harmon Killebrew, their great home run hitting slugger who hit more home runs during the 1960s than any other player in major-league baseball. Killebrew came up with the Senators in 1954 but never got a chance to play every day until 1959 and soon became the American League's most prolific right-handed home run producer. It is ironic to learn that 1965, when the Twins finally won the pennant, was one of Killebrew's worst seasons. He hit only 25 home runs in 1965, best on the team but his lowest output since joining the team as a regular player. The success of the Minnesota Twins came from unexpected sources.

The leader of the Twins' offense was Zoilo Versalles, the American League's Most Valuable Player. Zoilo hit only .273 but he led the league in runs scored, doubles, triples, and, sad to report, strikeouts. Jimmie Hall, Bob Allison, and Don Mincher all had 20-plus home run years and Tony Oliva led the league in hitting at .321. It was a good, though not great, hitting club. But it was better than most.

The big news for the Twins was pitching. Their star pitcher, Camilo Pascual, lost a chunk of the season due to a back injury but Jim "Mudcat" Grant, who came over to Minnesota from Cleveland in 1964, had his best season ever, winning 21 games to lead the Twins and the American League.

Lefty Jim Kaat posted 18 victories and reliever Al Worthington starred with 10 wins of his own and 21 saves. The Twins won the American League with surprising ease, beating out the Chicago White Sox by seven games.

The Los Angeles Dodgers were back atop the National League and they didn't do it with hitting. Sandy Koufax had become baseball's most dominating pitcher, picking up his fourth consecutive ERA title and leading the league with 26 wins and 382 strikeouts. Don Drysdale was the second half of the Dodgers' great one-two punch on the mound, winning 23 games.

The Dodgers' offense was all about speed and timely hitting. They did not have a single .300 hitter, unless you choose to count Don Drysdale, the perennial good-hitting pitcher who batted exactly .300 that year and was an occasional pinch hitter for manager Walt Alston. Maury Wills, who posted the highest batting average of the regular starting lineup at .286, also engaged in a campaign of grand larceny by swiping 94 bases. As for home runs, the Dodgers didn't believe in them. They were last in the majors with 78 homers, about half of what the Twins hit in 1965. Their leading "sluggers" were Jim LeFebvre and Lou Johnson, who muscled out a mere 12 round-trippers each, tying them for thirty-seventh in the National League's home run race.

The World Series started on Yom Kippur, the most sacred of the Jewish High Holidays, and the Dodgers' ace, Sandy Koufax, would not pitch. He didn't make a big deal of it but there was no way he was going to work on a day that meant so much to his faith. Don Drysdale opened for Los Angeles and the Twins tagged him for seven runs in less than three innings on their way to an easy 8–2 win. When Koufax returned for Game Two, the Twins were ready for him, beating Sandy and the Dodgers, 5–2. Koufax pitched well enough to win, giving up only one earned run in six innings, but the Dodgers' offense could do nothing against Jim Kaat and his defense betrayed him.

Down two games to none, the Dodgers returned home and found the pitching that had got them to the World Series. Claude Osteen shut down the Twins in Game Three, 4–0. Don Drysdale pitched a complete-game win in Game Four, 7–2. Sandy Koufax was back in peak form for Game Five, shutting out the Twins on only four hits while striking out ten, 7–0. And just like that, the Dodgers were up, three games to two and going back to Minnesota.

The home-field advantage remained intact, as the Twins stayed alive in Game Six. Mudcat Grant held the Dodgers to a single run and slugged a three-run homer to set up Game Seven. It was Don Drysdale's turn to pitch but manager Walt Alston wanted his ace lefty, Sandy Koufax, on only two days of rest.

Sandy's fastball was as good as ever in the Seventh Game. The Twins heard the pop of the catcher's mitt and that's how they figured out that Koufax had zipped another by them. But eventually, given a little time, big-league ballplayers will catch up to a pitcher's fastball, especially when they are looking for it. It became painfully clear to the Dodgers and their fans, delightfully clear to the Twins and theirs, that Koufax could not get his curveball over the plate. He was a one-pitch pitcher that day.

And it did not matter. Sandy Koufax threw fastball after fastball, without shame or hesitation, and the Twins could do nothing with it. They managed three hits all day. Zoilo Versalles singled in the third, Frank Quillici doubled in the fifth, and Harmon Killebrew singled in the ninth. That was the beginning, middle, and end of Minnesota's success against Sandy Koufax. After walking two batters in the first inning, Koufax settled down and gave up only one more walk all day. During one stretch, from the fifth to the ninth inning, Sandy set down a dozen Twins in a row. The only question for the Dodgers was whether their anemic hitting attack could deliver a run or two in support of their great left-handed pitcher.

Lou Johnson led off the fourth inning against Twins starter Jim Kaat with a line drive down the left-field line. It was not hit that far and it was not hit that straight but it was deep and true enough to hit the foul pole for a solo home run. For good measure, Ron Fairly followed with a double down the right-field line and scored on Wes Parker's single. That was enough for Koufax. A succession of Minnesota relievers kept the Dodgers off the board for the rest of the contest but it didn't matter. Game Seven of the 1965 World Series belonged to Sandy Koufax. After Harmon Killebrew singled with one out in the ninth inning to give the home fans a glimmer of hope— false hope—Koufax struck out Earl Battey and Bob Allison to end the game with a typical Koufaxian flourish. He finished the game with 10 strikeouts, tying him with another dominating lefty, Hal Newhouser, for most strikeouts in a Seventh Game. But Koufax did it with a pitch that the Twins knew was coming, each and every time. And they couldn't do a thing about it.

With his dominating performance in the 1965 World Series—one earned run in 24 innings—Sandy Koufax was perched high atop the baseball world. No one imagined that after one more brilliant season (27–9, 1.73 ERA), an arthritic elbow would force him to retire from the game he loved so much. There have been other shutouts in World Series Seventh Games, six before and two after, but no pitcher dominated a Game Seven as did the lefty from Brooklyn.

October 16, 1965

	1	2	3	4	5	6	7	8	9	R	H	E
LOS ANGELES (NL)	0	0	0	2	0	0	0	0	0	2	7	0
MINNESOTA (AL)	0	0	0	0	0	0	0	0	0	0	3	1

PITCHERS: LAD: Koufax (W); MIN: Kaat (L), Worthington, Klippstein, Merritt, Perry

DOUBLES: Fairly, Roseboro, Quillici

TRIPLES: Parker

HOME RUNS: Johnson

ATTENDANCE: 50,596

TIME OF GAME: 2:27

1967

Too Much Gibson, Not Enough Rain

St. Louis Cardinals   7
Boston Red Sox   2

Music was everywhere in 1967. You can close your eyes and hear the unmistakable sounds of the "Summer of Love." Procol Harum's "A Whiter Shade of Pale." Bobbie Gentry's "Ode to Billie Joe." The 5th Dimension's "Up, Up and Away." Smokey Robinson and the Miracles, with "I Second That Emotion." Van Morrison's "Brown-Eyed Girl." Wow! Turn up the stereo! Can you think of 1967 and *not* remember the psychedelic sounds of the Jefferson Airplane with "White Rabbit" and "Somebody to Love"?

Millions of Americans tuned in to watch the final episode of "The Fugitive." Was it the "one-armed man" or was Dr. Richard Kimball a cold-blooded murderer? It was also a grand year for the movies. *In the Heat of the Night*, *Bonnie and Clyde*, *Cool Hand Luke*, and *The Graduate* dazzled America with tales of wonder and excitement in the summer of 1967.

It was also a grand year for the baseball fans of New England, whose Boston Red Sox scripted their own tale of wonder and excitement by winning the American League pennant, their first flag since 1946. They called it "the Impossible Dream," because few had given the Red Sox, ninth-place finishers in 1966, any chance at supremacy in the American League.

MVP Carl Yastrzemski led the Red Sox with the best year of his Hall of Fame career—44 home runs, 121 runs batted in, and a .326 batting average. It was the last Triple Crown performance baseball has seen. Pitcher

Around the Horn in 1967

- A rookie outfielder for the Kansas City A's appeared in 35 games and dazzled nobody with his .178 average and one home run. His name was Reggie Jackson.
- The Chicago White Sox finished only three games out of first despite having no everyday player hit higher than .241.
- At the age of forty, Lew Burdette finished his career with the California Angels, pitching in 19 games and going 1–0 with a save. The man who broke open the Seventh Game of the 1958 World Series against Lew with a three-run homer, Bill Skowron, ended up with the Angels that year as well.

Jim Lonborg won 22 games and seemed invincible when the Red Sox needed him most.

The Red Sox knew they could rely on Yastrzemski but at the beginning of the season they were also counting on a right-handed slugger who had already amassed more than 100 career home runs by the tender age of twenty-two. Tony Conigliaro was the new hope and promise of the Fenway faithful; he was the handsome local boy, from nearby Swampscott, Massachusetts, and his talents seemed unlimited. Tragedy struck when he could not get out of the way of a Jack Hamilton fastball on a steamy August night and his season was over. He would try a comeback a few years later but Tony C. never really recovered from the beaning; he died in 1990. The Red Sox refused to weaken and won the pennant in dramatic fashion, by beating the Minnesota Twins on the last day of the regular season.

That pennant-winning game would prove instrumental in the World Series, because Boston used their best pitcher, Jim Lonborg, in that final game of the regular season. It meant that Lonborg could not possibly start the Series, which began only three days later.

The St. Louis Cardinals provided their fans with no such excitement in winning the National League pennant by a comfortable 10½ games over the San Francisco Giants. Orlando Cepeda led the Cardinals with an MVP year nearly equal to that of Yastrzemski. Lou Brock, Curt Flood, and Tim McCarver put up impressive seasons, too.

The biggest question mark for St. Louis was pitching, a punctuation mark made by Pittsburgh's Roberto Clemente when he hit a vicious low line drive directly back at Cardinals star pitcher Bob Gibson on July 15. Gibson was out for 56 games with a broken leg, but the rest of the staff, led by Dick Hughes, Nelson Briles, and twenty-two-year-old Steve Carlton, picked up the slack. When Gibson returned in September, he was well rested and ready for the World Series. By clinching the pennant more than two weeks before the end of the regular season, manager Red Schoendienst could plot his World Series pitching rotation to ensure that Bob Gibson would not only start the Series but possibly even start a Seventh Game, if one were necessary.

So it was that the St. Louis Cardinals had their best pitcher, Bob Gibson, on the mound in the opening game of the 1967 World Series. The Boston Red Sox could not match the Cardinals with their ace; manager Dick Williams knew that Lonborg needed at least one more day of rest to be at his best. But what of it? This was the year of the Impossible Dream, and magic was in the air at Fenway Park.

The Red Sox countered with Jose Santiago, who in his second year with Boston had compiled a 12–4 won-lost record. Santiago was impressive in the Series opener, giving up only two runs and hitting a solo home run himself off of Gibson. That was Gibson's only mistake of the game, as the Cardinals beat the Red Sox, 2–1.

A rested Jim Lonborg started Game Two for Boston and shut out the Cardinals on one hit, an eighth-inning double by Julian Javier. This was Lonborg at his best. Unfortunately, the delayed start of Lonborg in the Series meant that baseball fans could only speculate as to the excitement of a Gibson-Lonborg duel.

The Series moved to St. Louis and Game Three saw the Cardinals win, 5–2, as mere mortal pitchers, Gary Bell for Boston and Nelson Briles for St. Louis, faced off. It was now time for more Bob Gibson; Jim Lonborg was a mere spectator as Gibson shut out the Red Sox in Game Four on five hits, 6–0. The bad news for Boston was that its beloved team was down three games to one, facing elimination. The good news was that it was Jim Lonborg's turn to pitch.

Lonborg again sparkled in Game Five, holding the Cardinals scoreless on just two hits into the ninth inning with a 3–0 lead. His streak of 17 consecutive scoreless innings ended when Roger Maris hit a solo home run, but the Red Sox were alive. Two questions remained: (1) could Boston force a Seventh Game and (2) who would pitch against Bob Gibson in that Seventh Game?

The Red Sox answered the first question with an 8–4 win in Game Six; home runs by Rico Petrocelli (a pair, no less), Carl Yastrzemski, and Reggie Smith led Boston into a Seventh Game and a chance to avenge its Game Seven loss to the Cardinals back in 1946.

Red Sox fans across the country prayed for rain, hoping against hope that one more day off would deliver a rested James Lonborg to the mound at Fenway Park. The rain never came and the Red Sox gambled that two days of rest would be enough for their star pitcher.

For a short time, it appeared that the Impossible Dream would continue. Although it was evident early that Lonborg was not the dominating pitcher he was in Games Two and Five (he gave up singles in each of the first two innings), the game remained scoreless into the third inning. But Bob Gibson was overpowering, striking out three in the first two innings and not allowing a hit. And the Impossible Dream came to an abrupt end.

Dal Maxvill, a .227 hitter during the season, opened the third inning with a triple off the center-field wall. Lonborg was not ready to give in, retiring the next two batters and keeping Maxvill at third base. He needed only one more out, but Curt Flood singled to score Maxvill and came around to score the second Cardinals run on a Roger Maris single and a wild pitch. The score was 2–0, Cardinals.

Although the Cardinals did not score in the fourth inning, the Red Sox showed no signs of getting through to Gibson, who allowed only one base runner—a walk to Joe Foy to lead off the game—and struck out seven of the first thirteen men to face him. Nevertheless, the lead was only two runs and impossible dreams had a way of coming true in Boston that year.

Lonborg was tired. After inducing Dal Maxvill to ground out to start the fifth inning, he faced his pitching rival. Bob Gibson had gained a reputation as a good-hitting pitcher over the course of his career but had not yet gotten a hit in the 1967 World Series. That changed when he blasted a Jim Lonborg pitch for the first and only home run by a pitcher in a World Series Seventh Game. The unraveling of Jim Lonborg and the Red Sox was just beginning. Lou Brock singled, stole second and third, and scored the fourth Cardinals run on a Roger Maris sacrifice fly. The Red Sox were down by four runs and had not registered a hit off Gibson.

A glimmer of hope came over the crowd in Boston when George Scott led off the Red Sox fifth inning with a triple and scored on an errant relay throw. Bob Gibson was human after all; it was the first hit and the first run for the Sox and maybe, just maybe, they could pull it off. Gibson responded by retiring Reggie Smith, Rico Petrocelli, and Elston Howard and the score was 4–1, going into the sixth inning.

Jim Lonborg was running on empty. Tim McCarver led off the sixth with a double to right field. After Mike Shannon reached on an error, Julian Javier came to the plate. This was the same Julian Javier who had broken up Lonborg's no-hit attempt in Game Two. He then proceeded to break the hearts of the loyal Red Sox fans by hitting a three-run homer into the screen above the left-field wall to make the score 7–1. It was over and everyone knew it.

Jose Tartabull batted for Jim Lonborg in the bottom of the sixth inning and struck out. Boston scored one more run in the bottom of the eighth inning but never threatened a serious comeback. Carl Yastrzemski led off the Boston ninth with a single but was erased when Ken Harrelson hit into a double play. George Scott ended the game by striking out. Bob Gibson had allowed only three Boston hits and won his third game of the 1967 World Series. He became the first pitcher—and is still the only pitcher—to win two World Series Seventh Games.

The Seventh Game of the 1967 World Series was close only in spirit for die-hard Red Sox fans. The truth manifested itself early: Gibson had it and Lonborg did not.

Would another day of rest for Jim Lonborg have made a difference? What if Tony Conigliaro had gotten out of the way of the Jack Hamilton fastball? What if the Red Sox had not sold Babe Ruth to the Yankees?

October 12, 1967

	1	2	3	4	5	6	7	8	9	R	H	E
ST. LOUIS (NL)	0	0	2	0	2	3	0	0	0	7	10	1
BOSTON (AL)	0	0	0	0	1	0	0	1	0	2	3	1

PITCHERS: STL: Gibson (W); BOS: Lonborg (L), Santiago, Morehead, Osinski, Brett

DOUBLES: McCarver, Brock, Petrocelli

TRIPLES: Maxvill, Scott

HOME RUNS: B. Gibson, Javier

ATTENDANCE: 35,188

TIME OF GAME: 2:23

1968

The Unexpected Duel

Detroit Tigers   4
St. Louis Cardinals   1

It was the year that brought more tears to America than we ever thought possible. Martin Luther King and Bobby Kennedy fell victims to assassins' bullets. Dion's "Abraham, Martin and John" showed that American pop music could respond to real life. Other songs took on a more melancholy tone as well. Mary Hopkins made a hit out of an old Russian folk tune with "Those Were the Days" and Hugo Montenegro struck an icy chord with his instrumental theme from the film *The Good, The Bad and the Ugly.*

There was also plenty of mirth and merriment in American culture. Jeanie C. Riley's "Harper Valley P.T.A." and Marvin Gaye's "I Heard It Through the Grapevine" were the talk-about tunes of the year. As for the movies, the big flick was Stanley Kubrick's *2001: A Space Odyssey.* CBS launched its legendary news magazine show "60 Minutes," and a British Kafkaesque import, "The Prisoner," found a niche following among those either too smart for their own good or too stoned to know the difference. It almost seemed as if there was no room for baseball anymore. But there has always been room for baseball, especially when we think there isn't.

The 1968 season was dominated by pitching. Some even say it was ruined by pitching. The pitching staffs of thirteen of the twenty major-league teams compiled team earned run averages under 3.00. Batting aver-

Around the Horn in 1968

- It was definitely the year of the pitcher. For the first and only time in history, every team's pitching staff had at least 10 shutouts. Twenty-nine players with 100 or more at-bats hit under .200.
- The pain was finally too much for Mickey Mantle, who played his last year in New York. He never failed to hit double-digit home runs in every one of his brilliant seasons.
- The Chicago White Sox lost nine 1–0 games (tying the American League record set by New York in 1914).

ages were at record lows. Boston's Carl Yastrzemski spared the American League the embarrassment of having a sub-.300 batting champ when he hit .301 to win the AL batting crown, almost by default. In the American League, there were many outstanding pitchers but one stood above the rest: Denny McLain.

Dennis Dale McLain won 31 games for the Detroit Tigers. Most baseball experts figured that the 30-win season was a thing of the past. If Koufax couldn't do it when he was at the top of his game, no one would. The last player to achieve that lofty plateau was Dizzy Dean in 1934. Denny McLain had put together three fine seasons with Detroit from 1965 to 1967, including a 20-win season in 1966. But in 1968, one thing was certain: Denny McLain was the best pitcher in the American League and he led his Tigers to the pennant by a comfortable 12-game margin over the Orioles and the rest of the frustrated junior circuit.

Besides McLain, Detroit had starters Joe Sparma, Earl Wilson, and a stocky left-hander by the name of Mickey Lolich. But with his 31 wins, Denny McLain was the man Tigers fans figured would lead them to a championship. The Tigers' offense was based on the home run ball. Detroit led all of baseball with 185 homers and the next closest team, Baltimore, was more than 50 behind in that department. The other side of the offensive coin, speed, was a different story. With 26 stolen bases, not only were the Tigers the slowest team in baseball, they established a record that stands today: fewest stolen bases by a pennant-winning team. Willie Horton led the offense with his .285 average and 36 home runs (but no steals) and Norm Cash, Jim Northrup, and Bill Freehan each contributed 20 or more long balls.

Without belaboring the point about weak hitting, and not intending to offend anyone, the left side of the Tigers' infield was as anemic as it got. Third baseman Don Wert needed every hit he got to bat .200 on the nose. The shortstop position was filled by the dynamic duo of Ray Oyler (.135 average) and Dick Tracewski (.156). There were serious holes in that lineup.

In sharp contrast to the Detroit Tigers were the St. Louis Cardinals, repeating as National League champions with a nine-game bulge over the San Francisco Giants. Orlando Cepeda led the Cardinals in home runs with 16, which would have been good enough for only the fifth spot in the power category at Detroit. The Cards hit a grand total of 73 home runs. They manufactured their runs with extra-base hits of the lower denomination and with speed. Their superstar left fielder, Lou Brock, led the league in doubles, triples, and stolen bases. It was, though, pretty much the same offense the Cardinals had put on the field to win the World Series from Boston the year before. Pitching, however, was a little different.

Denny McLain may have been the best pitcher in the American League but even with his 31 wins, he may not have been the best pitcher in baseball. The Cardinals' Bob Gibson won "only" 22 games but dazzled the baseball world with an earned run average of 1.12. Only two other pitchers in history ever posted a lower ERA, Dutch Leonard in 1914 (1.00) and Three Finger Brown in 1906 (1.04). Those were in the days of the dead ball, when teams struggled mightily to score runs and eight or nine homers made you a bona-fide slugger.

In addition to his microscopic earned run average, Gibson posted 13 shutouts, second highest in major-league history and the most since Pete Alexander notched 16 whitewashes back in 1916. He struck out 268 batters, most with his fastball but some just through intimidation. The other St. Louis starters, Nelson Briles, Ray Washburn, Steve Carlton, were capable but pitched only because Bob Gibson could not pitch every day.

The 1968 World Series featured the matchup that everyone wanted to see: Denny McLain versus Bob Gibson. That's what they got in Game One but it was no contest. Gibson struck out seventeen, a World Series record that still stands, and shut out the Tigers on five hits. McLain looked good until the fifth inning, when he walked Roger Maris and Tim

McCarver. Mike Shannon and Julian Javier combined to knock in three runs and Gibson had all that he needed.

Game Two was a battle of the number-two starters, Mickey Lolich and Nelson Briles. Again it was no contest but this time the Detroit Tigers came out on top, 8–1. Three Tigers homers, including Mickey Lolich's first and only major-league home run, led the way. With the Series tied at a game each, the number-three starters took their turns and the Cardinals came out on top, 7–3. Game Four was a highly anticipated rematch between Gibson and McLain with the same result, albeit more extreme. Gibson again dominated, striking out ten and giving up only five hits, while the Cardinals knocked McLain out in the third inning. The Cardinals won, 10–1, and were in command of the Series, leading three games to one. For Detroit it was a simple but formidable task: join the 1925 Pirates and 1958 Yankees as the only teams to come back from a 3–1 deficit to win the World Series.

Mickey Lolich was the Game Five starter for Detroit and many gave Detroit up for dead when Orlando Cepeda capped off the Cardinals' first inning with a two-run homer to stake St. Louis to a quick 3–0 lead. After that, Lolich teased and taunted but gave up no more runs. The Tigers scored two in the fourth and took the lead for good with three in the seventh. The 5–3 win kept Detroit alive but they would have to win the next two games in St. Louis to take the Series. And they knew that they would have to find a way to beat Bob Gibson in one of those games. But it would not be Game Six, as Cardinals manager Red Schoendienst decided to go with Nelson Briles as his starter and hold a fully rested Gibson for Game Seven, if necessary.

Detroit manager Mayo Smith had to make a difficult choice. He needed a pitcher to get him to Game Seven. The only pitcher he could not realistically use was Mickey Lolich, who had just won Game Five. Earl Wilson was available, but he had been totally ineffective in his only Series appearance. Applying the strategy of "Go with your best, even if your best hasn't been too good," Smith called on Denny McLain to stop the Cardinals. It was a good choice, because McLain found his regular-season form and pitched a complete-game victory. The Detroit offense came alive with 10 runs in the third inning and the Tigers coasted to a 13–1 win. Detroit had forced a Game Seven but would have to beat Bob Gibson to win the Series.

The Game Seven pitching choice for Detroit was obvious. Mickey Lolich had come through with two solid performances and had emerged as the Tigers' most effective pitcher in the Series. Lolich was pitching on two days' rest, but Mayo Smith was unwilling to trust anyone else with the task. It was a duel that few expected when the Series began: Bob Gibson versus Mickey Lolich. The Tigers were also facing a team with history on its side; no one had ever defeated the St. Louis Cardinals in six previous Seventh Games.

The game was everything the fans expected, a tense pitching duel between two pitchers who refused to budge. Through six innings, Bob Gibson allowed only an infield single to Detroit's Mickey Stanley in the fourth inning. Lolich pitched his more typical game, allowing occasional base runners through hits and walks but giving up no runs.

The top of the seventh started in classic Gibsonian style. Mickey Stanley struck out and Al Kaline grounded out to short. Bob Gibson had retired twenty of the first twenty-one batters to face him. Then on came the Tigers. Norm Cash and Willie Horton singled. Jim Northrup, who had homered against Gibson in Game Four for the only Tigers run off the Cardinals' ace in his first two games, hit a fly ball to deep center field. Curt Flood misjudged the ball and Northrup was on third base with a two-run triple—the thirteenth and last triple hit in a Seventh Game. Bill Freehan followed with a double to left center and the Tigers had a three-run lead.

Mickey Lolich continued to keep the Cardinals off stride and, for the most part, off base. They got a runner on by an error in the seventh and one via a walk in the eighth but the Cardinals were staring at their first-ever Game Seven loss with only three outs to go. Manager Red Schoendienst must have had faith in his team because he let Gibson hit for himself in the eighth inning; he struck out. It is hard to fault Schoendienst because Gibson was an excellent hitter and had already hit a home run earlier in the Series.

Gibson had to be tired, because there is no other explanation for the way Detroit scored a run in the ninth inning. With two out and two on, Don Wert, the Tigers' .200-hitting third baseman, singled home a run.

It was the bottom of the ninth inning, and Mickey Lolich was looking at a shutout as well as his third win of the Series and a miracle comeback for the Tigers. St. Louis was looking for its own miracle.

Curt Flood lined out to start the inning and Orlando Cepeda fouled out to the catcher. For Cepeda, this was his eleventh Seventh Game at-bat, spanning three World Series, without a hit. Mike Shannon was the Cardinals' last hope. Shannon lined a shot to left, into the stands for a home run. The Cardinals had busted up the shutout and were looking to keep their hopes alive. Tim McCarver, who had already singled once against Lolich, stepped to the plate and lifted a high foul pop that Tigers catcher Bill Freehan snared to end the game, the Series, and the comeback.

Bob Gibson may have been the most intimidating pitcher to play the game and is rightly enshrined in the Hall of Fame. Mickey Lolich was not nearly as intimidating as Bob Gibson and, despite a solid career that included two 20-win seasons, is not in the Hall of Fame. But on that one bright fall day at Busch Stadium, Mickey Lolich outpitched the great Bob Gibson.

October 10, 1968

	1	2	3	4	5	6	7	8	9	R	H	E
DETROIT (AL)	0	0	0	0	0	0	3	0	1	4	8	1
ST. LOUIS (NL)	0	0	0	0	0	0	0	0	1	1	5	0

PITCHERS: DET: Lolich (W); STL: Gibson (L)

DOUBLES: Freehan

TRIPLES: Northrup

HOME RUNS: Shannon

ATTENDANCE: 54,692

TIME OF GAME: 2:07

1971

The Blass Slipper

Pittsburgh Pirates 2
Baltimore Orioles 1

In 1971, the enterprising but not always so scrupulous Michael Milken started trading in "junk bonds." We saw the first digital quartz watch and wondered how we had lived without it. An upstart company called MCI thought it might compete with AT&T.

John Lennon and the Plastic Ono Band recorded "Imagine," and John Denver had a hit with "Take Me Home, Country Roads." We first met Archie and Edith Bunker in 1971 when "All in the Family" made its televison debut. At the movies, we saw *A Clockwork Orange* and *The French Connection*. It was a serious year, as the war in Vietnam dragged on and we looked anywhere and everywhere for comfort and solace. It's a good thing we had baseball.

The Baltimore Orioles were doing their best to make everyone forget about the old New York Yankee dynasty and establish their own. They won their third straight American League pennant and were aiming to repeat as world champions. Manager Earl Weaver was four times blessed with a quartet of 20-game winners. Dave McNally, Pat Dobson, Mike Cuellar, and Jim Palmer were the stalwarts of the staff and the envy of every other big-league manager, not only winning 81 but also starting all but 16 of the Orioles' games. They had a bullpen but it wasn't overworked, as the O's led the league with 71 complete games.

Around the Horn in 1971

- In 549 official plate appearances, San Diego's Enzo Hernandez drove in only 12 runs. He had more than 120 hits, including a dozen extra-base hits, but knocked in only 12. Can someone explain how that is possible?
- Even though they won their division, the San Francisco Giants led the major leagues in errors with 179. Three different Giants—Willie McCovey, Tito Fuentes, and Chris Speier—led the National League in errors at their position.
- The Milwaukee Brewers finished last in the American League West but somehow managed to lead all of baseball in staff shutouts with 23.

Baltimore had won the World Series in 1970, beating the Cincinnati Reds in only five games, and won the American League pennant in 1971 with virtually the same offense as the year before. Boog Powell and Frank Robinson fell off slightly in their run production but it was a solid lineup, top to bottom. The defensive strength of the team was the left side of the infield, where Brooks Robinson and Mark Belanger ate up ground balls like starving artists and spit them across the diamond to capable first baseman Powell. But going to the World Series with four 20-game winners? That was a baseball first.

Baltimore's starting pitching had no trouble with the suddenly successful Oakland Athletics in the League Championship Series (LCS), sweeping the A's in three games and needing only two innings from the Baltimore bullpen. "Bring on the National League," said Earl Weaver.

The Pittsburgh Pirates had won the National League East in 1970 but lost in the LCS to the Reds. The Pirates were back in 1971 with an even stronger team and had little trouble winning the East again by seven games over the Cardinals and made their date with the Orioles by beating the Giants, three games to one, in the LCS.

Who were these Pirates, returning to the World Series eleven years after Bill Mazeroski's ninth-inning home run beat the Yankees at old Forbes Field? They were in a new stadium with mostly new faces but the same old dream. Roberto Clemente was the lone member of the old Bucs still on the team, and even at the age of thirty-six he was as good as, even better than, he was in 1960. With his .341 average and shotgun arm in right field, Clemente had gained the recognition he always deserved.

There was ample power in the Pirates' lineup but no slugger so mighty as Wilver Dornel Stargell, who won baseball's home run derby with 48. Along with Willie Stargell, free swingers Manny Sanguillen, Al Oliver, and Richie Hebner delivered solid performances.

The Pirates' starting pitching couldn't compare with Baltimore's. Earl Weaver had his four 20-game winners, and Pittsburgh manager Danny Murtaugh had none. Dock Ellis came close with 19 wins, Steve Blass came in with 15, and many others contributed where they could. But the Pirates had a deep bullpen, led by closer Dave Giusti and his league-leading 30 saves, and that was a good thing because Murtaugh went to the pen often.

The Orioles jumped out in front in the World Series by winning the first two games at home, 5–3 and 11–3. When the Series moved to Three Rivers Stadium in Pittsburgh, the shell-shocked Pirates gave the ball to their seven-year veteran Steve Blass. Although Blass was Danny Murtaugh's number-two starter during the regular season, he had pitched poorly in the LCS, giving up 14 hits in only seven innings and running up a frightening 11.57 earned run average. But Blass tossed a brilliant three-hitter in Game Three and the Pirates won, 5–1, to get back in the Series. Pittsburgh tied the Series when relievers Bruce Kison and Dave Giusti combined for eight shutout innings after the O's had jumped to an early 3–0 lead; Milt May's pinch single in the seventh inning gave the Pirates the victory, 4–3.

The Pirates won Game Five, 5–0, behind veteran Nelson Briles's two-hit gem and the Series moved back to Baltimore, where the Orioles came from behind to win Game Six in 10 innings, 4–3. The Pirates, winners of their three previous Game Seven appearances in 1909, 1925, and 1960, were looking to make it a perfect four for four behind the right arm of Steve Blass. Baltimore, in its first Seventh Game ever, placed its hopes on the left arm of Mike Cuellar.

Everything looked good for Baltimore through the first three innings. Mike Cuellar set down all nine Pirates who dared to stand in against him. Steve Blass held the Orioles scoreless, but gave up a single and two walks in those same three innings. Then came the first heroics of the evening. After Cuellar set down Dave Cash and Gene Clines to make it eleven in a row to start the game, Roberto Clemente homered over the left-field wall.

The perfect game was gone, the no-hitter was gone, and the shutout was gone.

Cuellar settled down after the Clemente home run but his mates were having no success against Steve Blass, who recovered from his early inning wobblies. From the fourth through the seventh innings, the Orioles could get only one base runner, on a one-out double from catcher Elrod Hendricks in the fifth. After seven innings the score remained 1–0.

Willie Stargell led off the Pirates' eighth with a single. To the plate came the veteran Jose Pagan, no stranger to the pressure of Seventh Games. Pagan had been the shortstop for the San Francisco Giants in the 1962 thriller against the Yankees. Although Jose went hitless in his two trips to the plate in that Seventh Game, he had been the Giants' leading hitter in the Series, batting .368. That was in 1962. Pagan came to the Pirates during the 1965 season and filled in adequately as a part-time player. He was never an all-star, never a leader in any offensive category, never the hero. During the 1971 season, Pagan appeared in only 57 games, batting .241 with only one double, five homers, and 15 runs batted in. The name Jose Pagan and the term *offensive threat* rarely appeared together in the same sentence.

Nevertheless, Jose Pagan doubled off the wall in left-center field to score Willie Stargell with the second Pirates run. It was only the second double of the entire 1971 season for Jose but it was the biggest hit of his career, for it proved to be the game-deciding hit when the Orioles came back with a run in the bottom of the inning. On October 17, 1971, Jose Pagan was a hero—his lifetime batting average of .250 be damned!

Mike Cuellar recovered from the Pagan double by retiring the Pirates before any more runs could score. He left for a pinch hitter in the bottom of the eighth, having pitched eight innings of four-hit ball and not allowing a walk. On most days that would have been good enough for a win. Except on most days in Mike Cuellar's career he never had to face Roberto Clemente, Willie Stargell, or a destiny-driven Jose Pagan. And he never had to pitch against Steve Blass, who was pitching the game of his life.

The Orioles' lone run came in the bottom of the eighth. Ellie Hendricks and Mark Belanger singled but only one could score, on an infield groundout.

It came down to Steve Blass facing Boog Powell, Frank Robinson, and Merv Rettenmund in the bottom of the ninth. How far would Danny Murtaugh let him go? We will never know, because Boog, Frank, and Merv

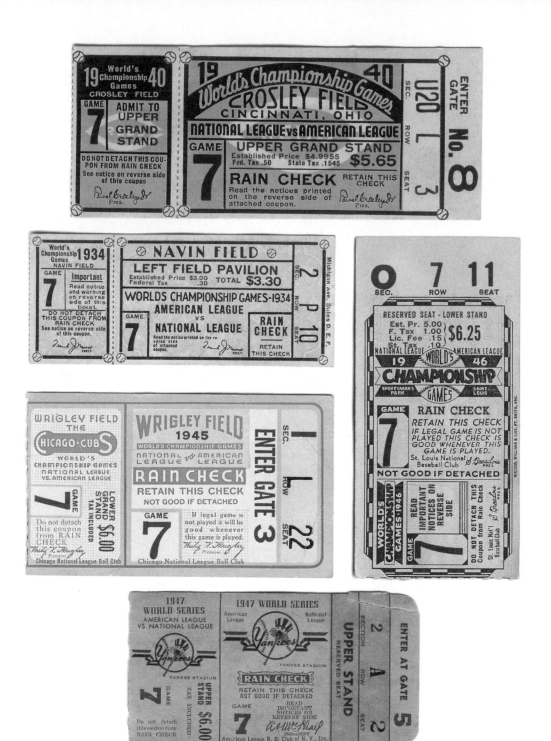

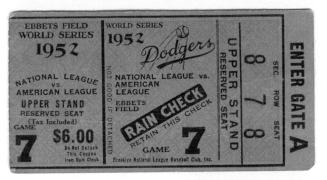

EBBETS FIELD
WORLD SERIES
1952

NATIONAL LEAGUE
vs.
AMERICAN LEAGUE
UPPER STAND
RESERVED SEAT
(Tax Included)
GAME
7 $6.00
Do Not Detach
This Coupon
from Rain Check

WORLD SERIES
1952
Dodgers
NATIONAL LEAGUE vs.
AMERICAN LEAGUE
EBBETS
FIELD
RAIN CHECK
RETAIN THIS CHECK
GAME
7
NOT GOOD IF DETACHED
Brooklyn National League Baseball Club, Inc.

UPPER STAND RESERVED SEAT
SEC. ROW SEAT
8 7 8
ENTER GATE A

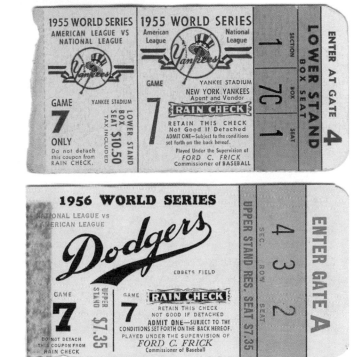

1955 WORLD SERIES
AMERICAN LEAGUE VS
NATIONAL LEAGUE
GAME
7
ONLY
Do not detach
this coupon from
RAIN CHECK.

1955 WORLD SERIES
American
League
Yankees
National
League
YANKEE STADIUM
NEW YORK YANKEES
Agent and Vendor
RAIN CHECK
RETAIN THIS CHECK
Not Good If Detached
ADMIT ONE—Subject to the conditions
set forth on the back hereof.
Played Under the Supervision of
FORD C. FRICK
Commissioner of BASEBALL

YANKEE STADIUM
LOWER STAND
BOX
SEAT $10.50
TAX INCLUDED

SECTION BOX SEAT
1 7C 1
LOWER STAND
BOX SEAT
ENTER AT GATE 4

1956 WORLD SERIES
NATIONAL LEAGUE vs
AMERICAN LEAGUE
Dodgers
EBBETS FIELD
GAME
7
UPPER
STAND
$7.35
DO NOT DETACH
THIS COUPON FROM
RAIN CHECK

GAME
7
RAIN CHECK
RETAIN THIS CHECK
NOT GOOD IF DETACHED
ADMIT ONE—Subject to the
CONDITIONS SET FORTH ON THE BACK HEREOF.
PLAYED UNDER THE SUPERVISION OF
FORD C. FRICK
Commissioner of Baseball

UPPER STAND RES. SEAT $7.35
SEC. ROW SEAT
4 3 2
ENTER GATE A

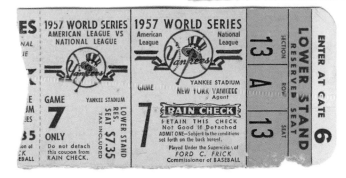

ES 1957 WORLD SERIES
AMERICAN LEAGUE VS
NATIONAL LEAGUE
GAME
7
ONLY
Do not detach
this coupon from
RAIN CHECK.

1957 WORLD SERIES
American
League
Yankees
National
League
YANKEE STADIUM
NEW YORK YANKEES
Agent
RAIN CHECK
RETAIN THIS CHECK
Not Good If Detached
ADMIT ONE—Subject to the conditions
set forth on the back hereof.
Played Under the Supervision of
FORD C. FRICK
Commissioner of BASEBALL

YANKEE STADIUM
LOWER STAND
RES.
SEAT $7.35
TAX INCLUDED

SECTION ROW SEAT
13 A 13
LOWER STAND
RESERVED SEAT
ENTER AT GATE 6

went down without a ball getting to the outfield. A grounder, a pop-up, and one more easy grounder ended the game. The Pirates were now perfect in their four Seventh Game tries. Baltimore had lost its only Game Seven but would look forward to another chance, eight years later, against the same Pittsburgh Pirates.

As for Steve Blass, he had another good season left in him. The 1972 season was his best, as he won 19 games and finished second to Steve Carlton in the balloting for the Cy Young Award. He won a game in the 1972 League Championship Series, and pitched well enough to win the fifth and deciding game but his bullpen blew it in the ninth. After that, baseball was not kind to Steve Blass. He went 3–9 in 1973, pitched in only one game in 1974, and was gone.

Willie Stargell would hang around long enough to haunt the Orioles in one more Seventh Game. Roberto Clemente, the best hitter in the 1971 Series with his .414 average, would play one more year for Pittsburgh and collect his 3,000th career hit on the last day of the 1972 season. Then on December 31, 1972, on a relief mission to Nicaragua, Clemente died in a plane crash.

October 17, 1971

	1	2	3	4	5	6	7	8	9	R	H	E
PITTSBURGH (NL)	0	0	0	1	0	0	0	1	0	2	6	1
BALTIMORE (AL)	0	0	0	0	0	0	0	1	0	1	4	0

PITCHERS: PGH: Blass (W); BAL: Cuellar (L), Dobson, McNally
DOUBLES: Hendricks, Pagan
TRIPLES: None
HOME RUNS: Clemente
ATTENDANCE: 47,291
TIME OF GAME: 2:10

1972

Tenace, Anyone?

Oakland A's   3
Cincinnati Reds 2

Historians will look back at 1972 and remember President Richard Nixon's historic visit to China. Music lovers will recall Don McLean's "American Pie," Helen Reddy's pop anthem "I Am Woman," and the Moody Blues' "Nights in White Satin." Cinema buffs will summon up images of *The Godfather*, *Cabaret*, and *Deliverance*. Couch potatoes were content to watch "M*A*S*H" and "Kung Fu" on TV.

Scientists talked about "black holes" and they were not referring to the defensive weaknesses of any particular baseball teams. Susan Lynn Roley and Joanne Pierce completed their training at Quantico, Virginia, to become the first female FBI agents. And a little baby was born who would soon not be so little—Shaquille O'Neal. It was also a grand year for baseball.

Does the 1972 World Series stand out in anyone's mind as one of the game's greatest? Probably not, but it should, as six of the seven games, including the deciding Seventh Game, were decided by a single run.

The A's franchise had not been in a World Series since 1931, when they lost to the Cardinals in seven games. Their journey from Philadelphia to Oakland, with an intervening stop in Kansas City, had provided their fans with few thrills and even fewer reasons to cheer over four decades of mediocrity. In those forty years, the A's recorded only eight winning seasons and

Around the Horn in 1972

- ⋗ Not a single Texas Rangers pitcher posted even a .500 record, including their ace Mike Paul, who had a 2.17 ERA.
- ⋗ Hank Aaron homered in the All-Star Game in front of the home fans in Atlanta. The National League won, 4–3, in 10 innings.
- ⋗ For the first time in baseball history, a batting champion hit no home runs. Rod Carew led the American League with a .318 average despite hitting not a single long ball.

finished last sixteen times; had it not been for the hapless Washington Senators of the 1950s and early 1960s, they would have claimed twenty-one last-place finishes in forty years. No rational fan ever confused the A's team with a good baseball club.

When Oakland's flamboyant and sometimes outlandish owner Charles O. Finley started to sign some genuine new talent, the fortunes of A's fans—those that remained and the new ones who did not know any better—turned around. It was no longer a legion of likable losers but rather a team of determined winners—future Hall of Famers Reggie Jackson, Catfish Hunter, and Rollie Fingers were only three reasons for the American League to stand up and take note of this new West Coast challenge.

Depending on how you look it at, the 1972 season was dominated either by very good pitching or very weak hitting. The Tigers won the American League East despite having no regular player bat higher than .262 or club more than 22 home runs. Rod Carew was the league's best hitter at .318, but did not hit a single home run. The A's were neither the league's best hitting team (their .240 average was sixth out of twelve teams) or the best pitching team (close—their 2.58 ERA was second only to Baltimore), but they had balance and bravado. They beat the Tigers in a tough five-game League Championship Series to advance to the World Series, but with a nagging question mark. How would they fare without Reggie Jackson, victim of a season-ending hamstring injury in the final game of the LCS?

The Cincinnati Reds had their own core of future Hall of Famers. Offensive stars Johnny Bench, Joe Morgan, and Tony Perez, plus Pete Rose, with his undeniable Hall of Fame credentials despite his flaws of character, flourished under the direction of manager Sparky Anderson, a Coop-erstown inductee himself in 2000. Cincinnati's pitching was adequate, if not inspiring. Youngsters Gary Nolan and Ross Grimsley were the top winners but the strength of the staff was the bullpen. Tom Hall, Pedro Bor-bon, and Clay Carroll appeared in 174 games, winning 24 and saving 56. Cincinnati advanced to the World Series by coming from behind in the last game of the LCS with two runs in the bottom of the ninth to beat the Pirates, 5–4.

The A's stunned the Reds by winning the first two games of the World Series in Cincinnati, each by a single run. In Oakland, the Reds won Game Three by one run and were on the verge of tying the Series when Oakland scored two in the bottom of the ninth in Game Four to win the game, again by a single run, and forge ahead in the Series three games to one.

Facing elimination on enemy turf and down by a run entering the eighth inning in Game Five, the Reds staged their own heroics and came back to win, 5–4. It was a first: five one-run games to open a World Series.

After five close games, the Reds' mighty hitters were frustrated but relieved to be heading back to Cincinnati. They came alive in Game Six, busting open a close contest in the seventh inning with five runs on four singles and three walks. Another Game Seven was at hand.

Oakland manager Dick Williams tapped his young righty John "Blue Moon" Odom to get the A's pitching back on track. Odom had lost Game Three even though he pitched well. Sparky Anderson went with Jack Billingham, who had not allowed an earned run in his two previous Series outings that year. Sparky didn't know it at the time, but Billingham would appear in two more World Series (1975 and 1976) and retire with the low-est earned run averge—0.36—of any player hurling 25 or more innings in World Series play. That's lower than Christy Mathewson, lower than Sandy Koufax, lower than everybody else who ever played the game.

With one gone in the first inning of Game Seven, Oakland's Angel Mangual flied to Bobby Tolan in center. It should have been the second out, but when Tolan misplayed the ball, Mangual found himself on third base and the A's had the game's first golden opportunity. Cincinnati nearly escaped when Joe Rudi popped to short left field, but Gene Tenace nudged a bad-hop single to third base, scoring Mangual. Tolan's error was the Reds' fifth error of the World Series and it was the costliest. Sal Bando struck out to end the inning but the A's had taken an early lead on the only unearned run of the Series. It was not a good sign for the Reds, for in each of the previous six games the team that scored first emerged as the winner.

Billingham did not let the unearned run get to him. He allowed a walk and a single in the second inning but no runs. He retired the A's in order in the third, fourth, and fifth innings. Meanwhile, Blue Moon Odom was baffling the Reds with his own outstanding performance through four innings, allowing only an infield single and a pair of walks.

The Reds finally broke through with the tying run in the bottom of the fifth, but it cost them their starting pitcher. Tony Perez led off with a stinging double down the left-field line. After Dennis Menke struck out, Cesar Geronimo walked. Odom fell behind in the count to Dave Concepcion, two balls and one strike, and manager Dick Williams decided he had seen enough of Blue Moon. It wasn't that the Reds were teeing off on Odom, but with the relief pitching available to Williams it was almost a no-brainer kind of move. In came Jim "Catfish" Hunter, ace of the staff during the regular season and winner of Game Two. It was not a typical situation for Catfish, because he had relieved only once during the season. But in the Seventh Game of the World Series, all pitchers are potential relievers, even in the middle of an at-bat.

Hunter allowed two more balls to Concepcion, completing the walk. The bases were now loaded with one out and it was decision time for manager Sparky Anderson. His Reds were down a run and his pitcher was due to hit. Jack Billingham had been Sparky's best pitcher in the Series, giving him almost 14 innings without an earned run. It was too early to panic but opportunities like the one before him, especially against Oakland's talented bullpen, were not likely to appear again. Although there were many ways the tying run could score without a hit, Jack Billingham was a notoriously bad-hitting pitcher. His regular-season average of .070 left no doubt as to that flaw in Jack's game. Besides, the Reds' bullpen had been more than adequate all year and Sparky needed to score some runs. The hot-hitting Hal McRae, with four hits in nine at-bats in the Series, pinch-hit for Billingham.

The Reds needed a hit from McRae but Hal gave them the next best thing, a fly ball to deep center field that allowed Tony Perez to score the tying run. It was up to Pete Rose to give the Reds the lead but Catfish Hunter won the battle, getting Rose to fly out to Angel Mangual. Pete hit it well but it was the third out. Sparky Anderson now needed a pitcher.

For the sixth time in the Series, Pedro Borbon took the mound for Cincinnati. Borbon had allowed only one earned run in his previous five outings. He had been one of Sparky's most dependable pitchers during the season. But this time Pedro faltered.

Bert Campaneris singled to lead off the sixth inning. Angel Mangual sacrificed Campaneris to second base and Joe Rudi grounded to second base, moving Campy to third. Gene Tenace came to the plate. Before the 1972 World Series, few had heard of Gene Tenace and even fewer feared him. As Oakland's backup catcher and occasional reserve first baseman, Tenace batted a profoundly unremarkable .225 during the regular season. He was born October 10, 1946, on the day the St. Louis Cardinals were banging out 20 hits on the way to a decisive win over the Boston Red Sox in the fourth game of their World Series. Maybe that was an omen.

Gene Tenace came alive in the 1972 Series. His four home runs in the first five games tied him with Babe Ruth and Duke Snider for most homers in a World Series. His first-inning run-scoring single in Game Seven was his eighth RBI of the Series. The Reds could no longer take Gene Tenace for granted. But what were the odds of this low-average, second-string catcher coming through again?

As improbable as it may have seemed to all in baseball, Gene Tenace did it again. He doubled home Bert Campaneris with the go-ahead run. When Allen Lewis came in to pinch run for Tenace, the sportswriters had already filled out their ballots for Series MVP: Fiori Gino Tennaci. The A's were not done. Sal Bando whacked a run-scoring double, putting the A's up by two runs. Clay Carroll relieved Borbon but the damage had been done.

Catfish Hunter got out of a minor jam in the bottom of the sixth inning and set the Reds down in order in the seventh. Only six outs to go for the upstart A's, who had finished their scoring for the day but seemed in control with Catfish Hunter on the mound.

When Pete Rose opened the Cincinnati eighth with a single, Dick Williams brought in his left-handed starter, Ken Holtzman, to face the Reds' most dangerous left-handed hitter, Joe Morgan. Williams had lost his top left-handed reliever, Darold Knowles, to a late-season injury and Holtzman had to be the Game Seven lefty out of the bullpen. Holtzman had pitched well in the Series, winning Game One, and was notoriously tough on left-handed batters. Joe Morgan, though, was notoriously tough on all pitchers and doubled to right, sending Rose to third. The lefty-lefty strategy backfired on Dick Williams and the Reds had the tying run in scoring position with nobody out. It was time for the chess match to begin.

George Foster was due to hit. Foster had entered the game in the seventh inning when Sparky Anderson removed Bobby Tolan and moved Cesar Geronimo to center. George Foster had great years ahead of him but he was not any kind of offensive threat in 1972. In came Julian Javier to pinch-hit. And out went Ken Holtzman. Dick Williams brought on his star reliever, Rollie Fingers.

Sparky Anderson countered with a different pinch hitter, leaving Julian Javier with the distinction of not appearing in the 1972 Seventh Game except for the official scorer's notation of "announced for Foster." To the plate marched left-handed Joe Hague, a .246 hitter during the season and hitless in his two plate appearances in two earlier World Series games. Hague did not have a chance against the future Hall of Fame reliever. He popped weakly to short.

He did not know it, but Rollie Fingers had two future Hall of Famers to face. Johnny Bench came to bat with Tony Perez waiting on deck. Pitch to Johnny Bench, the National League's leading RBI producer? It was not to be. Fingers intentionally walked Bench to load the bases and bring up Tony Perez. It was no less of a challenge. Tony Perez had been the Reds' best hitter during the Series, collecting 10 hits in his previous 23 at-bats and slamming two home runs. One swing could change the outcome of the game, but not the swing that Tony Perez delivered. He hit a fly ball to right field, hit well enough to score Pete Rose but not well enough to overcome Oakland's lead.

Joe Morgan took third on the sacrifice fly. Johnny Bench stole second base and the pressure was on the Reds' Dennis Menke. A single would give Cincinnati the lead, an out would all but extinguish their hopes against the best reliever in baseball. Menke did not have much of a regular season, batting only .233. He was having even less of a World Series, picking up only two hits in his previous 23 at-bats. Despite his puny performance, the A's remembered that one of Menke's two hits had been a home run in Game Five and that he nearly had another in the bottom of the ninth in Game Two. Fingers did not take Menke lightly and bore down. Fingers won the battle, inducing an easy fly ball for the third out. The Reds had narrowed the lead to one run and the first-inning error by Bobby Tolan was looming large.

The A's went down in order in the top of the ninth. It was up to Rollie Fingers to preserve the lead. He quickly retired Cesar Geronimo and Dave Concepcion, and all of Cincinnati's hopes rested on pinch hitter Darrel Chaney, with Pete Rose standing impatiently behind him. The home-team crowd prayed for a miracle: if only Chaney could get on, the Reds would have a chance! But Darrel Chaney? He was a .250 hitter during the season and hitless in his seven at-bats in the Series. The chances of Darrel Chaney (who retired after the 1979 season with a lifetime .217 average) getting on base were slim. Then came the unexpected. Chaney "took one for the team." An inside pitch from Rollie Fingers nicked Chaney and the Reds had the tying run aboard with Pete Rose at the plate. It was an opportunity few Reds fans believed they would get. It came down to legend versus legend, Fingers against Rose. One would make it to the Hall of Fame, the other would be barred from it.

So it was that Pete Rose made the final out of the 1972 World Series. He lofted a fly ball to Joe Rudi and the game was over. The Reds had their chances, coaxing six walks but only four hits off a quartet of Oakland pitchers. Both teams hit a meager .209 for the Series but the A's won the four one-run games they needed to win.

The Oakland A's had begun their own mini-dynasty, as they returned to the World Series in 1973 for another Game Seven. But 1972 was the first Seventh Game win in the A's long history, going back to their days in Philadelphia under Connie Mack. Their only other Seventh Game appearance, a loss to the 1931 Cardinals, seemed so distant.

October 22, 1972

	1	2	3	4	5	6	7	8	9	R	H	E
OAKLAND (AL)	1	0	0	0	0	2	0	0	0	3	6	1
CINCINNATI (NL)	0	0	0	0	1	0	0	1	0	2	4	2

PITCHERS: OAK: Odom, Hunter (W), Holtzman, Fingers (SV); CIN: Billingham, Borbon (L), Carroll, Grimsley, Hall

DOUBLES: Bando, Morgan, Perez, Tenace

TRIPLES: None

HOME RUNS: None

ATTENDANCE: 56,040

TIME OF GAME: 2:50

1973

Too Much Knowles and
Too Many Fingers

New York Mets   2
Oakland A's   5

Spiro T. Agnew resigned as vice president of the United States and that was only the beginning of the political drama that would unfold in 1973. One historic event would even try to upstage the World Series.

Scientists began talking about "recombinant DNA," and if you understood what they were talking about, you were very smart. It sounded scary, but not nearly as scary as the hit movie *The Exorcist*, a movie that had nothing to do with the Boston Red Sox and the "Curse of the Bambino." A horse named Secretariat won the Triple Crown of racing. Roberta Flack's "Killing Me Softly" was a huge hit and baseball was going strong, but with a wrinkle.

Half of baseball changed radically in 1973. The American League adopted the "designated hitter rule," allowing managers to substitute a hitter into the lineup in place of the usually weak-hitting pitcher without the pitcher having to leave the game. Purists protested but to no avail.

The Oakland A's repeated as West Division champions. Gene Tenace's heroics in the 1972 World Series earned him a place in the starting lineup and he responded with 24 home runs. Reggie Jackson was back from his hamstring injury and even more productive, leading the league in home runs and runs batted in. Catfish Hunter, Ken Holtzman, and Vida Blue were all 20-game winners and the bullpen was as tough as any in the league. Rollie Fingers was back and so was the lefty Darold Knowles. In

Around the Horn in 1973

- ☉ A utility infielder ended his six-year major-league career with a .199 batting average and no home runs. He went on to be one of the game's most respected managers. His name: Tony LaRussa.
- ☉ Bob Gibson won his eighth straight Gold Glove Award as the best-fielding pitcher in the National League. Pitcher Jim Kaat picked up his eighth straight Gold Glove in the American League.
- ☉ It was future Hall of Famer Mike Schmidt's first full season, but not a promising one as Mike hit just .196 for the Phillies.

the League Championship Series, the A's took the East Division champion Baltimore Orioles to the limit and won the finale behind Catfish Hunter's shutout. Although Reggie Jackson and Darold Knowles would not have to miss the 1973 World Series, as happened in 1972, the A's would be without their speedy new outfielder, Billy North, whose 53 stolen bases were an integral part of their regular-season offense.

The Cincinnati Reds repeated as West Division champs in the National League and were heavily favored to win the pennant. They had baseball's best record, the league's top hitter in Pete Rose, more good pitching from Jack Billingham and Don Gullett, and were facing a clearly inferior team in the East Division's New York Mets. Division play had produced a curious imbalance and the Mets won the East with only 82 wins, just three more games than they lost.

The Mets, the Amazing Mets, were back. They had stunned the baseball world in 1969 with their improbable World Series win over the Baltimore Orioles and were trying for another upset in 1973. Many of the same names were there—Seaver, Koosman, Kranepool, and Cleon Jones. But it would take a near miracle to get by the obviously superior Cincinnati Reds in the LCS. And that is exactly what the 1973 Mets did, winning the National League pennant in five games.

The star of the Mets was Tom Seaver, winner of 19 games and the National League's ERA leader. The next two starters, lefties Jerry Koosman and Jon Matlack, won 14 games apiece but each lost more than he won (15 and 16). As for hitting, there wasn't much. Not a .300 hitter on the team. John Milner was their "slugger" with 23 home runs. And they didn't win with speed either; the entire team stole 27 bases, more than a hundred fewer than the Oakland A's. It would take another near miracle—no, a full-blown miracle of epic proportions—for the Mets to win the World Series again. By some accounts, avoiding a sweep would be miraculous enough. The Mets did have one advantage in the Series. There would be no use of the designated hitter in the Fall Classic, so American League pitchers would find themselves in an unfamiliar place, the batter's box. Of course, as the Series would reveal, that advantage was purely theoretical.

After Oakland won Game One, 2–1, the Mets achieved their first minor miracle with a 12-inning, 10–7 win in Game Two. The sweep was off and the Series, a good one, was on. The teams went to New York for more thrills and more minor miracles.

Oakland took Game Three in 11 innings, 3–2. The Mets refused to acknowledge their inferiority and tied the Series with an easy 6–1 win in Game Four. Then they shocked the A's and everyone else by shutting out Oakland in the fifth game, 2–0, behind Jerry Koosman's masterful three-hitter. The A's were going back to Oakland facing elimination and New York's ace starter, Tom Seaver, in Game Six. Suddenly Oakland needed miracles.

What a matchup it was for Game Six: Tom Seaver against Catfish Hunter. Seaver pitched well but Hunter and his relievers pitched better; the A's won, 3–1, setting up the third World Series Seventh Game in as many years.

The Game Seven pitching matchup was not as glamorous as Game Six's and neither team could claim any real advantage. Ken Holtzman and Jon Matlack had already squared off in Games One and Four. Each had won a game and each had lost a game.

Neither team scored in the first two innings. The Mets picked up the game's first hit in the third on Don Hahn's leadoff single. After Bud Harrelson flied out, pitcher Jon Matlack, normally a good bunter (he was even among the top ten in sacrifice hits during the season), tried to sacrifice but bunted into a double play. Then everything that could have gone wrong went wrong for Jon Matlack and the Mets.

In the bottom of the third, Oakland pitcher Ken Holtzman doubled down the left-field line. It was Holtzman's second double of the Series and the third for A's pitchers. Mets pitchers had collected only two singles. So much for the advantage that the Mets' pitchers supposedly enjoyed over their American League counterparts, unfamiliar as they were to batting.

Leadoff hitter Bert Campaneris stepped to the plate. His speed was already legendary but few paid any attention to his power, what there was of it. During the regular season, Campaneris had hit only four home runs. Reggie Jackson must have been giving little Campy some pointers in the postseason because he slugged two homers in the League Championship Series. So it should not have come as that big of a surprise when Bert Campaneris ripped a two-run homer to right field off of Jon Matlack. The A's had a lead and a bullpen ready to protect it. But they were not finished with Matlack.

Joe Rudi followed with a single to center. Things must have looked secure for the Mets after Sal Bando popped to second for out number two and Reggie Jackson came to bat. Matlack had faced Reggie eight times in the Series and allowed only a walk and a single. The lefty-lefty advantage was clearly working in favor of the Mets. He had not yet picked up the nickname "Mr. October," but Reggie Jackson did what Mr. October was supposed to do. He crushed a two-run homer deep to right field, sending Jon Matlack to the showers and giving Oakland a 4–0 lead.

Harry Parker relieved for New York and the A's were content to leave the inning with their four-run margin. In the fourth inning, the Mets threatened to come back when Rusty Staub singled and Cleon Jones walked. But nothing came of the two runners when John Milner bounced to second to end the inning. Ken Holtzman gave up a leadoff single to Jerry Grote in the fifth inning but set down the next three Mets, two on strikeouts.

In the bottom of the fifth, Bert Campaneris dispensed another hit, a single to left. When Cleon Jones had trouble fielding the ball, Campy scooted to second and later scored on Joe Rudi's single. The score was 5–0, and no team had ever bounced back from a five-run deficit in a World Series Seventh Game. But the Amazing Mets had never been in a Seventh Game, so why couldn't they be the first?

The Mets made a move in the sixth inning. With one out, Felix Millan and Rusty Staub hit successive doubles to finally plate a run. Oakland manager Dick Williams wasted no time in going to his bullpen. There was no reason to let any miracles begin to grow. Into the game came Rollie Fingers, and he quickly smothered all hopes of any miracle. At least in the sixth inning.

In the seventh inning, the Mets' Don Hahn singled with one out. After Bud Harrelson made the second out with a fly to center, pinch hitter Ken Boswell singled to bring Wayne Garrett to the plate. Garrett had been one of the major power sources for the Mets during the regular season, hitting 16 home runs. He had homered twice in the World Series but was otherwise struggling in the postseason. He had struck out ten times and was within one strikeout of tying the record for most strikeouts in a World Series. The "feast or famine" Series of Wayne Garrett continued when he looked at a called strike three. At least he was in good company, because his 11 strikeouts tied the record held by another third baseman, Hall of Famer Eddie Mathews.

The A's were done with their scoring. Their lead seemed secure, especially when Rollie Fingers set down Felix Millan, Rusty Staub, and Cleon Jones in the eighth inning. The ball never left the infield. Fingers was in fine form.

The Mets were down but not out. Not yet. John Milner started the ninth inning with a walk. After Jerry Grote flied out, Don Hahn slapped a single, his third of the day. Bud Harrelson grounded out, advancing the two runners. The Mets were down to their last out and were desperate for a miracle. Any miracle. When pinch hitter Ed Kranepool bounced to Gene Tenace at first base, it seemed as if the miracles had run dry. But the hero of the 1972 World Series muffed the easy grounder, allowing Milner to score and bringing the tying run to the plate. It was a miracle, although the official scorer ruled it an error.

The tying run stood at home plate in the person of Wayne Garrett. He had one last chance to redeem himself for his 11 strikeouts and overall weak World Series. He also had the chance to set a new record for most strikeouts in a World Series. Even though Garrett had struck out against Fingers in the seventh inning, Dick Williams wanted the lefty-lefty pitching advantage and summoned Darold Knowles from the bullpen. For Knowles it was a new World Series record, pitching in all seven games.

Wayne Garrett hit 61 homers over the course of his ten-year career in the big leagues. He hit 3 more in the postseason, but unfortunately for the Mets of 1973, none were in the ninth inning of the Seventh Game of the 1973 World Series. At least he did not set any new record for World Series strikeouts. Instead, he made the final out by popping up to the A's little slugging shortstop, Bert Campaneris.

The story of Game Seven was the same as the other three Oakland wins. The one-two punch of Fingers and Knowles—sometimes it was Knowles and then Fingers—was too much for the Mets. The two relievers saved the four victories and allowed only one earned run in 20 innings of work. That kind of pitching tends to squeeze the life out of miracles.

Reggie Jackson would return to the World Series four more times, once with the A's in 1974 and three times with the New York Yankees. He would hit nine more World Series home runs but never even have a chance to hit another one in a Seventh Game. As for the Mets, they would have another chance at a Seventh Game victory, but it would take a different kind of miracle to get them there, thirteen years later.

So what other political drama unfolded during the 1973 World Series? The night before the Seventh Game, President Richard Nixon fired Watergate Special Prosecutor Archibald Cox, an event that came to be known as the "Saturday Night Massacre." Nixon obviously had no respect for baseball, for if he did he would have waited until the Series was over. Curiously, on the same night before Game Seven Americans watched the premier of a new TV series, "The Six Million Dollar Man," never dreaming that one day that title would describe mediocre ballplayers and their inflated salaries.

October 21, 1973

	1	2	3	4	5	6	7	8	9	R	H	E
NEW YORK (NL)	0	0	0	0	0	1	0	0	1	2	8	1
OAKLAND (AL)	0	0	4	0	1	0	0	0	X	5	9	1

PITCHERS: NYM: Matlack (L), Parker, Sadecki, Stone; OAK: Holtzman (W), Fingers, Knowles (SV)

DOUBLES: Holtzman, Millan, Staub

TRIPLES: None

HOME RUNS: Campaneris, Jackson

ATTENDANCE: 49,333

TIME OF GAME: 2:37

1975

A Hard Act to Follow

Cincinnati Reds   4
Boston Red Sox   3

There was plenty of entertainment at the movies in 1975. Jack Nicholson starred in *One Flew over the Cuckoo's Nest* and Al Pacino was brilliant in *Dog Day Afternoon*. Hollywood came up with a new term to describe the biggest hit of the year—*blockbuster*—because that was the only word that could come close to explaining the power and popularity of *Jaws*. Olivia Newton John asked the musical question, "Have You Never Been Mellow?"

Teamsters boss Jimmy Hoffa disappeared. The best comedy on television was "The Mary Tyler Moore Show." Arthur Ashe and Billie Jean King won at Wimbledon and if you missed it on the tube, there would soon be VHS technology to let you record your favorite sporting event and watch it whenever you wanted to. For many, especially in 1975, the favorite sporting event was baseball because baseball put on a great show that year.

Game Seven of the 1975 World Series faced an impossible challenge: how could the teams hope to top the drama and heroics of the Sixth Game, which has since become etched in the collective memory of baseball fans as arguably the greatest game every played? On October 21, 1975, Boston Red Sox fans thought they had found the stairway into paradise when Carlton Fisk capped off a magical night of comebacks and marvelous defensive plays with his twelfth-inning body-English home run off the left-field foul

Around the Horn in 1975

- ☉ It was a sorry day at Wrigley Field in September when the Pirates throttled the Cubs 22–0, the most lopsided shutout in major-league history. Rennie Stennet went seven for seven for Pittsburgh.
- ☉ So much for the value of speed in 1975. The California Angels, last in the American League West Division, topped the AL in steals with 220, more than three times the number of thefts committed by the pennant-winning Red Sox, who had 66.
- ☉ The National League record for most consecutive hits before the first out of a game is eight, and it has been accomplished only twice, both times in 1975 (by Philadelphia and Pittsburgh).

pole in Fenway Park to force a Seventh Game. That was Game Six, and there was no way Game Seven could measure up.

In truth, Game Seven did not measure up to Game Six, but no game before or since has been equal to that task. Game Seven was a diamond gem in its own right and suffers only by an unfair comparison with a game that still warms the hearts of Red Sox fans—and all fans of the game—whenever they begin to wonder why they so love baseball.

How did the Red Sox get to the World Series in 1975? They had finished third in the American League East in 1974 but took charge of the division in 1975 with two superstar seasons from two superstar rookies, Jim Rice and Fred Lynn. Lynn's year was the more remarkable, as he won both Rookie of the Year and Most Valuable Player honors. The Sox led all of baseball in hitting and that made up for a pitching staff that was average in talent but long in inspiration. The cigar-smoking Luis Tiant, "El Tiante," dazzled the opposition with his unorthodox pitching delivery in which he turned to stare at second base—and far beyond—before releasing the ball. When they swept the defending World Series champion Oakland A's in the LCS to take the pennant, everyone knew that the Boston Red Sox were for real.

No one even questioned whether the Cincinnati Reds were for real. With the best record in all of baseball, the "Big Red Machine" won the N.L. West by 20 games and dispatched the N.L. East–winning Pirates in three games to advance to the World Series. Joe Morgan, Johnny Bench, Pete

Rose, Tony Perez, and Ken Griffey provided the offense and manager Sparky Anderson got the most out of a talented but no-name pitching staff. Three 15-game winners spread the wealth for Sparky and he had two fine relievers, lefty Will McEnaney and righty Rawly Eastwick, who combined for 37 saves.

Boston was seeking its first World Series win since 1918 and would have to get it without their star rookie Jim Rice, who had broken his wrist in early September and was out for the rest of the year. With or without Rice, no one could have foreseen the Series that was about to unfold.

Luis Tiant shut out the Reds in Game One before an ecstatic crowd at Fenway Park in the opener. It looked as if the Red Sox were going up two games to none when they took a 2–1 lead into the ninth inning of the second game, but Boston starter Bill Lee could not smother a Cincinnati rally that evened the Series.

The Series switched to Riverfront Stadium in Cincinnati, where the teams split a pair of one-run thrillers before the Reds took the pivotal Game 5 by a 6–2 margin. Boston fans bitterly remember Game Three for the sacrifice bunt by Cincinnati's Ed Armbrister in the tenth inning, a play in which the Fenway faithful still think Armbrister should have been called out for batter interference but instead was instrumental in the Reds' victory. Boston returned home in need of two wins against the Big Red Machine. To get to a Game Seven they would have to first win Game Six. They did, in a game that continues to resonate for the ages.

This is a book about Seventh Games, not about sixth games. If the game played in Boston on October 21, 1975, were the Seventh Game of the 1975 World Series and not the sixth game, it would have rendered pointless any debate as to the greatest Seventh Game in World Series history. The story of Game Six has been told many times but a brief summary is necessary as a bridge to the Seventh Game. The danger here is evident: to summarize Game Six in one paragraph is like describing the Mona Lisa as "a picture of a girl with a quirky smile" or reducing a Michael Jordan slam dunk to "a tall guy takes a running start and stuffs a ball into a hoop." But here it is.

The Red Sox scored three in the first inning but the Reds stormed back to take a 6–3 lead into the bottom of the eighth. Pinch hitter Bernie Carbo tied the game with a three-run home run. Boston nearly won it in the bottom of the ninth, but George Foster gunned down Denny Doyle at home. In the eleventh inning, Dwight Evans robbed Joe Morgan of a home run with a sensational running catch at the right-field wall. Carlton Fisk led off the bottom of the twelfth with a long fly ball to deep left. The only question was whether it would stay fair. Helped by Fisk's imploring body gyrations and the prayers of all New England, the ball plunked the foul pole for a game-winning home run. John Kiley, organ master at Fenway Park, broke into Handel's "Hallelujah Chorus" and Red Sox fans get the chills (some even cry) when they watch replays of it. End of summary.

So how could the teams, emotionally drained from the four-hour ordeal of Game Six, treat the fans to a Game Seven worthy of the first six games? Somehow they did.

Lefty Don Gullett, the loser in Game One but the winning pitcher in Game Five, got the nod from Sparky Anderson. For Boston, it was Bill "Spaceman" Lee, the strange and unpredictable southpaw who had pitched so well in Game Two only to see the Reds storm back and snatch the victory away from Boston.

The Spaceman set down Pete Rose, Joe Morgan, and Johnny Bench to open the game. How many pitchers can make that claim? Boston came out flying, as Bernie Carbo doubled off the wall in left. Denny Doyle failed to advance Carbo to third and the Red Sox squandered the scoring opportunity when Carl Yastrzemski and Fisk went down.

Cincinnati threatened in the third. Ken Griffey singled, but the Sox defense rose to the occasion with a nifty double play, made even more significant when pitcher Don Gullett followed with a single. Pete Rose ended the inning with a routine ground ball and the game was shaping up to be a classic.

The Red Sox scored in the bottom of the third. After Bill Lee struck out, Bernie Carbo walked. Denny Doyle singled and Carbo scampered to third. Yaztrzemski drilled a single to right, scoring the first run of the game. Doyle hustled to third and Yaz alertly took second on the throw to third. The Reds were in no mood to pitch to Carlton Fisk and, on orders from Sparky Anderson, issued the Game Six hero an intentional walk. The strategy looked brilliant when Gullett struck out Fred Lynn. It swiftly blew up in the Reds' faces when Gullett suddenly lost his control and walked both Rico Petrocelli and Dwight Evans with the bases loaded. It was 3–0 and the bases were still loaded for the Boston shortstop, Rich "the Rooster" Burleson. This was the Red Sox chance to break the game open. Burleson had been having a good Series, with seven hits in the first six games. This was the time for one of those lazy Fenway fly balls off the fabled Green

Monster. But the Rooster did not even make contact as Gullett struck him out. Three more runners left on base but Boston had a three-run lead.

Joe Morgan beat out a bunt to open the fourth. After Bench flied out, Morgan stole second but never came home as pitcher Bill Lee was too tough for the Reds. Meanwhile, Boston squandered another good scoring chance in the bottom of the fourth. Bill Lee stunned the crowd with a single to open the inning and took second on a wild pitch. Bernie Carbo moved Lee to third on a ground ball to the right side but neither Doyle nor Yastrzemski could bring home that fourth Boston run.

Cincinnati then showed Boston how to really squander a scoring opportunity. Dave Concepcion reached first on an infield single. Ken Griffey got a break when Denny Doyle's error allowed him to reach first, and it also sent Concepcion to third. First and third, nobody out—that is a golden opportunity for runs in the big leagues. But Bill Lee was just toying with the Reds. He struck out Cesar Geronimo and then faced Merv Rettenmund, pinch-hitting for Don Gullett. The pitcher's best friend, the double-play ball, came out and the Red Sox lead was intact.

Not to be outdone, Boston showed Cincinnati that it was not through wasting good scoring prospects. Fred Lynn drew a one-out walk against the Reds' new pitcher, Jack Billingham, and Rico Petrocelli followed with a single. Dwight Evans caught hold of a Billingham offering and sent it deep to center field. Deep, but not deep enough. Rick Burleson walked to load the bases, bringing up Bill Lee with a chance to help his own cause. Of course, Red Sox manager Darrell Johnson could have brought in a pinch hitter with a far better probability of delivering a hit. Lee hit for himself and flied out to end the threat. As it turned out, the Red Sox would squander no more chances because they would get no more.

Pete Rose always found a way to make things happen. He singled to right to start the Cincinnati sixth. After Joe Morgan flied out, Johnny Bench rapped what should have been an inning-ending double-play ball to Rick Burleson. The Rooster fielded the ball cleanly, flipped it to Denny Doyle, and Doyle threw the ball away trying to double up Bench. Everyone knew it—Boston should have been out of the inning. Instead, Bill Lee had to face Tony Perez. He had already faced Perez twice, with complete success. This time Lee had something special in mind for Perez.

The scouting report on Tony Perez was to never pitch "off speed" to Tony, meaning never to throw slow stuff. Bill Lee was the master of the slow curve and decided to throw him something more akin to a blooper pitch, a very, very slow curveball. It was more than "off speed," it was "no speed." The problem was that it didn't curve. Perez jumped out of his socks and whacked the ball over the left-field wall for a two-run homer. Just like that, the Boston lead was down to a single run. Denny Doyle's bad throw cost the Sox dearly. Lee was annoyed at Doyle's inability to turn the double play and lost his focus for a fatal instant. He recovered to retire George Foster for the third out but a sense of foreboding fell upon Fenway Park.

Boston went down in order in the bottom of the sixth. With one out in the top of the seventh, Bill Lee walked Ken Griffey and then unexpectedly left the game because of a blister. Except for the mistake to Perez, Lee had pitched remarkably well. In six innings, he got the Reds to hit into two double plays and, as all Red Sox fans will tell you, there should have been three of them. Into the fire walked Roger Moret, the skinny (some might even say emaciated) lefty who had seen limited action in the previous six games. During the season, Moret was one of Boston's best pitchers, compiling a sparkling 14–3 record. He got Geronimo to pop out but could not close the inning. After walking pinch hitter Ed Armbrister, he gave up a run-scoring single to Pete Rose. Cincinnati had completed its comeback and tied the game, 3–3.

The Red Sox got out of the inning without further scoring, just barely. Joe Morgan walked to load the bases and the seldom-used Jim Willoughby came in to get Johnny Bench to foul out. In the bottom of the inning, the deflated Red Sox went down in order. But so did the Reds in the top of the eighth. Now it was Boston's chance to take the lead and Dwight Evans enticed a walk out of Clay Carroll to start the Boston eighth. Rick Burleson tried to bunt Evans over to second but failed on two attempts and then swung away. He grounded into a double play. Cecil Cooper, the talented first baseman who had put together a solid year for Boston but who was having a dreadful World Series (one hit in 18 at-bats) pinch-hit for Jim Willoughby and fouled out to end the inning.

Boston needed a new pitcher to hold the Reds in the ninth inning. They called on Jim Burton, a rookie left-hander who had won only one game in his big-league career. Only one pitcher on Boston's World Series roster had pitched fewer innings than Burton and that was the man he was replacing, Willoughby. On the other hand, Burton was the only member of the Boston pitching corps with an earned run average under 3.00. But those who understood the game knew that Burton had one glaring weakness: he tended to walk a lot of batters. And he walked Ken Griffey to lead off the ninth inning.

Cesar Geronimo did what Rick Burleson could not do a half inning earlier. He laid down a good sacrifice bunt. Dan Driessen grounded out to second and Ken Griffey moved to third base. Burton walked Pete Rose. He needed one more out, just one more out to preserve the tie. In his way stood Joe Morgan. Jim Burton made a great pitch to Morgan, a down-and-away slider. Morgan swung and did not hit the ball well. It was a weak bloop pop fly to short center field, beyond the reach of the infield and not far enough for Fred Lynn to catch. It dropped for a hit and the Reds had taken the lead. Reggie Cleveland came in to pitch but the Reds were in front. No one hit the ball hard off Jim Burton but the Reds showed that they could use their fundamental skills to squeeze out one little run as adeptly as they could use their power to blast out bunches of them.

Boston needed a miracle finish, as they had found in Game Six, but there were no miracles left in Boston that night. Reds reliever Will McEnaney made sure of that. Pinch hitter Juan Beniquez flied out. Pinch hitter Bob Montgomery grounded out. Carl Yastrzemski was the last hope for the Red Sox. More than anyone else in Fenway Park, Yaz wanted to keep the game going, to somehow find a way to bring victory to Boston. But he flied out to center field and the 1975 World Series was over.

For the Red Sox, it was their third trip to the World Series since selling Babe Ruth to the Yankees in 1920. It was also the third time they lost in seven games. Whispers of the "Curse of the Bambino" were spreading like a noxious weed. It would get even worse eleven years later.

October 22, 1975

	1	2	3	4	5	6	7	8	9	R	H	E
CINCINNATI (NL)	0	0	0	0	0	2	1	0	1	4	9	0
BOSTON (AL)	0	0	3	0	0	0	0	0	0	3	5	2

PITCHERS: CIN: Gullett, Billingham, Carroll (W), McEnaney (SV);
BOS: Lee, Moret, Willoughby, Burton (L), Cleveland

DOUBLES: Carbo

TRIPLES: None

HOME RUNS: Perez

ATTENDANCE: 35,205

TIME OF GAME: 2:52

1979

Pops

Pittsburgh Pirates 4
Baltimore Orioles 1

It was a difficult year, 1979. Even though Jimmy Carter helped negotiate the Camp David Accords (does anyone even remember them?), the international scene turned ugly when a militant government in Iran held sixty-six Americans hostage. It was the year of the Three Mile Island scare, when a Pennsylvania nuclear reactor came close—how close we may never know—to a catastrophic meltdown. It was a tragic summer for baseball too. Yankees catcher Thurman Munson, captain and emotional leader of the New York squad, died in a plane crash in early August.

Even the movies took on a more sober tone. *Apocalypse Now*, *Norma Rae*, and *Kramer vs. Kramer* made us think more than we wanted to. We needed something uplifting from baseball that year and baseball delivered.

Although the Baltimore Orioles could not boast of a single .300 hitter in its daily lineup, manager Earl Weaver's team had no trouble winning the American League East Division by a comfortable eight games over Milwaukee's Brewers. The Orioles' pitching staff dominated the league, led by Cy Young winner Mike Flanagan (23–7, 3.08 ERA) and youngsters Dennis Martinez and Scott McGregor. Eddie Murray, Ken Singleton, and Al Bumbry led the capable Orioles offense but there was no doubt as to where Baltimore's strength lay: pitching.

Around the Horn in 1979

- ☽ Bobby Cox's Atlanta Braves finished last in their division but boasted baseball's last "20-20" pitcher. Phil Niekro won 21 and lost 20 for the Braves.
- ☽ For the first and only time in history, relief pitchers won both Cy Young Awards. Bruce Sutter of the Cardinals and Rollie Fingers of the Brewers took home the honors.
- ☽ In the wildest game of the year, the Cubs rallied from a 17–6 deficit to tie the Phillies at 22–22, only to lose 23–22 in 10 innings at Wrigley Field.

As expected, the Orioles defeated the California Angels in the LCS to advance to the World Series, where they would have the chance to avenge their loss in 1971 to the Pittsburgh Pirates, who had defeated them in seven games.

When you recall the Pittsburgh Pirates of 1979, one name comes to mind: Willie Stargell. His regular-season stats of 32 home runs and 82 runs batted in does not begin to tell the story of Stargell's worth to the Pirates and their fans. They called him "Pops," because he was the grand old man of Pittsburgh. With gentle grace and timely hitting, Willie led his team to a pennant as no other player had led before.

The Pirates offered a potent lineup in addition to the aging slugger Stargell. Dave Parker, Bill Robinson, and mid-season acquisition Bill Madlock anchored an offense that was ripe with talent. The pitching staff, however, was a different story. It had no 20-game winners; it did not even have a 15-game winner. The staff leader in wins was John Candelaria (14–7). For the first time in history, a team without even a single 15-game winner was in the World Series. Baltimore certainly owned the pitching advantage.

After splitting the first two games of the Series at Baltimore, the Orioles stunned the Pirates by winning Games Three and Four in Pittsburgh. If the Pirates were to win the Series, they would have to win three games in a row, the last two in Baltimore. Fortune smiled upon the Pittsburgh Pirates when the Orioles' bats grew silent: they scored a total of one run in

Games Five and Six, bringing another Seventh Game to Baltimore's Memorial Stadium. It was 1971 all over again.

This much can be said of Game Seven of the 1979 World Series: it was one of the best eight-inning games in a World Series. Unfortunately for Baltimore fans, the game of baseball was, as it had been for over a century and continues to be, a nine-inning affair.

Baltimore had the clear pitching advantage in Game Seven. Earl Weaver started lefty Scott McGregor, who had already pitched a complete-game win in Game Three. Pirates manager Chuck Tanner called upon Jim Bibby, who had been unimpressive in the Game Four loss in Pittsburgh.

When the Pirates squandered good scoring opportunities in the first two innings, Scott McGregor seemed to gain strength and momentum. The Orioles stunned the Pirates when second baseman Rich Dauer, who over the course of his ten-year career hit only 43 home runs (and never more than 9 in a season), lined a Jim Bibby offering into the left-field stands for a 1–0 lead after three innings.

The Pirates had a splendid chance to tie the game in the fourth. With one out, Stargell doubled to left. Madlock followed with a sharp ground ball to shortstop Kiki Garcia. Stargell tried to take third base—an obvious baserunning mistake—but made it when Garcia's errant throw pulled Doug DeCinces off the bag. Runners were on first and third with only one out. But McGregor escaped when Steve Nicosia lined out to second base and Phil Garner popped harmlessly to first baseman Eddie Murray. Harmlessly? Perhaps not.

Phil Garner's pop fly to Murray should have been a routine out to end the inning. Although it did end the inning, it did so in a way that was anything but routine and may have affected the outcome of the game in a totally unexpected way. The high pop fly sent Murray into foul territory near the first-base bag. But the ball drifted back into fair territory and Murray drifted with it, directly into the path of Garner. As Murray reached for the ball, Garner slammed into him, forcing the ball loose in fair territory. The first-base umpire called Garner out for interfering with Murray's attempt to catch the ball; no one disputes that it was the correct call. But did the jarring collision affect Murray's concentration later in the game, when he would need it most?

McGregor nursed the one-run lead into the sixth inning. He began the inning by jamming Dave Parker and inducing a weak ground ball for the first out. Bill Robinson then sent a sharp grounder to shortstop Garcia's right. It glanced off of Garcia's glove for a hit and up to the plate walked Willie Stargell.

Stargell had already reached McGregor for two hits, a bloop single to left in the second and a bloop double to left in the fourth inning. Hits they were, but in all fairness to McGregor, they were good pitches that Stargell did not hit very hard. In Earl Weaver's mind, this was a confrontation that favored Baltimore: the left-handed McGregor against the left-handed Stargell.

McGregor's first pitch to Stargell was a fastball, down in the strike zone. With a smooth and powerful stroke, Stargell sent the ball over the right-field fence for a two-run home run. Silence fell over the Baltimore crowd. The score was 2–1, the final score of the 1971 Seventh Game, eight years ago to the day.

The Stargell home run did not shake Scott McGregor. He stayed in the game and pitched well through the eighth inning. Stargell doubled in the eighth but did not score. McGregor needed only one run from his mates to tie the score and another to win it. The opportunity came in the bottom of the eighth inning, when the Orioles loaded the bases and put matters onto the shoulders of Eddie Murray. The game was on the line and Murray could only send a fly ball to Dave Parker, ending the inning. What effect did the fourth-inning collision with Phil Garner have on Murray? Murray has never used the jarring collision as an excuse. We can only wonder. The Orioles would have one last chance in the bottom of the ninth inning and they were still down by only one run.

Then came the complete collapse and unraveling of the Baltimore Orioles.

Tim Stoddard replaced Scott McGregor in the top of the ninth inning. Phil Garner greeted the hard-throwing righty with a double to left. Pirates star reliever Kent Tekulve, who had entered the game in the bottom of the eighth, was unable to bunt Garner to third. Out came Earl Weaver for a pitching change. Lefty Mike Flanagan came in to pitch to the left-handed-hitting Omar Moreno. Flanagan had been effective against Moreno earlier in the Series but now Moreno singled to center, scoring Garner. It was now a two-run game.

Weaver made another pitching change, bringing in Don Stanhouse to pitch to Tim Foli. Choking up high on the bat, the bespectacled Foli laced a single to center, sending Moreno to third. It was time for another pitching change. Conventional baseball wisdom dictates that right-handed pitchers have the advantage when facing right-handed batters (with the same advantage holding true for lefty versus lefty) and Earl Weaver played the ninth inning in strict obedience to that wisdom. He brought in the left-hander Tippy Martinez to face the left-handed Dave Parker.

Tippy promptly hit Parker to load the bases and bring up the dangerous—and right-handed—Bill Robinson. It was time for yet another pitching change. In came the righty Dennis Martinez (no relation to Tippy), who responded by hitting Robinson to force in another run. Two hit batsmen in a row by two unrelated pitchers with the same last name—that is a record that may stand for centuries.

The score was now 4–1, and the game was utterly out of control. Five pitchers in one inning could not stem the Pirates tide, and Earl Weaver bowed his head in disbelief. So much for conventional wisdom!

The bases remained jammed with one out and Willie Stargell at the plate. He had already collected four hits, joining Max Carey and Ripper Collins as the only men to accomplish that feat in a Seventh Game. Weaver had run out of managerial gymnastics and let the left-handed Stargell have his licks against the right-handed Dennis Martinez. Willie knew it didn't matter; after all, he had gotten his four hits against the lefty McGregor. And as if to add the final insult to Weaver's managerial injuries, Stargell bounced into an inning-ending double play.

The bottom of the ninth inning was a whimper. Gary Roenicke and Doug DeCinces struck out on outside pitches and Pat Kelly ended the game with a fly ball to center.

President Jimmy Carter joined Baseball Commissioner Bowie Kuhn in presenting the championship trophy to the Pirates. Willie Stargell was named Most Valuable Player of the Series. Lovers of the Seventh Game will remember him for many things, including his four hits and the fact that he is the only player in major-league history to score the winning run in two different Seventh Games.

The Pittsburgh Pirates were perfect: five wins against no losses in Seventh Games. The Baltimore Orioles were also perfect: zero wins against two losses in Seventh Games.

October 17, 1979

	1	2	3	4	5	6	7	8	9	R	H	E
PITTSBURGH (NL)	0	0	0	0	0	2	0	0	2	4	10	0
BALTIMORE (AL)	0	0	1	0	0	0	0	0	0	1	4	2

PITCHERS: PGH: Bibby, D. Robinson, Jackson (W), Tekulve (SV);
BAL: McGregor (L), Stoddard, Flanagan, Stanhouse,
T. Martinez, D. Martinez

DOUBLES: Stargell (2), Garner

TRIPLES: None

HOME RUNS: Stargell, Dauer

ATTENDANCE: 53,733

TIME OF GAME: 2:54

1982

The Cardinals—Again!

Milwaukee Brewers   3
St. Louis Cardinals   6

The year 1982 marked the historic breakup of the AT&T monopoly. John Updike won the Pulitzer Prize for *Rabbit Is Rich* and the best play on Broadway was *The Life and Adventures of Nicholas Nickleby*. The "Wow!" movie of the year was Steven Spielberg's *E.T. the Extra-Terrestrial*, but a lot of us got off on the brilliant slice of life in the Baltimore comedy *Diner*, directed by Barry Levinson (no relation).

There was plenty of music to remember from 1982. Huey Lewis and the News had a hit with "Do You Believe in Love?" Stevie Wonder scored with "That Girl." The theme from *Chariots of Fire* by Vangelis was everywhere. One of the first modern TV hospital dramas, "St. Elsewhere," made its debut and the year was ripe for baseball. As always.

When the Braves left Milwaukee after the 1965 season, fans in the beer city wondered whether they would ever see baseball again. When the expansion Seattle Pilots folded their tent after only one season and relocated in Milwaukee for the opening of the 1970 season, the new Milwaukee Brewers provided a degree of entertainment for the locals but little hope of postseason play. In their first eight seasons, the Brewers always lost more games than they won. In 1978, Milwaukee posted its first winning season and then kept getting better. They finally won a pennant in 1982, with great hitting from Robin Yount, Paul Molitor, Cecil Cooper, and Gor-

Around the Horn in 1982

- Minnesota's Terry Felton set the all-time record for most losses by a pitcher without a win in a single season. Felton went 0–13 for the hapless Minnesota Twins.
- Dave Kingman led the National League in home runs with 37, despite hitting only .204; it is the lowest average ever posted by a league's home run champion.
- Manny Mota, then baseball's all-time pinch-hit leader, played his last season, retiring with 150 pinch hits. Lenny Harris broke Mota's record when he delivered his 151st pinch hit in 2001.

man Thomas. Their pitching was thin but good enough. It was a tough finish, as the Brewers had to beat the Baltimore Orioles on the last day of the season to clinch the American League East Division title. They did nothing the easy way in 1982. They won the pennant by spotting the West Division champion California Angels a two-game head start in the best-of-five League Championship Series before coming back to win the pennant before the home crowd in Milwaukee.

In the National League, St. Louis manager Whitey Herzog pieced together a team well suited to the artificial turf at Busch Stadium. Speedsters Lonnie Smith, Willie McGee, and Ozzie Smith discovered that they could manufacture runs the old-fashioned way. The Cardinals hit the fewest home runs in baseball but scored bunches of runs whenever they needed them. No Cardinals starting pitcher won more than 15 games but the staff pulled together as a team. Bruce Sutter, baseball's best relief pitcher with 36 saves, was a big plus. The Cardinals had no difficulty sweeping the West Division champion Atlanta Braves to set up a World Series matchup of baseball's home run leaders against baseball's home run losers. Never before had the Series seen such a disparity in home run power—the Brewers had slugged 216 homers compared with the Cardinals' laughable 67. It would take the full seven games to see who would have the last laugh.

The teams split the first two games in St. Louis by scores that reflected the character of the teams. The Brewers crushed the Cardinals, 10–0, in the opener, and the Cardinals edged the Brewers, 5–4, in Game

Two. The Brewers won two of three in Milwaukee to send the Series back to St. Louis, where the slugging Brewers needed only one victory to win their first World Series.

The Cardinals forced a Seventh Game by turning the tables on the Brewers with a 13–1 rout in Game Six. To start the Seventh Game, the Cardinals called on their quick-tempered ace, Joaquin Andujar. He had not lost a game in his last dozen starts but had caught a wicked line drive on the leg off the bat of Ted Simmons in Game Three. How well he could pitch in the forty-four-degree chill of the St. Louis night air was manager Whitey Herzog's biggest concern.

The Brewers had their own concerns with starter Pete Vuckovich. Pete had lost his last five starts of the regular season and was having shoulder problems. But he had been the Brewers' best pitcher over the past two seasons. Even though he was the loser in Game Three, no one could blame him as the Brewers' defense had betrayed him with three errors. Brewers fans knew they would be in for a cardiac challenge, as Vuckovich was known for giving up lots of hits and walks en route to his victories.

When the Cardinals took the field in the first inning, shortstop Ozzie Smith electrified the crowd with his trademark acrobatic front flip and back flip. NBC's Joe Garagiola quipped, "We may need a big mustard jar before this day is over with all the hot dogs we've seen so far." Joe did not realize how prophetic his comment was.

Neither team scored in the first three innings but they went about their business in totally different ways. Not a single Brewer reached base against Andujar. The Cardinals, on the other hand, had plenty of scoring chances, leaving one runner on base in the first, the bases loaded in the second, and two runners on in the third. Baseball is a game of opportunities and these were opportunities lost that could come back to haunt the Cardinals.

The Brewers finally got a runner and threatened to score in the fourth inning. With one out and Robin Yount on first, Cecil Cooper roped a single to right field. Right fielder George Hendrick fielded the ball cleanly and with poker-faced efficiency fired a perfect strike to third baseman Ken Oberkfell in time to catch Yount trying to take third base. Yount's headfirst slide gave him no chance and probably a throbbing headache as he slammed into Oberkfell's masterful blockade of the base.

In the bottom of the fourth, St. Louis pushed across a run on three singles to take the early lead. The Brewers, never a team to waste time or energy on stringing hits together as other teams often did, tied the game on a home run by Ben Oglivie in the top of the fifth inning. Then came the sixth inning, where the fortunes of the Brewers rose and fell. Jim Gantner led off with a double. Paul Molitor tried to move Gantner to third base with a bunt. Andujar pounced on the bunt and threw poorly to first base, hitting Molitor as he neared the bag. The ball ricocheted off Molitor. Gantner scored and Molitor took second base. The official scorer credited Molitor with a hit and charged Andujar with an error for the bad throw. The Brewers had the lead and another run in scoring position with none out.

Robin Yount tried to move Molitor to third by bouncing one to the right side of the infield. He succeeded beyond his wildest dreams when Andujar failed to cover first base on the grounder to Keith Hernandez and Yount was safe. It was officially a hit but as the whole world could see, it was a huge mental error by Andujar. In the three games that the Brewers had won, they had averaged nearly eight runs a game and that number now looked like a distinct possibility for Game Seven. First and third, nobody out, a run already in. The fans back in Milwaukee were salivating as the sweet-swinging Cecil Cooper strode to the plate. Cooper lofted a deep fly to left field, deep enough to score Paul Molitor with the second Brewers run of the inning. But that was all the Brewers could do. Ted Simmons and Ben Oglivie grounded out and Milwaukee had to be content with a two-run lead. It was not enough.

With one out in the bottom of the sixth, Ozzie Smith, known mostly for his defensive wizardry, smacked a single to left. The Cardinals had reached Pete Vuckovich for nine hits, all singles. Lonnie Smith changed the streak with a double down the right-field line, sending Ozzie to third base. Vuckovich was done for the day. Milwaukee manager Harvey Kuenn brought in the left-handed pitcher Bob McClure to face the left-handed batter Ken Oberkfell. Whitey Herzog countered with a pinch hitter, the veteran Gene Tenace. Tenace had been the star of the 1972 World Series but had not gathered a single hit in his previous six trips to the plate in the 1982 Series. The Cardinals needed a single to tie the game. McClure pitched carefully, too carefully, and walked Tenace to load the bases. The Brewers' two-run lead was in jeopardy.

There was no sense of panic in the Brewers' dugout because Bob McClure, always tough on left-handed batters, was facing the left-handed-hitting Keith Hernandez. For both McClure and Hernandez, it must have been a bittersweet moment, for they had been teammates in high school.

McClure fell behind in the count, three balls and one strike, and served up a fat one to his old buddy. Hernandez singled and two runs came home. Happy birthday, Keith—it was his twenty-ninth birthday and his high school buddy had delivered the present.

The score was tied and the Cardinals were threatening to blow the game apart. The dangerous right-handed hitter George Hendrick stepped to the plate. Moose Haas, ready and willing in the Brewers' bullpen, was the logical choice for this critical situation. For reasons never explained, Harvey Kuenn let McClure pitch to the Cardinals' leading RBI man. McClure almost escaped when Paul Molitor fielded Hendrick's ground ball and threw home to erase pinch runner Mike Ramsey. But the ball was ruled foul, by a matter of inches, and Hendrick had a second chance. Hendrick then singled to put St. Louis into the lead. McClure stayed in to face the left-handed hitter Darrell Porter but it was too late. After retiring Porter on a force-out, Moose Haas finally came in to pitch and got pinch hitter Steve Braun to end the inning.

Joaquin Andujar had a one-run lead and the Cardinals were one inning away from bringing in Bruce Sutter. Andujar fanned Gorman Thomas to start the seventh inning. After Roy Howell flied to deep left field, a play that Lonnie Smith made more spectacular than it should have been by running around in needless circles, Charlie Moore singled. Jim Gantner, who was two for two against Andujar in Game Three and had already doubled against Andujar earlier in the game, stepped in. Andujar induced a ground ball back to the pitcher. As Andujar stabbed the comebacker and threw to first, Gantner called Andujar a "hot dog" for his excessive showmanship. Perhaps Joe Garagiola knew something when he made his pregame comment about needing a big mustard jar. Andujar was incensed, threw off his glove, and was ready to have it out with the Brewers' second baseman. The home plate umpire jumped between the potential combatants and peace was restored.

The Cardinals went down in order for the first time in the game in the bottom of the seventh inning. If the Brewers were to make a comeback, they would have to do it against the bearded Bruce Sutter, baseball's top relief pitcher. Sutter, who looked more like an Amish wood-carver than a professional ballplayer, had mastered the split-fingered fastball, an apparent violation of all laws of physics. The pitch would approach home plate straight and true, just below the batter's waist. As the batter's eyes bulged in anticipation of the tremendous hit that would soon follow, the ball would, at the very last instant before reaching the contact zone, suddenly drop to the ground, as if flattened by an invisible sumo wrestler. The batter was hopelessly into his motion, unable to stop the embarrassing swing and miss. But Bruce Sutter had not been invincible in his previous three appearances in the Series. Cecil Cooper had even hit a home run off him.

The Brewers were desperate for a run. They sent up the top three batters in their order to face Bruce Sutter and all three failed. Molitor and Cooper grounded out, surrounding Robin Yount's swinging strikeout at a vintage Sutter splitter. The game had taken on all the markings of a classic—the home team clinging to a one-run lead against a mighty offense. Too bad, though, for the Cardinals shattered the suspense in the bottom of the eighth inning.

Lonnie Smith led off the Cardinals' eighth with his second double of the day. After Mike Ramsey struck out, the Brewers intentionally walked the birthday boy, Keith Hernandez. George Hendrick flied to center and Harvey Kuenn brought in the left-hander Mike Caldwell to face the left-handed hitters Darrell Porter and Steve Braun. Not only had Caldwell pitched brilliantly for Milwaukee in the Series, winning Games One and Five, it was obviously the correct move for the situation. Unfortunately for Milwaukee, neither Darrell Porter nor Steve Braun was paying attention to the lefty-lefty disadvantage by which managers live and die. Both delivered run-scoring singles and the Cardinals' lead ballooned to three runs going into the ninth inning.

The Brewers went down without a twitch. Ted Simmons and Ben Oglivie hit weak ground balls to the infield and Gorman Thomas struck out to end the game.

The St. Louis Cardinals had won their seventh Game Seven. For the Brewers, it was their first and last World Series appearance to date. At least they had the satisfaction of taking it to the limit, of experiencing the rare thrill of competing in a Seventh Game. The Cardinals celebrated deep into the night. In quiet villages elsewhere, others were celebrating, too. The night of the Seventh Game of the 1982 World Series marked the one hundredth anniversary of the birth of horror-movie star Bela Lugosi. Coincidence? Ask the Brewers.

October 20, 1982

	1	2	3	4	5	6	7	8	9	R	H	E
MILWAUKEE (AL)	0	0	0	0	1	2	0	0	0	3	7	0
ST. LOUIS (NL)	0	0	0	1	0	3	0	2	X	6	15	1

PITCHERS: MIL: Vuckovich, McClure (L), Haas, Caldwell;
STL: Andujar (W), Sutter (SV)
DOUBLES: Gantner, L. Smith (2)
TRIPLES: None
HOME RUNS: Oglivie
ATTENDANCE: 53,723
TIME OF GAME: 2:50

1985

Blowout from Bret and Brett

St. Louis Cardinals   0
Kansas City Royals   11

What do we remember about the year 1985? Lionel Richie had a huge hit on his hands, or on his lips, with "Say You, Say Me." Wherever you went, you heard "We Are the World." Movies were okay, but not great. *The Color Purple*, *Prizzi's Honor*, and *Kiss of the Spider Woman* just don't stick in our cinematic memories as do the hits of other years. But 1985 gave us something wondrous, something that would change America forever. It was the birth of the Home Shopping Network and as hard as baseball tried, the national pastime could do nothing to stop it. At least 1985 gave America another seven-game World Series.

The Kansas City Royals had been to the World Series in 1980 and lost in six games to the Philadelphia Phillies. George Brett and Dan Quisenberry, stars of the 1980 squad, were back in 1985, and these new Royals were one of the best-balanced teams of the 1980s. Willie Wilson and Lonnie Smith swiped 83 bases between them and the not-so-speedy Steve Balboni provided punch with 36 homers. But George Brett was the key to Kansas City's attack, with a rare mix of power and average, along with that even rarer commodity, fire in the belly.

Sophomore sensation Bret Saberhagen won 20 games and took the Cy Young Award for his efforts. Sidearm relief specialist Dan Quisenberry picked up 37 saves to provide manager Dick Howser with many restful

---

Around the Horn in 1985

- Dwight "Doc" Gooden was a harbinger of things to come for the New York Mets, earning Rookie of the Year honors for his 24–4, 1.53 ERA season for Davey Johnson's New York Mets. At the other end of the spectrum, Pirates pitcher Jose Deleon posted a 2–19 record.
- Kansas City's Willie Wilson led the American League with 21 triples, the most since Cleveland's Dale Mitchell hit 23 three-baggers in 1949.
- Wade Boggs won his first of four consecutive batting crowns, hitting .368 for the fifth-place Red Sox.

---

nights of contented sleep. It was hard to find flaws with the 1985 Royals, but they made their way into the World Series the hard way, falling behind three games to one against the Toronto Blue Jays before sweeping the final three, including the last two in Toronto. That turned out to be a good warm-up for the never-say-die Royals.

After a two-year absence, the St. Louis Cardinals were back in the World Series and the name of their game was speed. Manager Whitey Herzog wound them up and let them fly, and the Cardinals responded with 314 stolen bases, fourth on the all-time list for team steals in a single season. Vince Coleman led the world with his 110 swipes but four other Cardinals pilfered 30 or more bases. One reason they were able to steal so many bases is that they got on base so often, thanks to the highest batting average in the National League. Veteran Jack Clark gave the Cardinals just enough home run power to be respectable.

As for pitching, St. Louis was the only team in baseball with a pair of 20-game winners. John Tudor and Joaquin Andujar each notched 21 wins, with Danny Cox close behind at 18. Jeff Lahti and Ken Dayley were a talented tandem out of the pen, so Whitey Herzog had plenty of reasons to be confident about bringing home the tenth world championship in the history of the franchise. They survived a brief scare when the Dodgers won the first two games of the League Championship Series, but the Cardinals stormed back to sweep the next four games and set up a date with their cross-state cousins, the Kansas City Royals. If one team had an advantage, it was the Royals because they were healthy. St. Louis would have to do without the services of its premier speedster, Vince Coleman, sidelined due to a freak injury in the LCS.

When the Cardinals took three of the first four games to open the Series, Kansas City found itself in a familiar but unpleasant position. Four other teams, the 1925 Pirates, 1958 Yankees, 1968 Tigers, and the 1979 Pirates, had dug themselves out of the same hole and won the World Series but no team had ever performed that comeback act twice in a single post-season. The Royals won Game Five in St. Louis behind pitcher Danny Jackson's complete-game effort and took the Series back to Kansas City in hopes of duplicating their LCS comeback performance.

They still talk about Game Six, especially in St. Louis. The teams swapped zeroes for seven innings before the Cardinals scored on Brian Harper's two-out pinch single in the eighth. After Kansas City failed to score in the bottom of the eighth, the St. Louis clubhouse was prepping for media interviews and champagne. Royals pinch hitter Jorge Orta led off the bottom of the ninth inning with a bouncer to first baseman Jack Clark, who flipped to reliever Todd Worrell. It was a close play and television replays showed that Orta was out. But Umpire Don Denkinger called Orta safe. The Cardinals were livid but Denkinger had made his decision. Then came the comeback. The Royals loaded the bases and Dane Iorg delivered a two-run pinch single to win the game for Kansas City. "We wuz robbed," the Cardinals cried, and they were right. But Game Seven was on and at least the Cardinals had some history behind them. They had already been in eight Seventh Games since 1926 and won all but one. Of course, they never had to rebound from such a gut-wrenching and disappointing Game Six loss.

Game Six was a classic, flawed as it was by an umpire's bad call. But there is no way to spin Game Seven into anything other than what it was: an ugly and brutal massacre.

How often do baseball fans see an 11–0 game? It sounds more like a college football score, put together by a touchdown and two-point conversion, followed by a field goal. It does not happen very often. There have been entire seasons without an 11–0 score. Yet *two* of the thirty-five World Series Seventh Games were decided by that score. The St. Louis Cardinals punished the Detroit Tigers in an 11–0 rout in 1934 and the Kansas City Royals returned the shame upon the Cardinals in 1985. Neither game was pretty unless you were cheering rabidly for the winning team and cared not a whit for the grace and beauty of a well-played and evenly matched contest.

Bret Saberhagen pitched for Kansas City. He had allowed only one run and six hits in beating St. Louis in Game Three and was well rested for Game Seven. Whitey Herzog regrouped from Game Six and came back with his ace, John Tudor. Tudor had won the first and fourth games, giving up only one run in the two starts. It should have been a great pitchers' duel but the Royals had other plans.

After a scoreless first inning, Kansas City's Darryl Motley put the hometown boys ahead with a two-run homer, his only extra-base hit of the Series. The Royals added three more in the third and John Tudor was gone. St. Louis collapsed in the fifth inning when the Royals batted and batted and batted some more, scoring six runs to put the game out of reach. Whitey Herzog and Joaquin Andujar were also ejected from the game on successive pitches in the nightmare fifth.

George Brett singled four times to join Max Carey, Rip Collins, and Willie Stargell as the only players to collect four hits in a Seventh Game. Bret Saberhagen went the distance to join the exclusive group of seven other pitchers who have thrown Seventh Game shutouts. (There would eventually be one more member of the club.) The Cardinals paraded seven pitchers to the mound, also a Seventh Game record. If there is a motto to attach to the 1985 Seventh Game, it is this: the less said about it, the better. Especially if you are a Cardinals fan.

October 27, 1985

	1	2	3	4	5	6	7	8	9	R	H	E
ST. LOUIS (NL)	0	0	0	0	0	0	0	0	0	0	5	0
KANSAS CITY (AL)	0	2	3	0	6	0	0	0	X	11	14	0

PITCHERS: STL: Tudor (L), Campbell, Lahti, Horton, Andujar, Forsch, Dayley; KCR: Saberhagen (W)

DOUBLES: L. Smith

TRIPLES: None

HOME RUNS: Motley

ATTENDANCE: 41,658

TIME OF GAME: 2:46

1986

They Never Had a Chance

Boston Red Sox 5
New York Mets 8

Ben E. King's 1961 song "Stand By Me" made a comeback in 1986, perhaps foreshadowing other amazing comebacks in baseball that year. The hottest sounds came from Peter Gabriel, the Miami Sound Machine, Van Halen, and Janet Jackson. Televison's "L.A. Law" was an admirable attempt to show that lawyers are human. But for even better drama, Greg LeMond became the first American to win the Tour de France bicycle race.

Half a planet away, in the Russian town of Chernobyl, the core of a major nuclear reactor went into meltdown in April of 1986. The world held its breath as fears of a global nuclear disaster ebbed and flowed. Six months later, back in the United States, in an area known as Flushing Meadow, the Boston Red Sox baseball club went into a similar meltdown, losing the Sixth Game of the World Series in historic and ignominious fashion. The only good news coming from that disaster was that the baseball world would be treated to its thirtieth Seventh Game.

The Boston Red Sox were back in the hunt for the world championship that had eluded them since 1918. They won the American League East by a satisfying five and one-half games over their arch rivals, the New York Yankees. In only his third year in the league, young Roger Clemens staked his first of many claims to being the best pitcher in baseball with an overpowering 24–4 season for Boston. He was the Cy Young Award win-

Around the Horn in 1986

- Boston's Don Baylor not only provided home run power and valuable leadership for the Red Sox; he showed the baseball world what it meant to "take one for the team." Baylor led the majors in being hit by a pitch. Opposing pitchers nicked Baylor thirty-five times, more than twice that of the runner-up, California's Brian Downing.

- Roger Clemens set the record for most strikeouts in a nine-inning game—20. He would tie the record himself in 1996, as would Chicago Cubs pitcher Kerry Wood in 1998.

- Bob Brenly, playing third base for the San Francisco Giants, made four errors in one inning on September 14. Only two other third basemen have achieved that feat—in 1891 and 1901.

ner, the league's Most Valuable Player, and the main reason that Boston won the division.

There were other reasons for Boston's success. Wade Boggs hit .357 to win his third batting title, and Jim Rice put together his last outstanding season, batting .324 and driving home 110 runs. Another key player was a veteran first baseman who drove in more than a hundred runs. The Boston fans appreciated his hard-nosed spirit and loved his hustle. His name was Bill Buckner.

Getting to the World Series was not easy for Boston. They were down three games to one against the California Angels in the League Championship Series and down by three runs in the ninth inning of the fifth game when Dave Henderson became an instant Boston legend with a dramatic home run. The Sox pulled out a win and went on to claim the pennant back at Fenway. No one ever told Boston about the old adage: "He who lives by the dramatic comeback, dies by the dramatic comeback."

The New York Mets won the National League East with baseball's best pitching. They had four quality starters in Bob Ojeda, Doc Gooden, Sid Fernandez, and Ron Darling, and an effective bullpen duo of Roger McDowell and Jesse Orosco that combined for 43 saves. The offense was equally solid, led by sluggers Gary Carter and Darryl Strawberry, while infielders Keith Hernandez, Wally Backman, and Ray Knight hit near or above .300. The Mets got to the World Series after a dramatic six-game series with Houston that featured two marathon Mets wins in the final two games. They continue to buzz about the 16-inning finale at Shea Stadium.

The fans of New England were downright giddy about the chances for finally winning a World Series, especially after the heroics of the LCS. Only the most severe pessimists dared speak of "the Curse" when the Series started, and then only in hushed tones and among close friends. The optimism only increased when the Red Sox won the first two games in New York. Bruce Hurst shut out the Mets in the opener, 1–0. But did anyone realize that this was the second time a Red Sox pitcher opened a World Series with a 1–0 victory? The first was in 1918, when another lefty, Babe Ruth, shut out the Cubs en route to the last Red Sox championship. Depending on your point of view, that was either a good sign or a bad omen.

The Red Sox pounded out 18 hits in the Game Two win and then it was off to Boston, where the loyal hometown fans were ready to host a victory celebration for their surging heroes. Ex-Sox lefty Bob Ojeda silenced the fans in Game Three with a 7–1 Mets win and New York evened the Series with a decisive 6–2 win in Game Four. Boston reclaimed the momentum in Game Five behind another strong outing by Bruce Hurst, winning 4–2, and the Sox returned to Shea Stadium in need of only one more victory.

Repeating the mantra written about Game Six of the 1975 World Series, this book is about Seventh Games, not sixth games. Only so much about Game Six as is necessary to segue into the Seventh Game will be presented here, in one succinct paragraph. However, a brief summary of Game Six of 1986 presents the same problem that we had with Game Six of 1975. It cannot do justice to what transpired. It would be like reducing the *Hindenburg* disaster to "A big blimp caught fire and crashed," or compacting the Fall of the Roman Empire into "Speaking Latin couldn't save a bunch of fat emperors who ignored the home front and fought a bunch of stupid foreign wars." Some tragedies cannot be easily simplified, but that is what we must do.

Needing only one win to claim their first world championship since 1918, the Red Sox jumped to an early 2–0 lead but the Mets tied the game and forced extra innings. Boston scored two in the top of the tenth and, when the first two Mets went down in the bottom of the tenth, were on the verge of victory. Refusing to give up, Gary Carter, Kevin Mitchell, and Ray Knight singled off Boston reliever Calvin Schiraldi to cut the margin to one. Boston reliever Bob Stanley uncorked a wild pitch and the game was tied.

Mookie Wilson sent an easy grounder to first and it went through Bill Buckner's legs to score Ray Knight with the winning run. For Boston fans, it was the darkest hour. For Mets fans, it was the greatest comeback ever imagined.

As tragic as Game Six was for the Red Sox players and fans, it meant that another Game Seven would soon be in the books. After a day of rain— a day of mourning for some—Game Seven got under way at Shea Stadium. Boston fans would consume millions of glasses of flat champagne during that game, all from bottles opened prematurely two nights before. Whispers of "the Curse" filled the air and now they were neither circumspect nor soft.

Boston had its best World Series pitcher going for them in Game Seven. Bruce Hurst had given the Sox two outstanding performances and had two of the Boston wins to show for them. Ron Darling, winner of one game and loser of another, started for New York. Dwight Evans and Rich Gedman homered to lead off the Red Sox second and Wade Boggs drove in a third run to give Boston an early 3–0 lead. The optimistic Red Sox fans were jubilant, but the pessimists pointed to Game Seven of 1975, when Boston also took an early 3–0 lead, only to let it slip away.

Bruce Hurst was in command until the Mets came to bat in the sixth inning. To that point Hurst had allowed only one hit, but Lee Mazzilli started a rally with a one-out single. Keith Hernandez delivered the key blow, a bases-loaded two-run single, and when the inning was over, the game was tied. Just as in 1975, Boston's 3–0 lead had vanished.

Boston manager John McNamara then made one of many key moves that remain subject to intense criticism. He sent Tony Armas in to pinch-hit for Bruce Hurst in the top of the seventh. Armas struck out, the Red Sox scored nothing, and their ace lefty was gone. McNamara needed a pitcher and his ace righty, Roger Clemens, was ready. Instead, he called on Calvin Schiraldi, the hard-luck loser of Game Six. Ray Knight, the first batter to face Schiraldi, homered. Two more Mets runs came across in the bottom of the seventh and the Mets had a three-run lead. Boston was six outs away from another crushing Game Seven defeat.

In the Boston eighth, Bill Buckner and Jim Rice singled and scored on a Dwight Evans double. It was the second hit of the night for Buckner, goat of the sixth game. But that was all Boston could do, and the game moved to the bottom of the eighth with the Sox trailing by one run. They had the ninth inning before them and everyone knew what they had done to California when facing elimination in the ninth inning of Game Five in the LCS only fifteen days ago. And against California they were down by more than one little run.

The Sox looked ahead to the ninth inning but the Mets stayed focused on the bottom of the eighth. In another of John McNamara's questionable moves, Al Nipper took the mound. Nipper had been Boston's fourth starter during the season and the American League had little trouble getting to him. Neither did the Mets in Game Four, when they knocked Nipper around for seven hits in six innings. Was Al Nipper really the man to hold the lead? Where was Clemens?

Darryl Strawberry was not complaining about the sight of Al Nipper on the pitcher's mound. He homered to give the Mets that all-important "insurance run." Even Jesse Orosco was not complaining about seeing Al Nipper. The Mets' reliever, hitless in his six at-bats during the regular season, drove in a run with a single. The New York lead was back to three. The Red Sox went quietly in the ninth inning, with Marty Barrett striking out to end the misery.

Blame it on the "Curse of the Bambino." Blame it on Bill Buckner. Blame it on John McNamara. Or give some credit to the New York Mets.

In the years following the 1986 Game Six collapse and Game Seven loss, Red Sox fans believed that it could never get worse. How wrong they were. In 2003, the Red Sox took a 5–2 lead into the eighth inning of the seventh game of the American League Championship Series against the New York Yankees and found a way to lose. It was not a World Series seventh game, but the Red Sox proved that when it came to seventh games of any dimension, no Boston lead was, is, or will ever be safe. Speak of "the Curse" if you will; Boston fans can only weep.

October 27, 1986

	1	2	3	4	5	6	7	8	9	R	H	E
BOSTON (AL)	0	3	0	0	0	0	0	2	0	5	9	0
NEW YORK (NL)	0	0	0	0	0	3	3	2	X	8	10	0

PITCHERS: BOS: Hurst, Schiraldi (L), Sambito, Stanley, Nipper, Crawford; NYM: Darling, Fernandez, McDowell (W), Orosco (SV)

DOUBLES: Evans

TRIPLES: None

HOME RUNS: Evans, Gedman, Knight, Strawberry

ATTENDANCE: 55,032

TIME OF GAME: 3:11

1987

Sonata in A for Viola and Twins

St. Louis Cardinals 2
Minnesota Twins   4

In 1987, Paul Simon won a Grammy for his song "Graceland." A Victor Hugo novel was the basis for the year's best musical, *Les Misérables*. Cher won an Oscar for Best Actress as Loretta Castorini in *Moonstruck*. But the real story in America came six days before the end of the World Series. The stock market crashed on Monday, October 19, 1987, "Black Monday," as it would be forever known. Millions of people lost a lot of money. Could baseball do anything about it? Not really, but it did what baseball had always done when America needed it. It gave a full-throttle World Series worth watching.

When the dust finally settled in the American League in 1987, the Minnesota Twins were going to the World Series. They won only 85 games during the season, with a modest winning percentage of .525. Their opponents had outhit them, outscored them, out-everythinged them, but manager Tom Kelly's boys won enough games at the right times to capture the American League pennant. Playing at home in the Hubert H. Humphrey Metrodome, where the right-field wall looked like a giant baggie, didn't hurt their cause either, because the Twins had the best home record in baseball.

Kent Hrbek, Gary Gaetti, and Tom Brunansky hit a bunch of home runs for Minnesota but a lot of guys were hitting home runs in 1987. Some believed that a "juiced-up" baseball was responsible for the great power

Around the Horn in 1987

- It was Phil Niekro's last season, ending a twenty-four-year career in which he won 318 games. When brother Joe retired a year later, the two had posted 539 wins, the most by any pitching siblings in history.
- Rob Deer, the feast-or-famine outfielder for the Milwaukee Brewers, set the American League record for strikeouts in a season with 186. But he did hit 28 home runs.
- Detroit's Jack Morris tied a seventy-five-year-old American League record when he uncorked five wild pitches in one game.

surge of 1987. Some blamed it on inferior pitching. Whatever the reason, twenty American League batters swatted 30 or more home runs that year. Home runs were certainly part of the Twins' success but there was more. Kirby Puckett, in only his fourth year of an all-too-short twelve-year Hall of Fame career, led the team in hitting and in inspiration. Frank Viola led the pitching staff with 17 wins and Jeff Reardon was there to put out the fires, notching 31 saves.

The National League was a different story. The St. Louis Cardinals were the only team in baseball to hit fewer than 100 home runs but relied on speed, pitching, and defense to claim their fifteenth pennant in franchise history. Jack Clark gave them some decent power with 35 home runs, but the long ball was not manager Whitey Herzog's game. Vince Coleman epitomized the Cardinals' attack with his league-leading 109 stolen bases. Ozzie Smith, the great defensive wizard, pitched in with the best offensive year of his career, batting .303.

The Cardinals won with pitching but it was never clear whose pitching it was. No one on the staff won more than 11 games and they were next-to-last in the majors in complete games. Finishing games was a task that fell to their hard-throwing reliever, Todd Worrell, who saved 33 games for St. Louis.

The Redbirds had more than their share of problems as they entered the World Series. Jack Clark was scratched from the Cardinals' postseason roster due to an injury and Terry Pendleton, also hurting, was available only for pinch-hitting duty. At least Vince Coleman, who had missed the 1985 World Series due to a freak accident, was ready to run around the bases.

The teams split the first six games in predictable and unexciting fashion. The home team won all six games and there wasn't a single one-run game among them. The battered Cardinals were just glad to have made it to another Seventh Game, their tenth in franchise history. The Twins were looking for one more home-field victory to bring them the championship and hoping for a World Series first: never in a seven-game Series had the home team won all seven games.

Frank Viola, winner of Game One at home but loser of Game Four at St. Louis, was Tom Kelly's starter. Rookie Joe Magrane, who had lost to Viola in the first game, was on the mound for Whitey Herzog's Cardinals. The Cardinals jumped out with two runs in the second inning on singles by Tony Pena and Jim Lindeman, but Twins fans were not rattled. They knew that in four of the first six games, the losing team had scored first. There was no reason to panic.

In the bottom of the second, the Twins came back with a run but it should have been more, as the home plate umpire called Don Baylor out on a bad call. Would this be a game determined by the umpires? Perhaps the umpires were evening the score when the first-base umpire later ruled the Twins' Greg Gagne safe on a play that on replay showed that Joe Magrane's foot had indeed brushed the bag before Gagne crossed it. The Twins tied the game in the fifth and might have taken the lead were it not for Cardinals catcher Steve Lake's courageous block of the plate and tag on a charging Gary Gaetti.

A third bad call by the umpires cost the Cardinals dearly. With Tommy Herr on first, Twins pitcher Frank Viola threw to first and caught Herr leaning the wrong way. Herr was caught in a rundown and desparately tried to return to first. The final throw to nail Herr came from the second baseman to Viola covering first. But Minnesota first baseman Kent Hrbek was in the base path, slowing up Herr in his effort to get back to first. Because Hrbek did not have the ball, he had no business impeding Herr and interference, awarding Herr the base, should have been called. It wasn't. Instead, Viola applied the tag and Herr was called out. But to compound matters, replays show that Herr was in ahead of the tag anyway and should have been called safe. For the Cardinals, it was a case of two wrongs making an out. For the second time in three years, an umpire's "suspect" call had damaged the Cardinals' chances at a world championship.

In the bottom of the sixth, the Twins broke the tie on Greg Gagne's bases-loaded infield single with two outs. The Cardinals' last decent chance came in the seventh inning when Tony Pena doubled to right but was stranded on the base paths when Jose Oquendo struck out and Tom Lawless flied to center. The Twins put the game out of reach when Dan Gladden doubled home Tim Laudner in the eighth.

Frank Viola spun a masterful game, allowing six hits and walking none in eight innings. Jeff Reardon pitched a perfect ninth for the save and the Twins had finally brought a championship to Minnesota.

For the first time in a seven-game World Series, the home team had won every game. And for the second time in a row, the St. Louis Cardinals failed to pick up Seventh Game win number eight. But with seven wins in their ten Seventh Games, they remained baseball's most successful Seventh Game team.

October 25, 1987

	1	2	3	4	5	6	7	8	9	R	H	E
ST. LOUIS (NL)	0	2	0	0	0	0	0	0	0	2	6	1
MINNESOTA (AL)	0	1	0	0	1	1	0	1	X	4	10	0

PITCHERS: STL: Magrane, Cox (L), Worrell; MIN: Viola (W), Reardon (SV)

DOUBLES: Puckett, Pena, Gladden

TRIPLES: None

HOME RUNS: None

ATTENDANCE: 55,376

TIME OF GAME: 3:04

1991

A Jack of All Trades

Atlanta Braves	0
Minnesota Twins	1 (10 Innings)

Whatever happened in America in 1991 was only prelude to the greatest drama of the year, the Seventh Game of the World Series. Amy Grant's hit song "Baby, Baby" was only a preview of what they would be saying about this game. America was riveted to the Clarence Thomas Supreme Court confirmation hearings in the Senate during the middle of October, but by the end of the month everyone was talking about baseball.

The Minnesota Twins had gone from world champions in 1987 to cellar dwellers in only three years. The 1990 version of the Twins finished a whopping 29 games behind the first-place Oakland A's. But the 1991 Twins rose up from the depths of last place to surprise everyone by capturing the American League West by eight games over their nearest rivals. They had the same manager, many of the same players, but produced totally different results. The most noticeable difference was the addition of veteran pitcher Jack Morris, a feisty right-hander who brought with him fourteen years of big-league winning experience, including three postseason wins for the champion Detroit Tigers of 1984.

The Atlanta Braves began their string of eleven consecutive years in the postseason by winning the National League West Division by one game over the Los Angeles Dodgers. The hallmark of the great Atlanta

Around the Horn in 1991

- ◔ Montreal's Dennis Martinez pitched a perfect game, beating the Dodgers 2–0 on July 28.
- ◔ On May 23, Kirby Puckett collected six hits in a game, the second time he did so in his career. Although there have been more than 100 six-hit performances in baseball history, only Kirby has done it twice.
- ◔ The Toronto Blue Jays became the first team to draw over 4 million fans in one season. Only the 1993 Colorado Rockies have done it since.

teams of the 1990s was pitching, and the first edition set the mark. Lefty Tom Glavine was the ace of the staff and Steve Avery, Charlie Liebrandt, and John Smoltz gave the Braves the most solid starting rotation in all of baseball. Terry Pendleton led the offense with a .319 average, tops in the National League, while Ron Gant and David Justice provided the power for Bobby Cox's balanced crew.

Getting to the World Series was no easy task for the Braves. They went the full seven games in the National League LCS against Pittsburgh and needed shutout wins from Steve Avery and John Smoltz in the final two games to bring the first World Series to Atlanta. But to bring home a World Series championship, the Braves would have to win at least one game in Minnesota, where visiting teams had never fared well. The 1987 St. Louis Cardinals, losers of all four games in the Twins' domed stadium, could vouch for that.

True to their 1987 championship form, the Twins won the first two games at home, 5–2 and 3–2. The Braves treated the Twins to a taste of southern inhospitality by winning the next three games in Atlanta, winning Games Three and Four by a single run scored in their final at-bat. Atlanta won the only blowout of the Series, 14–5, in Game Five.

The Twins were in a familiar situation, on the verge of World Series elimination but in the warm and comfortable surroundings of their Metrodome. They had done it in 1987 and they were ready to do it again in 1991—force a Game Seven by winning Game Six. And win Game Six they did, in classic and dramatic fashion, prevailing in 12 innings on a Kirby

Puckett home run. Four of the first six games had been decided by one run and baseball fans recognized that this had the potential to be one of the greatest World Series ever. If only Game Seven could live up to the first six.

All of baseball knew that it was going to be a memorable Seventh Game when Atlanta leadoff hitter Lonnie Smith shook hands with Minnesota catcher Brian Harper moments before Jack Morris threw his first pitch. Almost three and a half hours later, the final score of the Seventh Game of the 1991 World Series stood at 1–0, in 10 innings. There are those who assume that a 1–0 baseball game is boring, without a hint of drama or excitement. The story of this game extinguishes that assumption.

There are also those who assume that a 1–0 baseball game, although potentially thrilling, is by definition no more than a tight pitching duel. Although both teams' pitchers prevented opposing batters from scoring through the first nine innings, by no means did they dominate the hitters. In the first nine innings the teams put twenty-one runners on base (fifteen hits, five walks, a hit batsman) but could not push a single run across home plate. Never before in the course of the World Series had two teams collected so many hits and scored so few runs.

The story of this Seventh Game is one of clutch pitching and solid defense, but it is also the story of an oft-neglected fundamental skill, baserunning. When the dust finally settled at home plate at the Metrodome that night, one team found itself victimized by a baserunning blunder while the other team emerged victorious by virtue of baserunning excellence.

Starting pitchers Smoltz and Morris each retired the only three batters they faced in the first inning. After that, it was a case of scoring threat after scoring threat, with the pitchers rising to the occasion. The Braves had a runner in scoring position in each of the next four innings but failed to score. The Twins had a runner as far as second base in the second and third innings and runners on base in each of the next three innings but tallied not a single run.

Leading off for Atlanta in the eighth, designated hitter Lonnie Smith singled. The National League's leading hitter, Terry Pendleton, stepped to the plate. He had been hitless in his three previous plate appearances, two of them with Braves runners in scoring position. This time he did not fail, ripping a hit to the gap in left-center field, a sure double. Smith, a runner with above-average speed, should have had no trouble scoring. Braves fans held their breath as they watched the ball bounce high toward the outfield wall; if the ball went over the wall, it would have been an automatic ground-rule double with Smith awarded third base and no more.

Luckily for Atlanta, the ball took a high bounce up against the wall and came back into play. The entire stadium expected to see Lonnie Smith racing across home plate with the first run of the game. Instead, Smith had to stop at third base because he fell prey to one of the oldest tricks in the baseball book, the "decoy" play.

As little kids on the rough grass fields and sandlots across America, we all tried to fool the other team with the decoy play. Of course, unless you were lucky enough to have a very gullible runner on first base, it never worked. If you are not familiar with the decoy play, here is how it goes: A runner is on first base. The batter hits the ball safely to the outfield. The runner should be racing around second base without hesitation. If the ball is hit hard enough and deep enough, the runner should score. The "decoy" comes when the second baseman pretends that the ball is hit to him. He mimes a catch of the ball and a throw to the shortstop. The shortstop mimes a catch of the second baseman's throw to second base, as if the runner were being retired on a ground-ball out.

If the runner is taken in by the decoy catch and throw of the infielders, he either slides into the base, or stops, or at least hesitates at second base. Of course, the decoy play never works at the major-league level. Almost never.

It worked in Game Seven in 1991. Minnesota infielders Chuck Knoblauch and Greg Gagne went through the motions of fielding a ground ball that wasn't there and Lonnie Smith fell for it. Perhaps it was the noise of the Metrodome crowd that caused Smith to think for a moment that Pendleton's hit was a ground ball to Knoblauch instead of the long double to left-center field. Whatever the cause, Lonnie Smith ended up on third base listening to a coach's instructions instead of in the dugout hearing his mates' congratulations.

Even though the Braves had missed one scoring opportunity, they had another directly before them because they had runners on second (Pendleton) and third (Smith) and no outs. It was baseball's best opportunity for at least one run, a run that would make everyone forget about Lonnie Smith's baserunning blunder.

The Twins brought their infielders in to try to cut off Smith in any attempt to score on a ground ball. Jack Morris bore down and induced Ron

Gant to stroke a ground ball to first, hit sharply enough that Smith could not even try to score. One out.

The Twins issued an intentional walk to cleanup hitter David Justice, loading the bases with one out. The Braves had so many ways of scoring a run—a hit, an error, a walk, a hit batsman, a wild pitch, a long fly ball, a slowly hit ground ball, etc. The Twins rested their hopes on pitcher Jack Morris's ability to retire first baseman Sid Bream without a run scoring. Morris triumphed, inducing Bream to hit into a nifty inning-ending double play.

The momentum of the game shifted to the Minnesota Twins. They had narrowly escaped from an enemy scoring chance in the top of the eighth inning and mounted their own threat in the bottom of the inning. A pinch-hit single by Randy Bush, a single by Chuck Knoblauch, and an intentional walk to Kirby Puckett gave the Twins an opportunity identical to that of the Braves only a few minutes before—the bases were loaded with only one out. So many ways for Minnesota to score and so few ways of stemming the tide for Atlanta.

Twins first baseman Kent Hrbek faced Atlanta relief pitcher Mike Stanton with the chance to drive in the only run of the game. Hrbek had been a productive power hitter during the regular season but had had a difficult World Series to that point. His task was no less difficult by virtue of being a left-handed hitter; Stanton is a left-handed pitcher who was notoriously difficult on left-handed batters. Hrbek hit a soft line drive and the hopes of the Metrodome fans soared until Atlanta second baseman Mark Lemke caught it and stepped on second base for an inning-ending double play.

When is the last time you can recall two teams hitting into inning-ending double plays with the bases loaded in the same inning? The game remained scoreless after eight innings and everyone realized that this was indeed a special game in the history of the World Series.

Jack Morris retired the Braves in the ninth without a threat or a runner. The Twins could now become world champions with just one run in the bottom of the ninth. It seemed as if that was exactly what would happen, as Chili Davis and Brian Harper opened the inning with singles. Atlanta needed a miracle and got it when relief pitcher Alejandro Pena got a double play out of Shane Mack and, with the winning run on third base, struck out pinch hitter Paul Sorrento.

For the third time in World Series history and the first time in a Seventh Game, a game was scoreless after nine innings. Lonnie Smith's baserunning blunder in the eighth inning now took on momentous importance.

Extra innings began, for only the third time in Seventh Game history. In the previous two games (1912 and 1924), the home team came out the winner. Was this "home-field advantage" about to manifest itself again?

Jack Morris appeared to gain strength as the game wore on. He came out to the mound in the tenth inning, joining Hall of Famer Christy Mathewson as the only other pitcher to pitch beyond the regulation nine innings in a Seventh Game. Did no one tell the Twins that Mathewson had lost that game? Morris paid no heed to history, retiring the Braves in order in the tenth inning.

Dan Gladden led off the tenth inning for Minnesota. He had already singled and doubled earlier in the game but had garnered only four hits through the first six games. Alejandro Pena made a great pitch to Gladden, breaking Gladden's bat to produce a soft fly ball to short left-center field. Unfortunately for Atlanta, the ball fell to the ground behind shortstop Rafael Belliard and in front of outfielders Brian Hunter and Ron Gant.

Dan Gladden then showed the baseball world the meaning of great baserunning. Most hitters would have been content with a lucky bloop single. Gladden saw the ball take a high artificial-turf bounce and, without breaking stride as he turned first base, hustled into second base with a double. Yes, it was scored as a double, but it was really a bloop single that Gladden cunningly transformed into a double. Chuck Knoblauch followed with a perfect sacrifice bunt and the Twins had the championship run on third base with only one out. Atlanta had no choice but to intentionally walk Kirby Puckett and Kent Hrbek and pray for one more miraculous double play.

Alejandro Pena would not have to face the Twins' dangerous designated hitter, Chili Davis, because Davis had been replaced by a pinch runner, Jarvis Brown, in the ninth inning. Brown had assumed the role of designated hitter but manager Tom Kelly sent in Eugene Larkin to bat for Brown. The Braves brought their outfielders in close, in hopes of at least cutting off any bloop singles. Fly balls of any depth would score the winning run so there was no need to even consider a defense to catch them.

The Braves' magic evaporated into the night air as Gene Larkin entered baseball immortality with a fly ball to left field, over the head of Brian Hunter. Under ordinary circumstances it would have been a routine out, but it fell to the ground as a single, scoring a jubilant Dan Gladden with the only run of the game.

Does it get any better than that? Not if you are a Minnesota Twins fan. Or maybe just a fan of the game itself.

October 27, 1991

	1	2	3	4	5	6	7	8	9	10	R	H	E
ATLANTA (NL)	0	0	0	0	0	0	0	0	0	0	0	7	0
MINNESOTA (AL)	0	0	0	0	0	0	0	0	0	1	1	10	0

PITCHERS: ATL: Smoltz, Stanton, Pena (L); MIN: Morris (W)

DOUBLES: Pendleton, Hunter, Gladden (2)

TRIPLES: None

HOME RUNS: None

ATTENDANCE: 55,118

TIME OF GAME: 3:23

1997

The Florida Who?

Cleveland Indians   3
Florida Marlins   4 (11 Innings)

In 1997, Picasso's painting *Le Reve* sold at auction for $44 million. That staggering sum of money would have bought about half a baseball club that year. It was also the year of rapper Puff Daddy, the Spice Girls, the Backstreet Boys, and a whole lot of other surprises. Scientists cloned a sheep. Would the cloning of power-hitting shortstops be far behind?

The Seventh Game of the 1997 World Series featured a ninth-inning rally and a tenth-inning improbable victory by the home team but remains the great Seventh Game that baseball fans refuse to acknowledge. They bristle at any mention of the 1997 World Series because they refuse to accept the fact that a "wild-card" team won the championship. And not just any wild-card team. The upstart Florida Marlins, having rented a team of good ballplayers just for that season, beat a team that had been looking to win its first World Series in nearly fifty years.

From 1903 to 1968, the World Series of baseball meant a contest between the winner of the American League and the winner of the National League. The "pennant," the prize that went to the team winning its league, was decided by a most simple concept: the team that wins the most games in its league wins the pennant. That changed in 1969 when, as a result of expansion, the leagues were divided into divisions. The division winners

Around the Horn in 1997

- Twelve National Leaguers stole 30 or more bases. Only six American Leaguers pilfered as many.
- The Oakland A's pitching staff posted only two complete games and one shutout the entire season.
- The Boston Red Sox tied the major-league record for team doubles with 373, matching the 1930 St. Louis Cardinals.

would stage a playoff series—the League Championship Series, or LCS—to determine the pennant winner and, of course, the pennant winner went to the World Series. The LCS started as a best-of-five series but inflated to a best-of-seven format in 1985. Major League Baseball changed all that in 1994 but never saw the change in action until the following year.

At the beginning of the 1994 season, in a bold and controversial move, each league was divided into three divisions (East, Central, and West). In order to determine a pennant winner, the winners of the three divisions, along with a fourth team, would meet in a two-round series of playoffs. That fourth team was the "wild-card" team, the team with the best record of all the teams that did not win a division. Complaints that the new system was compromising the integrity of the game fell on deaf ears when fan interest increased with the greater opportunites for postseason play. But there were no wild-card teams in 1994, nor were there any division winners or league winners or winners of any kind. There were only losers. For the first time in history, a players' strike cancelled the postseason.

When baseball resumed in 1995, the new playoff system generated significant fan interest as baseball tried to regain what the strike had lost. The prospects of a wild-card team going to the World Series seemed remote, so the purists were satisfied. In both 1995 and 1996, no wild-card team made it to the Fall Classic. In 1997, the Cleveland Indians and Florida Marlins met in the World Series. The Indians had won their division by six games over the Chicago White Sox. In the playoffs, they defeated the wild-card Yankees and the Baltimore Orioles, winners of the American League East Division. The Marlins were a wild-card team and, despite finishing second in their division, stunned the National League

West Division champion San Francisco Giants and then beat the Atlanta Braves in the League Championship Series.

As horrible as the situation was for classicists of the game, one fact remained: the Florida Marlins were not just a lucky team, they were a good team. They even won more games than Cleveland during the regular season. But if the regular season is the measure of a team's worth, the best team in baseball, the Atlanta Braves, stayed home to watch the team they beat by nine games during the season now playing in the World Series. Who were these Florida Marlins and why did everyone resent them?

The Florida Marlins entered the National League in 1993. As an expansion team, they were expected to end their first season at or near the bottom of their division and they disappointed no one, finishing 33 games behind the Philadelphia Phillies. By 1996, owner Wayne Huizenga decided that he would buy himself a pennant-winning team and he spared no expense in going after some serious talent, like Al Leiter, Kevin Brown, and Devon White. In spite of these talents, the Marlins finished in third place. It took a few more dollars out of Huizenga's checking account before the Marlins had a winner. They picked up Moises Alou from Montreal, Alex Fernandez from the White Sox, and Bobby Bonilla from the Orioles. Cuban star Livan Hernandez defected at an opportune time and when the 1997 season was over, the Florida Marlins had snuck into the playoffs as the National League wild-card team. They had no .300 hitters, no 20 game winners, but were dangerous enough to make it to the World Series.

In the American League, everyone figured that the Seattle Mariners would finally get to the World Series. They set a new record for team home runs with 264, led by Ken Griffey Jr.'s monster year, and also had the most feared starting pitcher in baseball in Randy Johnson. But their pathetic bullpen failed them in the first round of the playoffs. The Cleveland Indians defeated the Baltimore Orioles in the LCS and advanced to the World Series.

What was so surprising about the Indians was not that they made it to the World Series but how they did it. The Indians won the Central Division with raw power and crushing offense. They hit 220 home runs, led by Jim Thome's 40. Sandy Alomar, David Justice, and Manny Ramirez all hit .300 and there were no weak spots in the lineup. The same could not be said for their pitching staff. Their team earned run average of 4.73 was the highest of any World Series participant in history.

Only two Cleveland starters won 10 or more games. What saved the Indians was their relief pitching. Jose Mesa was a menacing closer, and there were several other capable pitchers who chipped in with enough good short stints to make manager Mike Hargrove a winner. And when they needed it most, in the LCS, their starting pitching came alive. Chad Ogea shut out the Orioles in the opener and a committee of six Cleveland pitchers shut out the Orioles in the finale. The Indians were back in the World Series, where only two years before they had lost to the Atlanta Braves in six games.

The first six games of the 1997 World Series were not works of art. The Marlins won Game One, 7–4, but the score hardly reflects the game's utter lack of drama. Moises Alou and Charles Johnson homered for the Marlins and Livan Hernandez pitched five decent innings but was not a dominating force at all. The Indians came back to win Game Two, 6–1, another game devoid of any genuine excitement.

Game Three at Cleveland was the most entertaining of the first six games. For eight innings the teams slugged it out, swapping runs in bunches until the score stood tied at seven apiece. The Marlins broke the game open with seven runs in the top of the ninth. Three Cleveland errors and a wild pitch contributed to the farce. The Indians scored four in the bottom of the ninth to give the final score an air of closeness that was never really there.

Game Four saw snow falling at Jacobs Field in Cleveland, and that was the most exciting thing about the game. Florida teed off on a succession of Cleveland pitchers for an easy 10–3 win. Game Five's final score is misleading. Florida led 6–4 after six innings and added single runs in the last two frames for a comfortable 8–4 lead going into the bottom of the ninth. The Indians rallied but came up a run short, 8–7. Back in Florida, Cleveland forced a Seventh Game by winning Game Six 4–1 behind Chad Ogea's second start and help from a trio of relievers.

Is it no wonder that few expected much from Game Seven?

Surprise of surprises, Game Seven was a good one from start to finish. Young Jaret Wright, who had pitched six decent innings in Game Four, was on the mound for Cleveland. All Mike Hargrove wanted was five or six solid innings from Wright so that the Indians could start the procession out of the bullpen in time to hold on and escape with a win. Florida started Al Leiter, their talented lefty who started Game Three but did not last long enough to get credit for the bizarre 14–11 Marlins win. Florida manager

Jim Leyland knew that Leiter would have to pitch a lot better than he did in Game Three to give his team a chance to win.

It may not have seemed like much of a harbinger of a tight game, but for the first time in the Series neither team scored in the first two innings. Both Leiter and Wright looked sharp. In the third inning, Cleveland second baseman Tony Fernandez delivered a clutch two-run single to give the Indians the lead, 2–0. Meanwhile, Jaret Wright was brilliant, allowing only one Florida hit through six innings.

Bobby Bonilla, Florida's veteran slugger, led off the seventh inning. Jim Leyland had taken a chance on starting Bonilla because he was a defensive liability at third base. But at the age of thirty-four, Bonilla kept the quick bat that the Marlins needed. He had hit .297 during the regular season and was the team's number-two RBI man, behind Moises Alou. Bobby belted a solo home run to cut the Cleveland lead in half. After Charles Johnson struck out, Craig Counsell walked and the evening was over for Jaret Wright.

Wright had done his job. He had taken the Indians to the late innings with a lead and it was now up to the bullpen to hold that lead and present a World Series victory to the city of Cleveland, their first in forty-nine years. No one expected Wright to go much further. He had never pitched a complete game in the big leagues and that was fine with manager Mike Hargrove, whose starters had given him only four complete games all season. Lefty Paul Assenmacher kept the Marlins off the board and the score remained 2–1 in favor of Cleveland.

The Indians could do nothing with the Florida relievers that Jim Leyland used in a desperate effort to keep the game close. But the Indians' relievers, their "setup men" as they were called, did exactly what they were supposed to do—maintain the lead for the closer, Jose Mesa, who would surely secure the win for Jaret Wright and allow young Jaret the honor of becoming the first rookie to win a Seventh Game since Babe Adams back in 1909.

Cleveland had a chance for an "insurance" run in the ninth inning. With one out and Jim Thome on first and Sandy Alomar Jr. on third, Marquis Grissom hit a ground ball to Marlins shortstop Edgar Renteria. Renteria could have tried for the double play but instead went home and nailed Alomar trying to score. Had Renteria tried for the double play, it is likely that Grissom, a very fast runner, would have beat the throw from second base and the Indians would have had a two-run lead going into the bottom of the ninth. Instead, the Indians let an opportunity slip by. It would cost them dearly.

Moises Alou paid more dividends on owner Wayne Huizenga's investment when he singled off Jose Mesa to open the bottom of the ninth. Never in the history of the Seventh Game had a visiting team gone into the bottom of the ninth inning with a lead and lost. Not yet.

Things looked good for Cleveland when Mesa fanned Bobby Bonilla. The Indians were two outs away from the championship. Charles Johnson, a .250 hitter with moderate power, came to bat. C.J. also struck out a lot, 109 times in 416 at-bats during the season, so it appeared that Jose Mesa had the clear advantage. No matter, Johnson singled to right, sending Alou to third with the tying run.

The Indians needed a double play or some kind of out that would keep Alou from scoring. Craig Counsell had come to Florida during the middle of the season and proved to be one of Huizenga's most astute pickups, batting .299 in 51 games. He was not a feared power hitter but he consistently made contact with the ball—exactly the kind of hitter Jim Leyland wanted in the situation at hand. Mesa reared back and threw hard to Counsell. Craig did what he did best: he made contact. It was a fly ball that had no chance of clearing the fence in right field. But it was hit deep enough to let Moises Alou come home with the tying run. Jose Mesa had blown the save. The Indians were supposed to win this game, they had waited forty-nine years for this, they had paid their dues. (That was what it was all about.) The Marlins were the new kids on the block and weren't supposed to win it yet. They had not suffered enough.

Jim Eisenreich grounded out to end the ninth inning and for only the fourth time in World Series history, Game Seven was going into extra innings. Florida should have been elated, because in all three previous extra-inning Seventh Games, the home team had emerged victorious. Cleveland had to take comfort in the fact, for whatever it was worth, that in all three previous extra-inning affairs, the American League had come out with the win.

In the top of the tenth, Marlins reliever Robb Nen struck out Omar Vizquel, Manny Ramirez, and David Justice to work the crowd into a frenzy in anticipation of a great finish. The Marlins could not respond in the bottom of the tenth but the Indians could do nothing in the top of the eleventh.

Charles Nagy, the Indians' best starter during the season, had come in to pitch in the tenth. Manager Mike Hargrove had no idea how long the game would go on so Nagy was his best choice, especially since he had already gone through most of his good relievers. Bonilla led off the bottom of the eleventh inning with a single. The Marlins had removed Charles Johnson for a pinch runner in the ninth so they were stuck with Gregg Zaun, their backup catcher. Zaun was actually a better hitter than Johnson, posting a .301 average during the season, albeit in more limited playing time. It did not matter, because Zaun popped up. Next came the play that turned the game around.

Craig Counsell grounded what looked like a double-play ball to Cleveland second baseman Tony Fernandez. Fernandez, usually a steady and reliable fielder, never thought he had a chance for the double play but wanted to get the sure out at second base, the potential winning run. He got nothing, as he booted the ball for an error. The Indians intentionally walked Jim Eisenreich to set up a force play at home. Devon White, hitless in five trips, came to the plate and grounded to Fernandez. This time Tony fielded the ball cleanly and threw home to get Bonilla. White had missed the chance to be a hero and instead joined Travis Jackson as the only other player in Seventh Game history to go hitless in six at-bats. The Indians were one out away from the twelfth inning. All that stood in their way was sophomore shortstop Edgar Renteria.

Edgar Renteria hit .277 during the regular season and led the team in stolen bases, all at the age of twenty-two. The native of Colombia had not had either a good Division Series or League Championship Series but had come alive in the World Series with eight hits to that point. One more and he would be the hero. He took a good pitch from Charles Nagy and sent it up the middle on the ground into center field for a single and 67,204 fans began their celebration.

It was not long after that magical moment that Wayne Huizenga began his fire sale, selling off the players who had brought the world championship to Florida. By the time the 1998 season reached the all-star break, Moises Alou, Charles Johnson, Devon White, Bobby Bonilla, Kevin Brown, and Robb Nen were playing for other teams. By the middle of the 1999 season, Craig Counsell and Livan Hernandez were gone, too.

Maybe that's why baseball fans refuse to recognize the Seventh Game of the 1997 World Series as the truly great and exciting game that it was.

It's not that anyone begrudges an owner for buying a World Series—George Steinbrenner regularly digs deep into his pockets to stock the Yankees with superstars—but nobody likes the idea of short-term rentals.

Six years later the Florida Marlins finally made believers out of the rest of the baseball world. They beat the New York Yankees in six games to win the 2003 World series. True, they did it again as a wild-card team; but beating the Yankees goes a long way to establishing a team's credibility.

October 26, 1997

	1	2	3	4	5	6	7	8	9	10	11	R	H	E
CLEVELAND (AL)	0	0	2	0	0	0	0	0	0	0	0	2	6	2
FLORIDA (NL)	0	0	0	0	0	0	1	0	1	0	1	3	8	0

PITCHERS: CLE: Wright, Assenmacher, Jackson, Anderson, Mesa, Nagy (L); FLA: Leiter, Cook, Alfonseca, Heredia, Nen, Powell (W)

DOUBLES: Renteria

TRIPLES: None

HOME RUNS: Bonilla

ATTENDANCE: 67,204

TIME OF GAME: 4:11

2001

The Bottom of the Ninth

New York Yankees   2
Arizona Diamondbacks   3

There is no need to bring you back to the year 2001 with hints of popular culture, movies, songs, or television shows. You need only two words to find yourself firmly in the year 2001: *September eleventh.*

America had been attacked and experienced a fear that it had never known. Air traffic stopped. The stock market stopped. Even baseball stopped. Our grief was deep and seemingly without end. How could we even think of resuming the national pastime at a time like that? But we knew better: how could we think of *not* resuming the national pastime at a time like that? If baseball were to be of any worth, it would have to give us the drama and excitement that our parents and grandparents remembered. It had to give us a World Series that went the full seven games with a finale that would lift our spirits as no other had done. Could baseball meet that challenge?

When the games resumed, another drama was unfolding, the assault of Barry Bonds on Mark McGwire's single-season home run record, 70, set just three years earlier in 1998. Barry set a new mark, hitting his 73rd home run on October 7. Ho hum. There was plenty of real excitement left and everyone knew it would come later, maybe as late as November.

In the National League, the Arizona Diamondbacks, in only their fourth year, put together a mighty team led by the two best pitchers in base-

Around the Horn in 2001

- The Chicago Cubs set a new major-league record for most strikeouts by a pitching staff, 1,344. They were helped by their division mates the Milwaukee Brewers, who set a new record for most strikeouts by the offense, 1,399.
- Seattle's Ichiro Suzuki banged out 242 hits, the most since Bill Terry ripped 254 in 1930.
- The year 2001 saw major-league baseball's longest nine-inning game ever, a four-hour and twenty-seven-minute marathon between the Dodgers and Giants on October 5.

ball. Curt Schilling and Randy Johnson were both 20-game winners with earned run averages under 3.00. Their little Korean closer, Byung-Hyun Kim, anchored the bullpen with 19 saves. Luis Gonzalez led the offense with the best year of his career, slugging 57 home runs and driving home 142 runs. Who could have imagined anyone hitting 57 homers but finishing 16 behind the league's home run leader?

Arizona beat the pesky Cardinals in a close Division Series and easily disposed of Atlanta in the LCS to reach the World Series. Their opponent would be . . .

The events of September 11 brought America together in unexpected ways, and even some of the fiercest Yankees haters were rooting for New York to make it to the World Series. It would be poetic justice to see the pride of New York in the Fall Classic. If ever they belonged in the World Series, it was in 2001. They won the American League East Division but two major obstacles stood in their way, the Oakland A's and the Seattle Mariners.

After losing the first two games in New York in the best-of-five Division Series, New York traveled to Oakland in dire need of two victories on the road. They still talk about the 1–0 Yankees victory in Game Three, preserved by Derek Jeter's acrobatic catch of an errant throw from the outfield and subsequent shuffle throw to nail Jason Giambi at home plate. It was a thing of beauty, the catalyst that brought the Yankees back to win the series and go on to face Seattle in the LCS.

The Mariners had matched the major-league record for most wins in a season by going 116–46. They had great pitching, great hitting, great defense, and great momentum going into the LCS. The one thing they lacked was destiny, as the Yankees surprised the Mariners and the sportswriters by beating them handily, four games to one. This was what America wanted, the New York Yankees in the World Series. Baseball had delivered on part of its promise. Would it deliver on the rest and give America a World Series to remember?

The 2001 version of the New York Yankees was a delicate blend of youth and experience. Roger Clemens, at thirty-eight, astounded the baseball world when he ran his record to 20 wins against only one loss before losing his last two decisions to end at a still-amazing 20–3. The Yankees had the best closer in the game in slender Mariano Rivera, who recorded 50 saves. On offense, they put together a powerful lineup of veterans (Paul O'Neill, Bernie Williams, and Tino Martinez) and youngsters (Derek Jeter, Alfonso Soriano, and Jorge Posada). They were the three-time defending world champions and in 2001, more than ever before, they wanted one more championship. Even clusters of Red Sox fans around the country wiped away their tears with hopes of a Yankees victory in the World Series. Just this one time, of course.

Baseball made no promise that the Yankees would win but solemnly vowed that it would be a noble and unforgettable World Series. The commissioner of baseball never said so in so many words but that is what America so fervently desired. How could baseball *not* come through for its fans, for its country, and for the game itself?

That is not how the World Series started. Rested and ready, Arizona aces Schilling and Johnson gave up only one run in the first two games at home and Arizona crushed the Yankees, 9–1 and 4–0. Baseball had fallen down on its promise to America because, in truth, these two games offered little in the way of excitement and even less in the way of hope for Yankees fans. The Series moved back to New York, where the games would take on new meaning.

Seven weeks had passed since the devastation of the World Trade Center and now the city of New York was playing host to a World Series game. Yankees pride was one thing; it had fueled the success of the franchise for decades. This was different, a matter of New York pride, even national pride. The team that America had loved to hate for so many years was now the sentimental choice. There was only one problem: the Diamondbacks were beating up on them.

If there would be a Game Seven, the Yankees had to win three of the next four. It started with Game Three, as Roger Clemens allowed only three hits and New York held on to win, 2–1. Arizona fell apart with bad fielding and bad baserunning but nearly won behind an unknown starter, Brian Anderson. Game Four would present a much tougher challenge for the Yankees. Curt Schilling was the Arizona starter.

If you were there, you will never forget it. Curt Schilling pitched a masterpiece. The Diamondbacks led 3–1 in the eighth, when manager Bob Brenly brought in the usually reliable Byung-Hyun Kim to notch the save and give Arizona a commanding lead in the Series. Kim had already recorded three saves in the postseason and there was no reason to second-guess Brenly's move. Kim took the two-run lead into the ninth and Arizona began to savor the sweet taste of victory. Tino Martinez had no such appetite, tying the game on a two-out, two-run home run. This was pure Yankees magic. When Derek Jeter won the game with a home run in the tenth, also off Kim, Yankee Stadium found itself in a state of joy and euphoria that for a few—more than a few—wiped away all the sadness. This was the World Series that baseball had promised.

Game Five was equally unforgettable. With the Series deadlocked at two games each, one team and one team only would return to Arizona in need of a single victory for the championship. At Yankee Stadium, on November 1, 2001, the first time a postseason game was played in the month of November, Miguel Batista pitched the game of his life, holding the Yankees scoreless into the eighth inning. The Diamondbacks led by two runs going into the bottom of the ninth. Was there any more magic in the New York night air? Magic there was, as Scott Brosius homered to tie the game, again with two outs in the last of the ninth, again off Byung-Hyun Kim. This time all the world knew that New York would emerge victorious, and they pulled it out with a run in the bottom of the twelfth. Advantage: Yankees, three games to two.

Game Six: if you were there, you will never forget it, unless you are a Yankees fan, in which case you have already erased it from all memory banks. It was an old-fashioned whipping. Randy Johnson overpowered the Yankees and the Diamondbacks overpowered Andy Pettite and three other Yankees hurlers. The score was 12–0 after only three innings. When the score reached 15–2 after seven innings, Arizona manager Bob Brenly knew that there was no reason to keep Johnson in the game. No one cared about a complete game. It was more important to save what little bit of Randy Johnson might be left for the Seventh Game.

Although the sixth game was a rout, students of the game recognized that a Game Six blowout is usually a sign of a Game Seven classic. The 1960 World Series, in which the Pirates lost Game Six to the Yankees 12–0 before winning Game Seven on the Mazeroski home run in the ninth inning, was the best example of that possibility and was on everybody's mind. Bob Brenly knew that if the game was close, especially if the Yankees had any kind of lead late in the game, his Diamondbacks would have to win by beating the game's best postseason reliever, Mariano Rivera. In his previous twenty-three postseason save opportunities, Rivera was perfect. It was Bob Brenly's dream not only to win the World Series but to do it by beating baseball's best and most feared relief pitcher. He would have that chance.

It was the best pitching matchup of any Seventh Game. The two most dominating right-handed power pitchers in baseball, Roger Clemens and Curt Schilling, would treat the fans to a couple of virtuoso performances. Clemens was assured of a place in the Hall of Fame, while Schilling could join the Rocket with a few more years like the ones he had just posted.

Derek Jeter led off the game for New York and quickly returned to the dugout after Schilling buzzed three fastballs by him, the last clocking in at 97 mph. Next to bat was Paul O'Neill, the veteran right fielder who was rumored to be playing in his last game. O'Neill ripped a shot to right center, a sure extra-base hit. O'Neill headed to second at full speed and kept going, trying for a triple. It would take two good throws to nail him at third and the Diamondbacks obliged, with Craig Counsell's strike to Matt Williams nipping O'Neill by a cactus needle. The Paul O'Neill of old would have beaten the throw. But it is hard to criticize O'Neill's hustle and desire on a play that made Arizona execute two flawless throws. Bernie Williams flied out to end the inning and the Yankees had just missed out on the first good scoring chance of the game.

Roger Clemens had no trouble with the Diamondbacks in the first, allowing only one runner, by virtue of his own error. He was throwing as hard as ever and Arizona was not making good contact. In the top of the second, Shane Spencer crushed a Schilling pitch to deep center but Steve Finley made a fine running catch to retire Spencer and the Yankees. The

Yanks had tagged Schilling twice but had no runs to show for their efforts. But they had to be feeling good about being able to catch up with Schilling's fastball. They had plenty of time.

The Diamondbacks threatened to score in the bottom of the second, when Danny Bautista walked and Mark Grace singled. But Clemens struck out Damian Miller and Curt Schilling to get out of the jam. The only consolation that Arizona could take from their efforts was that Roger Clemens had thrown a lot of pitches in the first two frames. Maybe they could get to him soon.

Both Clemens and Schilling were strong over the next three innings. No one threatened, no one hit the ball very hard, and no one could take the upper hand.

Schilling was throwing 95-mph fastballs in the sixth inning and the bottom of the Yankees order walked meekly to the plate and turned back to the dugout. The Diamondbacks finally broke through off Roger Clemens in the bottom of the sixth. Steve Finley started it with a single, and Danny Bautista followed with a shot to left center that went all the way to the wall. Finley scored easily and it looked like a sure triple. Only a perfect catch and relay throw by Derek Jeter would have any chance of cutting down Bautista at third. Out at third! If any other shortstop had been there, Bautista would have been perched safely on third. Credit the athleticism of Derek Jeter with keeping the damage to one run, because Clemens retired the next three batters. New York now had to mount a comeback, something they had done twice in the Series already and countless times during the regular season.

Instead of waiting for the ninth inning, as they had done in Games Four and Five, the Yankees came right back in the top of the seventh inning. Derek Jeter and Paul O'Neill singled against Curt Schilling. Bernie Williams grounded to Mark Grace, who could only get Paul O'Neill at second base. One out, runners on first and third. Championship teams do not let such chances go by without scoring at least one run. Tino Martinez, playing in his last game with the Yankees (he didn't know it at the time), singled and the Yankees had answered. Jorge Posada popped up and Shane Spencer banged another long fly-ball out but the score was tied, 1–1. It was exactly the kind of game the fans knew that Schilling and Clemens would give them.

Bob Brenly had a well-rested bullpen to give him as many innings as he might need. He knew that his team needed a run and that he needed to get that run before New York scored, because a New York lead meant Mariano Rivera would enter the game. And Mariano Rivera, as all of baseball knew—especially those familiar with his last 23 postseason games—meant certain death. Curt Schilling had given Brenly seven exceptional innings but showed signs of weakness, giving up three hits in the top of the inning. Was there any good reason to let Schilling bat for himself leading off in the bottom of the seventh inning? He was not a good-hitting pitcher, batting only .133 during the season. But Schilling came out to hit. Roger Clemens struck him out.

Schilling's strikeout to start the seventh inning hurt because Tony Womack followed with a single. Yankees manager Joe Torre knew that Roger Clemens was finished and brought in Mike Stanton, his "situation" lefty. The Diamondbacks tried to manufacture a run by letting Womack, Arizona's best base stealer during the season, try to pilfer second. Jorge Posada cut him down and when Craig Counsell fouled out to Tino Martinez, the Diamondbacks had nothing to show for their efforts.

In the top of the eighth, Brenly's decision to keep Schilling in the game looked good for two pitches, as leadoff hitter Alfonso Soriano fell behind, 0-2. But on the next pitch, Soriano took Schilling deep to left field, far into the night, for a home run that silenced most of the 49,589 Diamondbacks fans. The Yankees had the lead. Mariano Rivera grabbed his glove and began to loosen his invincible right arm. The Yankees were not finished hitting, though. After Scott Brosius struck out, pinch hitter David Justice, playing in his third World Series Seventh Game for his third different team, cracked a pinch single. That was the end for Curt Schilling and the beginning of a classic World Series chess match between two astute and calculating managers.

Bob Brenly could not let the Yankees score again. A two-run lead for Mariano Rivera was more than anyone could hope to overcome. Brenly brought in Miguel Batista to pitch to Derek Jeter. Jeter hit a sharp grounder to Matt Williams, a perfect double-play ball. Craig Counsell took the throw at second base to retire Justice but juggled the ball in his attempt to transfer the ball from glove hand to throwing hand. Jeter was safe at first and the veteran Paul O'Neill was ready for his final at-bat in the big leagues. He yearned to make up for being thrown out at third base in the first inning. Bob Brenly could not let the righty Miguel Batista face Paul O'Neill. He needed a good lefty, a great lefty, and he found one. Randy Johnson, "the Big Unit," had pitched the night before but told Brenly that he could give him one or two innings. Removing Johnson after seven innings in Game Six proved to be the smartest move that Brenly ever made, although some criticized Brenly for not removing him even earlier.

Joe Torre knew how tough Randy Johnson was on lefties and that Paul O'Neill would have little chance against the wicked deliveries of the Big Unit. It must have hurt Joe Torre, who probably knew that O'Neill would never play another game. But the Yankees wanted one more run, that all important "insurance" run. He called back O'Neill and sent in Chuck Knoblauch to pinch-hit. Knoblauch had found a new home in the outfield for New York after his erratic throws as a second baseman proved to be too much of a liability for the Yankees. In truth, he did not have a great season, hitting only .250, and had an even more miserable World Series, with one hit in seventeen tries. But Knoblauch had a history of coming through when Torre needed him. Not this time. Randy Johnson won the battle and the Diamondbacks had six outs left.

Torre wasted no time in bringing in his indomitable closer in the bottom of the eighth. Mariano Rivera had saved 50 games for the Yankees during the regular season and 5 more in the 2001 postseason. If there was anything approaching a sure thing in baseball, it was Mariano Rivera in the postseason. The last time Rivera blew a save in the postseason was 1994. The 23 consecutive saves that followed made him a modern-day legend.

Although Rivera is a right-handed pitcher, left-handed batters have never held any advantage over him. The horrifying movement of his ball busting in on left-handed batters was more likely to shatter bats than produce hits. In the bottom of the eighth inning, Mariano Rivera broke no bats because he didn't have to. He struck out the heart of the Arizona order. Luis Gonzalez went down swinging. Matt Williams went down swinging. Steve Finley can tell his grandchildren that he got a hit off Rivera but it didn't matter because Danny Bautista went down swinging. The Diamondbacks had only three more outs left.

Randy Johnson had promised one or two innings to Bob Brenly and he made good on his word. One-two-three went the Yankees in the top of the ninth, Johnson ending it with a flourish by striking out Jorge Posada. Now all the Diamondbacks had to do was score against Mariano Rivera.

Former Cub Mark Grace led off the bottom of the ninth and hit a good pitch up the middle for a single. Not only did it bring a glimmer of hope to Arizona, it erased, once and for all, the myth of the "Cub factor," the theory (obviously concocted by cynical Cub fans who point to the Bill

Buckner error in 1986 and Mitch "Wild Thing" Williams's disastrous 1993 World Series) that former Cubs are a curse on any World Series team. Grace had done his part and the younger, faster Dave Dellucci came in to run for him. There was no reason for panic in the Yankees' dugout. After all, Mariano Rivera was on the mound. And if ever the country was rooting for New York, it was now.

Bob Brenly had to play it safe, play for one run and get into extra innings, where the home team had always come out on top in Seventh Games. He understood that playing for a tie in the bottom of the ninth inning is basic baseball strategy, so he called on Damian Miller to bunt. Although Miller was not exactly an accomplished bunter, with only seven sacrifice bunts in his five-year career, he must have been relieved because he had struck out in his previous three at-bats. The Arizona catcher bunted. It was a poor one, hit too hard and right back at Rivera. Rivera whirled and threw to second base, in plenty of time to get Dellucci. But Rivera's throw was wild, pulling Derek Jeter off the bag, and Dellucci was safe. Rivera's uncharacteristic error—he had committed only one error in his entire career to that point—gave Arizona more than just hope. This was a real break.

A sacrifice bunt now would mean runners on second and third with only one out. Big-league teams, especially good ones, are supposed to be able to score in that situation. Jay Bell, a skillful bunter, came in to bat for Randy Johnson. (Brenly never even considered letting Johnson try to bunt.) Bell bunted, and it was not a very good bunt either. Rivera pounced on it and threw to Scott Brosius in plenty of time to retire Dellucci at third.

Could Brosius have thrown across the diamond or to second base to complete the double play? Mariano Rivera would later accuse Brosius of failing to make the throw and not turning the double play. Of course, an errant throw by Brosius would have cost the tying run. But so what? The Diamondbacks had failed to move the runners and Mariano Rivera was in a much more comfortable situation. First and second with one out was a situation he had successfully faced dozens of times, probably even in his sleep. He needed only two more outs and the Yankees would again be world champions.

Rivera's next obstacle was Tony Womack, a .266 hitter during the season and not exactly Arizona's biggest threat. Tony ripped a single to right field, the hardest-hit ball off Rivera in the game, and the myth of Mariano Rivera's invincibility was gone. Pinch runner Midre Cummings scored the tying run, and Jay Bell was at third, representing the winning run. The Yankees brought in their infield, in desperate hope of getting a ground ball that would prevent the runner on third from scoring. Craig Counsell was the batter and Rivera hit him with a pitch. Was it a shortcut way of issuing an intentional walk? It did not matter, because neither Counsell nor the runner at second meant anything.

It was now Mariano Rivera against Luis Gonzalez. Lugo had come off his best season but those statistics meant nothing now. A long fly ball, a well-placed grounder through the drawn-in infield, even an inside pitch that he could "take for the team"—there were so many ways to score. Rivera made a great pitch and jammed Gonzalez. He popped it toward the edge of the outfield grass, just beyond where Derek Jeter might have caught it if he were playing at his regular shortstop position. The ball fell to the ground and Jay Bell crossed the plate with the winning run.

New York's Mayor Rudy Guiliani, America's mayor in our time of pain and distress, rose from his seat along the first-base line and cheered. He cheered for the effort that both teams had given. He cheered for the Arizona Diamondbacks, who had come back to win against the best relief pitcher in the game. And he cheered for the New York Yankees, who, although they took home no rings that year, did not lose. Even Red Sox fans could have handled a Yankees win in 2001, but instead they witnessed their rivals fall one game short with the kind of grace and dignity that no one would ever forget.

November 4, 2001

	1	2	3	4	5	6	7	8	9	R	H	E
NEW YORK (AL)	0	0	0	0	0	0	1	1	0	2	6	3
ARIZONA (NL)	0	0	0	0	0	1	0	0	2	3	11	0

PITCHERS: NYY: Clemens, Stanton, Rivera (L); ARZ: Schilling, Batista, Johnson (W)

DOUBLES: O'Neill, Bautista, Womack

TRIPLES: None

HOME RUNS: Soriano

ATTENDANCE: 49,589

TIME OF GAME: 3:20

2002

Another Giant Disappointment

San Francisco Giants   1
Anaheim Angels   4

America pondered three burning questions in October of 2002: (1) Will United Nations inspectors find weapons of mass destruction in Iraq? (2) Can interest rates fall any lower? (3) Will the Anaheim Angels pitch to Barry Bonds in the World Series? The history books will answer the first two. Anaheim manager Mike Scioscia answered the third by pitching to the most feared slugger in all of baseball when it suited his strategy and ultimately by winning the World Series.

Everybody was talking about Barry Bonds, veteran slugger for the San Francisco Giants. He had electrified the baseball world by smashing 73 home runs in 2001 but in 2002 Barry had the kind of year even the best of players can only imagine. Baseball fanatics will argue deep into the next century as to how great his 2002 season really was. He hit .370 to lead the National League and all of baseball in hitting. He hit 46 home runs and drove in 110 runs. The most impressive statistic of all is that he walked 198 times. That was the fear factor, the respect factor. Nobody wanted to pitch to Barry. Of the 198 walks, 68 were intentional, shattering the old record of 35 intentional walks in a single season. That is hard to fathom, intentionally walking a thirty-eight-year-old man because he is too dangerous.

When the Giants made it to the playoffs, critics were quick to point out that Barry Bonds had never performed well in postseason play. In his

Around the Horn in 2002

- Per order of Baseball Commissioner Bud Selig, the All-Star Game ended in a tie when both teams ran out of pitchers.
- Milwaukee's Jose Hernandez came within one whiff of tying the all-time record for most strikeouts in a season, 198, held by Bobby Bonds, father of Barry. Manager Jerry Royster benched Hernandez near the end of the season, taking away his chances at a new record.
- On May 23, Shawn Green of the Los Angeles Dodgers became the tenth player in history to hit four home runs in a game.

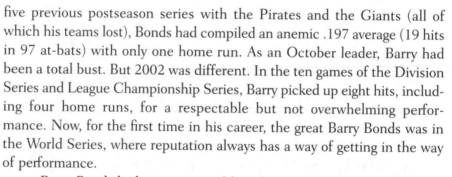

five previous postseason series with the Pirates and the Giants (all of which his teams lost), Bonds had compiled an anemic .197 average (19 hits in 97 at-bats) with only one home run. As an October leader, Barry had been a total bust. But 2002 was different. In the ten games of the Division Series and League Championship Series, Barry picked up eight hits, including four home runs, for a respectable but not overwhelming performance. Now, for the first time in his career, the great Barry Bonds was in the World Series, where reputation always has a way of getting in the way of performance.

Barry Bonds had teammates, although you might not have known it by the press coverage that Barry got. Jeff Kent was the most productive second baseman in the league, having posted his sixth straight year with 100 or more runs batted in. Rich Aurilia and J. T. Snow had subpar years but were accomplished players who had put up impressive numbers in earlier seasons. But the key player for the Giants was the man that manager Dusty Baker selected to bat behind Barry Bonds, veteran catcher Benito Santiago.

If Anaheim manager Mike Scioscia were to follow the lead of his National League counterparts, Barry Bonds would be receiving plenty of free passes to first base and the pressure would be on Benito Santiago to deliver the goods. Santiago, whose face seems to have been roughly hewn from the hardest wood of the forest, had been through the wars. He had come up with San Diego in 1986 and had made the rounds of both leagues, coming to San Francisco in 2001. He was no Barry Bonds but had driven home 74 runs during the 2002 campaign. He was MVP of the

League Championship Series, batting .300 and knocking in six against the Cardinals.

The Giants had a pitching staff, too, but it wasn't much. They had Russ Ortiz, who had won a pair in the Division Series against the Atlanta Braves, and veteran Kirk Rueter, who had an uncanny resemblance to the cartoon character Woody from the movie *Toy Story*. Each had won 14 games during the season but neither struck a whole lot of fear into the hearts of opposing batters. The Giants also had Livan Hernandez, the Cuban righty who was the MVP of the 1997 World Series when he won two games for the Florida Marlins. Hernandez may have had "big-game" experience but he had an entirely forgettable regular season for the Giants in 2002, winning only 12 games and losing 16.

That was what the National League had to offer for the 2002 World Series.

The big news in the American League was that the New York Yankees were not in the World Series. Despite gargantuan seasons from Alfonso Soriano and Jason Giambi, the defending American League champions ran into a bunch of hard-hitting overachievers from Anaheim in the Division Series and made an unexpected and unceremonious quick exit from postseason play. Who were these Anaheim Angels? What did they think they would accomplish?

They knew they would accomplish a lot more in 2002 than they did in 2001, when they finished 41 games behind the Seattle Mariners. They did not have a Barry Bonds on their roster. Instead, they had a bunch of young aggressive hitters like Garret Anderson, Tim Salmon, and Troy Glaus who learned that they could win ball games that others didn't think they could win.

The Angels had pitching, too. Jarrod Washburn was the ace of the staff, winning 18 games and losing only 6. Ramon Ortiz won 15 games but also gave up a lot of home runs, leading the American League in that dubious category, and veteran Kevin Appier chipped in with 14 wins. They also had the tough, squinty-eyed reliever Troy Percival, and no one liked to mess with Troy in the late innings. A youngster by the name of John Lackey came up in the middle of the year and won 9 games but no one figured he would be a factor in the postseason, if the Angels even got there.

They had one more thing: the "Rally Monkey," a toy monkey Angels fans brandished that seemed to bring wondrous miracles to the team whenever they needed them.

That's what Angels manager Mike Scioscia had to work with. But all the press wanted to know was whether the Angels would pitch to Barry Bonds. No one asked Dusty Baker if the Giants would pitch to Garret Anderson or Troy Glaus or Tim Salmon. Sure, Barry Bonds was the most dangerous offensive threat in baseball since Babe Ruth. But as dangerous as the Giants' slugger was, Scioscia knew that Barry Bonds could bat only one time for every nine San Francisco plate appearances because that is the law of baseball.

The teams split the first two games of the Series at Anaheim as balls soared out of Edison Field. The Giants edged the Angels in the opener, 4–3, on home runs by Bonds, Reggie Sanders, and J. T. Snow, overcoming a pair of homers by Troy Glaus. The Angels came back to nip the Giants in the second game, 11–10, despite four Giants homers, including one more by Bonds. This time it was Tim Salmon's turn to bang out a pair of home runs for the Angels.

Barry Bonds continued his home run barrage with yet another long one in Game Three at San Francisco but the Angels banged out 16 hits to win easily, 10–4. The Giants tied the Series with a 4–3 squeaker in Game Four, the only home run coming off the bat of Angels third baseman Troy Glaus.

The fifth game was all San Francisco. Jeff Kent led a 16-hit assault with two home runs and the Giants were one game away from their first world championship as residents of San Francisco and the first for the franchise since 1954. Barry Bonds crushed his fourth home run of the Series, Rich Aurilia slammed his second, and the Giants were rolling. When they took a 5–0 lead into the bottom of the seventh inning in Game Six back at Anaheim, the technical crew began laying cable for the Giants' postgame victory celebration. The champagne was ready for popping. There was one problem—Anaheim's Rally Monkey showed up. A three-run home run by Chris Spiezio at the end of a ferocious eight-pitch at-bat cut into the lead and got the technicians out of the Giants' locker room in a hurry.

Did the Angels make the greatest comeback in World Series history or did the Giants choke? No team down by five runs in an "elimination" game had ever rallied to win, but that was what the Angels did, edging the Giants 6–5 and setting up another World Series Seventh Game.

Who was going to pitch in Game Seven? Mike Scioscia had seen his ace, Jarrod Washburn, get walloped in Game Five and he had used Kevin Appier in Game Six. Why not the rookie John Lackey? No one bothered telling the Angels that it had been ninety-three years since a rookie had started and won a Seventh Game. That was the first Seventh Game, when Babe Adams blanked the Tigers in 1909. But Babe Adams had only Ty Cobb to face, not Barry Bonds.

Giants manager Dusty Baker had the same tough decision to make and tapped Livan Hernandez to start. The Angels shelled Hernandez in Game Two but Livan was the pitcher with "big-game" experience. He had won Games Two and Five for Florida in the 1997 World Series. Dusty should have checked more closely; in those two 1997 wins, Hernandez gave up eight earned runs and walked ten in 13-plus innings. Dusty should have checked one other statistic. Livan Hernandez had lost 16 games during the regular season. Only once in World Series history had a 16-game loser started a Seventh Game. Jon Matlack, 14–16 with the 1973 Mets, started the Seventh Game in 1973 and lost. History was not on the side of Livan Hernandez.

How could the Giants be emotionally ready for a Game Seven? After losing Game Six when they were five runs ahead with only eight outs to go, how could they possibly make a game of it? Remember the 1986 Boston Red Sox? They let their Game Six slip away in similar heartbreaking fashion and paid the ultimate price.

Chills ran down the spines of all 44,598 at Edison Field as four jet fighter planes screeched across the top of the stadium when Melissa Etheridge finished "The Star-Spangled Banner." Play ball! Play ball in the Seventh Game of the World Series for a thirty-fifth time. Dusty Baker and Mike Scioscia knew what was at stake because they had shared the dream as teammates in 1981, when the Dodgers beat the Yankees in six games. Only one would know that joy in 2002.

John Lackey came out firing, retiring the side in the first inning. He looked sharp, focused, in total command of his pitches. That was not the case with Livan Hernandez, who gave up a leadoff walk to the Angels' little gnat of a shortstop, David Eckstein. Sensing the importance of the first run, Scioscia called on Darin Erstad to bunt and Erstad moved Eckstein to second. Hernandez then walked Tim Salmon. Everyone could see it, that Livan Hernandez was not the right choice. Did Dusty Baker see it? If he did, what would he do about it?

The Giants caught a break when Garret Anderson caught hold of a Livan Hernandez offering and sent a screaming line drive to the outfield, directly at Kenny Lofton. Lofton caught the ball cleanly and threw to second base to double up Eckstein, who had wandered too far from the bag. Eckstein's baserunning blunder had bailed out Hernandez, but Livan was obviously more distressed with the home plate umpire's calls of balls and strikes than his own lack of stuff. From the dugout between the first and second innings came screams of protest from Hernandez. That, too, should have been a sign for Dusty Baker that his pitcher was not ready.

San Francisco broke through with a run in the second inning. After Barry Bonds lined out hard to David Eckstein, Benito Santiago singled, only his fifth hit of the Series. J. T. Snow, a former Angel, singled to right center and Santiago took third. Reggie Sanders, whose entire 2002 postseason had been more of a nightmare than the dream of every ballplayer, lofted a lazy fly ball deep enough to score Santiago with the first run of the game. In the thirty-four previous Seventh Games, the team that scored first had won twenty-two times. Advantage: Giants?

For a brief moment, Livan Hernandez looked good. He struck out Troy Glaus to start the bottom of the second inning. Brad Fullmer then crushed one to deep left center, but not deep enough, as Kenny Lofton hauled it in for the second out. Chris Spiezio, one of the Game Six heroes, coaxed another walk from Hernandez, the third in two innings. Benjie Molina was next and he ripped the ball to deep left center—no one was going to catch it. The ball bounced short of the wall. If it bounced over the wall, Spiezio would have been awarded third base on the "ground-rule" double. When the ball hit the turf it looked as if it would clear the wall. But luck was not with the Giants. The ball missed going over the wall by about a foot and came back in play, allowing Spiezio to score easily. Hernandez got the last out but the Angels had tied the game.

John Lackey retired the Giants in order in the top of the third and the struggling Livan Hernandez returned to the mound. Eckstein led off with a sharp single to left. No one was warming up in the San Francisco bullpen. Darin Erstad followed with another single. Still no one was warming up, although the whole world could see that Livan Hernandez was coming apart. Tim Salmon stepped to the plate. On a 2–1 pitch, Hernandez threw a terrific down-and-away slider to even the count at 2–2. It was Livan's last great pitch of the day. He then hit Salmon on the right hand to load the bases. Now the bullpen got busy.

But it was too late. Hernandez grooved a fastball, just above the waist and where all hitters like it, to Garret Anderson. Anderson yanked it into the right-field corner for a bases-clearing double. After an intentional walk to Troy Glaus, Dusty Baker took Hernandez out of the game but the Giants were down by three, 4–1. Chad Zerbe retired the Angels to escape further damage and San Francisco had to mount a comeback.

It would have been very easy for the San Francisco Giants to give up. They had been eight outs away with a five-run lead the night before. They had seen their "big-game" pitcher give up four quick runs to put them in a hole early in the Seventh Game. To their credit, they did not give up. With one out in the fourth, Barry Bonds and Benito Santiago singled but died on the bases when J. T. Snow and Reggie Sanders sent routine fly balls to the outfield.

In the bottom of the fourth, Kirk Rueter, whom many thought should have started the game, came in to pitch for the Giants and provided plenty of ammunition for the I-told-you-so crowd by retiring the Angels in order.

John Lackey needed one more inning to be the "pitcher of record" and be the first rookie to start and win a Seventh Game since Babe Adams in 1909. The way he was pitching, there was no way he should have had any problems. But leadoff hitter David Bell smoked a shot to left center in the top of the fifth, an apparent double to the gap. Darin Erstad raced in to make a brilliant diving stab, robbing Bell of a hit and the Giants of another chance to get into the game. After Pedro Feliz fanned, Kenny Lofton walked and the Giants had another base runner. When Rich Aurilia flied to right to end the inning, John Lackey had done his job.

Kirk Rueter pitched another strong inning for the Giants, strong but too late. Into the game for Anaheim walked burly relief pitcher Brendan Donnelly, the personification of big-league perseverance at its best. Donnelly had spent ten years in the minor leagues toiling with nine different organizations and was not even on the Angels' roster when the 2002 season started—but there he was, pitching in Game Seven of the World Series. He had picked up the win in Game Six and was there to contribute to the task of shutting down the Giants in the finale. Who says there are no more opportunities for the little guy, even if he is pretty big?

Donnelly retired Jeff Kent on a ground ball and got the better of Barry Bonds by inducing a towering pop fly to second. Benito Santiago drew a walk and J. T. Snow doubled to the right-field corner. Down by three with the slow-footed Santiago on base, the Giants could not afford to take a chance on scoring Benito and held him at third base. Dusty Baker called back Reggie Sanders, whose miserable Series made him a poor choice for batting in such a crucial situation, and nodded to the left-handed-hitting

Tom Goodwin. Pinch hitting had been a weak spot for the Giants in the 2002 postseason, no hits in seven tries. Make that no hits in eight tries, as Donnelly overpowered Goodwin with 91-mph fastballs. The Giants had let another opportunity go by.

Kirk Rueter continued his streak of scoreless innings. The critics were swarming down on Dusty Baker.

The Anaheim bullpen was busy, but not because Mike Scioscia lacked any confidence in Brendan Donnelly. Scioscia expected two innings from Donnelly, not a single pitch more. Donnelly knew his role and focused on giving Anaheim that one more good inning. With a little luck, he found that inning. David Bell, who had been robbed of a hit by Darin Erstad earlier in the game, ripped a shot to left that Garret Anderson hauled in on the warning track. Pedro Feliz, another of Dusty Baker's Game Seven hunches, struck out swinging. Kenny Lofton followed with a well-hit fly to deep right center, but it, too, was not deep enough. There were three outs on two well-hit balls and the Giants had only six outs left.

Kirk Rueter set down the Angels in order in the bottom of the seventh. He was no Sandy Koufax but he was also no Livan Hernandez.

Brendan Donnelly had done his job. Now it was time for twenty-year-old fireballer Francisco Rodriguez to give his one inning of hard work. The slender, baby-faced Rodriguez struck out Rich Aurilia and Jeff Kent to bring the Edison Field crowd into a state of total frenzy. Up to the plate came Barry Bonds, who had crushed a Rodriguez pitch 485 feet for a home run the night before. Rodriguez was not about to give Bonds a pitch to hit and issued him a walk, the thirteenth time Barry had walked in the World Series. Rodriguez then struck out Santiago to end the inning. The Giants were through. They did not have a chance. They would go quietly in the ninth against the Angels' dominating closer, Troy Percival. Or would they?

Todd Worrell pitched a perfect eighth for San Francisco and in came the squinty-eyed Percival, with six saves in six opportunities in the 2002 postseason. J. T. Snow started the inning with a single, his third hit of the game. Those Giants would not quit! After looking at a pair of 97-mph called strikes, Tom Goodwin bounced to second to force J.T. Two outs to go. David Bell, who had already hit the ball hard in his previous two appearances but had nothing to show for his efforts, drew a walk and the Giants were suddenly alive. The tying run came to the plate in the person of Tsuyoshi Shinjo, the first Japanese-born position player to appear in a World Series game. Shinjo had hit 19 home runs in his two seasons in the big leagues and was a good fastball hitter. He was perfectly capable of taking Troy Percival deep and tying the game. Percival made a mistake on a 1–2 pitch, serving up a fastball down the heart of the plate. But Shinjo just missed it, fouling the pitch back. He then chased a high outside fastball and the Giants were down to their last out.

Twelve-year veteran Kenny Lofton was San Francisco's last hope and Anaheim's last obstacle. He was not known as a home run hitter but had knocked out more than a hundred in his career. He had even slammed five home runs in his thirteen postseason series, including one for the Giants in the LCS against Atlanta only days ago. Kenny Lofton wasn't Barry Bonds but he was a big-league ballplayer who was no stranger to home runs. Lofton jumped on the first pitch and sent a fly ball to Darin Erstad in center field. It was not deep and not difficult but Erstad knew that it would be, could be, the biggest catch of his life. He remembered all his father had taught him—two hands, squeeze the ball—and made the catch that brought the Angels their first championship in their forty-two-year history.

Tearful fans began singing "Back in the Saddle," a tribute to the late longtime owner of the Angels, Gene Autry. It didn't matter that they were in a saddle they had never been in before. Victory was sweet, especially coming in the Seventh Game.

As for the Giants, they did manage to outhit the Angels, a feat accomplished only five times before by a losing team in a Game Seven. It may be a meaningless statistic for some but it shows that the Giants refused to quit. It was also the fourth time the Giants had gone down to defeat in a Seventh Game—twice when they were in New York, now twice in San Francisco. Their record in Seventh Games was 0–4. No other team has lost so many and won so few. Even the Red Sox have one victory to go with their four heartbreaks. Naturally, it came at the expense of the Giants, back in 1912.

And in the year the Giants and Angels hit more home runs through the first six games than had ever been hit in any World Series, no one bothered to hit one in Game Seven. It was just full of surprises, wasn't it?

October 27, 2002

	1	2	3	4	5	6	7	8	9	R	H	E
SAN FRANCISCO (NL)	0	1	0	0	0	0	0	0	0	1	6	0
ANAHEIM (AL)	0	1	3	0	0	0	0	0	X	4	5	0

PITCHERS: SFG: Hernandez (L), Zerbe, Rueter, Worrell; ANA:
Lackey (W), Donnelly, F. Rodriguez, Percival (SV)

DOUBLES: Snow, Anderson, Molina (2)

TRIPLES: None

HOME RUNS: None

ATTENDANCE: 44,598

TIME OF GAME: 3:16

Part 2

Deconstructing the Seventh Games

CHAPTER 36

Analysis: The Teams

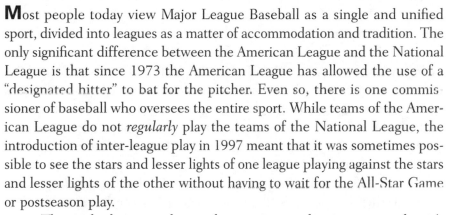

Most people today view Major League Baseball as a single and unified sport, divided into leagues as a matter of accommodation and tradition. The only significant difference between the American League and the National League is that since 1973 the American League has allowed the use of a "designated hitter" to bat for the pitcher. Even so, there is one commissioner of baseball who oversees the entire sport. While teams of the American League do not *regularly* play the teams of the National League, the introduction of inter-league play in 1997 meant that it was sometimes possible to see the stars and lesser lights of one league playing against the stars and lesser lights of the other without having to wait for the All-Star Game or postseason play.

The rivalry between the two leagues is not what it once was but it's still there. In 2003, for the first time in baseball history, the outcome of the All-Star Game will affect the World Series. The league that wins the All-Star Game will ensure that its champion hosts the first, second, sixth, and seventh games of the World Series. But does the "home-field advantage" mean anything in a Seventh Game?

In football and in basketball, the home-field or home-court advantage is purely psychological because the rules do not favor the home team. The goalposts are as wide for the home team as they are for the visitors and the three-point arc is as far away for the hometown shooters as it is for the visiting team. The home crowd may cheer for the home team and boo the visitors but the game itself favors neither side. The psychological advantage of sleeping in a comfortable bed at home versus an unfamiliar bed at some strange hotel is undoubtedly real but it has nothing to do with the game itself. Baseball is different.

The rules of baseball favor the home team in close games, in games that present the opportunity for extra innings. The home team bats last and that is a real and substantial advantage. In the ninth inning of a tie game, for example, a team's strategy will differ depending on whether it is the home team or the visitor. "Last ups" can mean a lot to a manager. It is the conventional wisdom of baseball that in the late innings of a close game, the visiting team plays to win at its first opportunity while the home team is content to try to tie the game and force extra innings. In extra innings, the home team knows what the visitor has done in its half of the inning and can map its offensive strategy accordingly. Knowing that your team will have a chance to respond to whatever the visitors have done can also shape defensive strategy. Students of baseball do not dispute the theory that the rules favor the home team. Do the results of the thirty-five Seventh Games support that theory?

At first blush, the results seem neutral. The home team has won eighteen Seventh Games while the visiting team has won seventeen. The difference is statistically insignificant. But consider the four extra-inning games and the one game that was tied going into the bottom of the ninth inning—the home team won them all. Do five games prove the point? Until a visiting team wins an extra-inning Seventh Game, the home-field advantage seems significant.

The most startling aspect of the home-field advantage in Seventh Games is that the advantage, if one really exists, has appeared only recently. From 1947 to 1958, the visiting team won six straight Seventh Games. The home teams have won the last eight Seventh Games. Until 1979, the record stood at 10 wins for the home team and 17 wins for the visitors. Did anything change with the 1982 World Series? Probably not.

That leaves open the question of league superiority. The numbers favor the National League by a 20–15 margin in Seventh Games. That may come as a surprise to many because the dominating Yankees, winners of twenty-six championships in the first century of the World Series, would seem to skew the results in favor of the American League. But as dominating as the Yankees have been in World Series play, they have been meek and totally beatable in Seventh Games. Their Seventh Game record is five wins against six losses. The strategy when playing the New York Yankees in the World Series is simple: extend the Series to seven games and there is a better than even chance of beating them. Conversely, in those Series involving the Yankees that do not go the limit, it is almost hopeless. The Yankees' record in World Series that are settled in less than seven games is 21 wins against only 6 losses.

The team standings in World Series Seventh Games:

American League

Team	W	L	Pct.
Anaheim Angels	1	0	1.000
Kansas City Royals	1	0	1.000
Oakland A's (Philadelphia)	2	1	.667
Minnesota Twins (Washington Senators)	3	2	.600
New York Yankees	5	6	.455
Detroit Tigers	2	3	.400
Boston Red Sox	1	4	.200
Baltimore Orioles	0	2	.000
Milwaukee Brewers	0	1	.000
Cleveland Indians	0	1	.000

National League

Team	W	L	Pct.
Pittsburgh Pirates	5	0	1.000
Arizona Diamondbacks	1	0	1.000
Florida Marlins	1	0	1.000
St. Louis Cardinals	7	3	.700
Cincinnati Reds	2	1	.667
New York Mets	1	1	.500
Los Angeles (Brooklyn) Dodgers	2	3	.400
Atlanta (Milwaukee) Braves	1	2	.333
Chicago Cubs	0	1	.000
San Francisco (New York) Giants	0	4	.000

One lesson from these standings rings clear: don't mess with the Pirates in a seven-game World Series. They are perfect in five tries. The Giants are another story. They are a perfect 0 for 4, losing twice while in New York, twice while in San Francisco. Their most recent loss in the 2002 Seventh Game was the only loss not decided by a single run. They lost two in extra innings and have showed their fans the meaning of heartbreak with alarming consistency. Who is missing here? Of the "original" sixteen franchises in the major leagues in 1903, when baseball hosted its first World Series, only the Chicago White Sox and Philadelphia Phillies have not played in a Seventh Game.

The Boston Red Sox, with one Seventh Game win before most readers of this paragraph were even born, also know something about heartbreak. Their four Seventh Game losses since 1946—their only World Series appearances since 1946—are a lead weight around the neck of all of New England.

The St. Louis Cardinals have won more Seventh Games than anyone else. Until 1985, their record was a blistering seven wins against one defeat. Losses in 1985 and 1987 brought them back to 7–3, still an impressive record by any standards.

What about scoring first? Teams generally claim an advantage to putting that first run on the board but does history support this assumption? In a purely statistical sense, scoring first has been an advantage. Scoring first has meant victory in twenty-two of the thirty-five Seventh Games. But there is something potentially misleading about this statistic. It is obvious that when a pitcher tosses a shutout, scoring first automatically means victory. There have been nine shutouts in the thirty-five Seventh Games; take away those games and the scoring-first advantage disappears. When both teams score, the team scoring first has won thirteen and lost thirteen. The moral of the story is this: if your opponent scores, just get on the board and you'll be fine.

More than a million and a half fans have attended the thirty-five Seventh Games (1,537,433, to be exact). The 1947 contest between the Dodgers and Yankees at Yankee Stadium drew the largest crowd, 71,548, and the 1912 game between the Red Sox and the Giants pulled in the smallest crowd, 17,034. (Why so few people at the new Fenway Park? See Chapter 2.)

The average Seventh Game has taken two hours and thirty-nine minutes but this is no longer a representative estimate of how much time you should budget for watching the game. Beginning with the 1986 Seventh Game, every game has lasted more than three hours. Before 1986, the only game taking three hours was the 12-inning marathon between the Senators and the Giants in 1924 (three hours, exactly). The 1997 11-inning game between Florida and Cleveland clocked in at four hours and eleven minutes, the longest Seventh Game. The shortest game was the 1940 pitchers' duel between the Reds and the Tigers, a mere one hour and forty-seven minutes. If you lined up all thirty-five Seventh Games, back-to-back, you could watch them all in just under four days. But it wouldn't be as much fun as enjoying them one at a time, inning by inning, pitch by pitch, as baseball was meant to be savored.

Analysis: The Offense (Hitting and Running)

You are a big-league manager about to bring your team onto the field for the Seventh Game of the World Series. The devil offers you a deal: in exchange for your soul, you may have the following Hall of Fame lineup (with their career statistics to remind you why it is such an enticing offer):

> First Base: Orlando Cepeda (.297, 379 HR)
> Second Base: Tony Lazzeri (.292, 178 HR)
> Shortstop: Travis Jackson (.291, 135 HR)
> Third Base: Brooks Robinson (.267, 268 HR)
> Catcher: Johnny Bench (.267, 389 HR)
> Outfield: Ty Cobb (.366, 117 HR)
> Outfield: Joe DiMaggio (.325, 361 HR)
> Outfield: Ted Williams (.344, 521 HR)
> DH: Mickey Cochrane (.320, 119 HR)

Do you accept the devil's offer? That's a lineup of nine star players with nearly 2,500 career home runs. Even if you don't value your soul, you should walk away from that deal. These nine sluggers have all appeared in Seventh Games and their composite batting average in those clutch games is .000. That is correct. They went hitless in their forty-nine trips to the plate in their forgettable Game Seven appearances. At the top of the list (or bottom) is Orlando Cepeda who, in three different Seventh Games, went 0 for 11. No player, Hall of Famer or not, has had more Seventh Game at-bats without a hit. It would not help to call on the likes of Bill Terry, Lou Gehrig, Jimmie Foxx, Al Kaline, Eddie Murray, or Gary Carter to pinch-hit for these all-star duds; they, too, went hitless in their trips to the plate in Seventh Games.

Do not jump to any conclusion about Hall of Famers. Many have excelled in their Seventh Game appearances and ten stand out above the rest:

> Lou Brock (5 for 11, 1 HR, 3 SB)
> George Brett (4 for 5)
> Max Carey (4 for 5, 3 doubles)
> Charlie Gehringer (4 for 8)
> Mickey Mantle (9 for 30, 2 HR)
> Bill Mazeroski (2 for 4, 1 HR)
> Phil Rizzuto (5 for 11)
> Babe Ruth (1 for 1, 1 HR, 4 walks)
> Willie Stargell (5 for 9, 2 doubles, 1 HR)

Wait! There are only nine Hall of Famers in this list. The tenth name is not yet in the Hall of Fame but I will avoid the controversy by listing his name with a commissioner-style asterisk:

> *Pete Rose (4 for 9)

You can decide whether he belongs with the Hall of Famers or not.

Mickey Mantle is tied with another Yankee for most hits (nine) in Seventh Games but it is not Yogi Berra, as most fans would suspect. Gil McDougald, who played his entire ten-year career in Yankees pinstripes, also collected nine Seventh Game hits in 22 at-bats for a sparkling .409 average. Curiously, McDougald has no Seventh Game RBIs to show for his hits.

It is not fair to judge a hitter by his performance in a single game. Batting is an art that readily forgives failure. A player with a .333 batting average is a star; only twenty-three men have retired with a lifetime batting average that high. A .333 average means that the player has been successful one out of every three attempts to hit and has *failed* two out of three times. How can one assess a player's worth on the basis of one game that may allow only four, maybe five, trips to the plate?

Fair or not, we expect our heroes to perform when the entire season is at stake. We remember the crucial hits of the Seventh Games far more vividly than we recall all other hits. So, too, do we remember the failures of Seventh Games more sharply than we remember all other failures. It is an opportunity for the all-star to be humbled and the everyday player to be immortalized.

Now comes a most subjective assessment, but here are a dozen of baseball's ordinary players (ordinary only in the sense that they are not in the Hall of Fame) whose Seventh Game batting performances stand out:

- **Ripper Collins.** Four hits and two RBIs in five trips in 1934. Only three other players have collected four hits in a Seventh Game and they are all Hall of Famers (Max Carey, Willie Stargell, and George Brett).
- **Bill Skowron.** "Moose" is only one of two players with three Seventh Game home runs and leads all players with nine Game Seven RBIs.
- **Roger "Doc" Cramer.** Why has nobody heard of Doc Cramer? He has more career hits (2,705) than Ted Williams, Reggie Jackson, or Mickey Mantle. He finished his career just a few points under .300 and rarely struck out. In two different Seventh Games, fourteen years apart (1931 and 1945), Doc picked up four hits in six at-bats, scoring two runs and driving home three.
- **Del Crandall.** Del is one of only four players with two or more Seventh Game home runs and he did it in back-to-back years. If there is a knock on Del's Seventh Game performances, it is that he twice left the bases loaded in 1958 before hitting his solo home run later in the game.
- **Bert Campaneris.** Five hits in eight trips, including a two-run homer, make Campy one of our favorite Seventh Game performers.
- **Lonnie Smith.** Hitting .500 is impressive enough over the course of one or two games, but going 6 for 12 in three games ranks as one of the top plate performances of the Seventh Games. Three of the hits were doubles and Lonnie drove in three runs and stole a base,

with three different teams. His baserunning is another story and will be discussed later.

- **Paul Richards.** Better known for his managerial stints with the White Sox and Orioles, Paul Richards played for four different teams in eight seasons, compiling a woeful .227 batting average. But he was the Cubs' worst nightmare in the 1945 Seventh Game, driving in four runs with a pair of doubles for the Tigers.

- **Ken Boyer.** Several players have collected three hits in a Seventh Game but when Ken Boyer did it in 1964, he made them all count: a single, a double, and a home run. He scored three runs and knocked in one. Brother Cletis didn't do so poorly either, hitting .333 (4 for 12) in three Seventh Games, including a double and a homer.

- **Gil McDougald.** We have already mentioned this versatile Yankee as the man who shares the all-time Seventh Game record for most hits, nine, with Mickey Mantle. Mickey banged out his nine hits in 30 at-bats but Gil needed only 22. Unfortunately, McDougald also holds the unenviable record of most Seventh Game errors (three).

- **Darryl Motley.** Darryl went three for four with a two-run home run in Kansas City's 11–0 pasting of the St. Louis Cardinals in 1985. His was a short career, though, six seasons, ending up with Atlanta and a lifetime batting average of .243.

- **Dan Gladden.** Twins fans remember him for his tenth-inning hustling double that became the winning run in the 1991 Seventh Game, but Dan went 4 for 10, including three doubles and an RBI, in two Seventh Games.

- **Andy High.** Other lightly regarded players had three hits in their only Seventh Game appearances (e.g., Ray Knight, Don Hahn, Omar Moreno, Phil Cavaretta, and Edgar Renteria) but Andy High did it when it was least expected. In 1931, he scored two of his team's four runs to lead St. Louis to an upset win over Connie Mack's A's. It was so unexpected because in that game, legends Al Simmons, Mickey Cochrane, Jimmie Foxx, and Frankie Frisch went hitless.

There have been 41 home runs in the thirty-five Seventh Games. Yogi Berra and Bill Skowron each have three and Mickey Mantle and Del Cran-

In a Pinch

Pinch hitters have been a part of every Seventh Game except the first one in 1909. How have pinch hitters fared in these tension-packed games? About as well as the regulars. Pinch hitters have gone 18 for 79, for a .227 average, only a few points lower than the aggregate Seventh Game batting average of .235.

There has never been a pinch home run in a Seventh Game. There have been five pinch doubles, but none since Bobby Brown's double in 1947.

The most significant pinch hit was undoubtedly Gene Larkin's pinch single to drive home the winning run in the bottom of the tenth inning in the 1991 Seventh Game. The most unlikely pinch-hit appearance was Allie Clark pinch-hitting for Yogi Berra in 1947. How often did anyone pinch-hit for Yogi? (Clark singled for Yogi.)

Pinch hitters went a combined 0 for 13 from 1952 to 1957. In the 1960 Seventh Game, the teams used three pinch hitters and they went 3 for 3, the most successful pinch hitting in any Seventh Game.

dall both have two. Skowron has the only Seventh Game grand slammer and, as the entire baseball world knows, Bill Mazeroski has the only game-ending home run in a Seventh Game.

Considering the talent that has played in Seventh Games, 41 home runs does not seem like a lot. And it isn't. If the players had hit home runs at the same pace they had hit them in the first six games of the Series, there should have been 52 round-trippers in the thirty-five Seventh Games. That leads to a greater question: how does the hitting in Seventh Games compare with the hitting over the first six games and with the teams' regular-season hitting?

We should expect that hitting in the Seventh Games (and in the entire World Series) would not be as robust as hitting in the regular season because the players are facing better pitching. With regard to Seventh Games, the statistics prove it. Add up all the Seventh Game hits and at-bats, and the players hit a modest .235. If you add up all the hits and at-bats from the pennant-winning teams in all thirty-five seasons in which the World

Series went a full seven games, you find a more hearty .269 average. Batters in Seventh Games hit nearly thirty-five points lower than they did in the regular season.

Of course, there are exceptions. The 10–9 free-for-all at Forbes Field in 1960 (in which nobody struck out) was the biggest hitting spree of any Seventh Game. But is there a difference between Seventh Game hitting and the hitting in Games One through Six?

Ah, statistics! They are the lifeblood of baseball controversy. In the games preceding Game Seven, the teams averaged eight runs per game. In Game Seven, the teams averaged seven runs per game. That may seem trivial to some but any big-league manager will tell you that one run per game can make all the difference. The average number of hits in Seventh Games is also lower than the average number of hits in Games One through Six, about one hit per game less.

Conclusion: despite the standout hitting by some, the Seventh Games have not been dominated by hitting.

What about baserunning, the often-neglected sidekick of batting? Most think of base stealing as the paradigm of baserunning, undoubtedly because it can be reduced to a simple statistic. Although there have been 38 stolen bases in the thirty-five Seventh Games, they have not figured prominently in the outcome of the games. The flip side is that a poor decision to try to steal second base ended one, the 1926 Seventh Game. With two out in the ninth inning, Babe Ruth walked and, with Bob Meusel up and Lou Gehrig on deck, was thrown out by the rifle arm of catcher Bob O'Farrell.

Baserunning, good and bad, figured prominently in the outcome of the 1991 Seventh Game. Atlanta's Lonnie Smith should have scored on Terry Pendleton's double in the eighth inning but fell prey to the old "decoy" play at second base. He never scored and the Braves lost, 1–0, in 10 innings. The Twins scored their only run on Dan Gladden's brilliant baserunning. He blooped a single to the outfield but stretched it into a double when he saw the ball take a high artificial-turf bounce.

So much for the offense, such as it was.

(For the complete batting records of all Seventh Game players, visit this book's companion website, theseventhgame.com.)

Analysis: Pitching

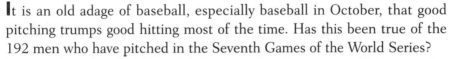

It is an old adage of baseball, especially baseball in October, that good pitching trumps good hitting most of the time. Has this been true of the 192 men who have pitched in the Seventh Games of the World Series?

During the regular season, pitching is generally measured by two statistics: wins and earned run average. Wins are, of course, meaningless in assessing the overall impact of pitching in Seventh Games because there have been 35 wins and 35 losses. Earned run average is more significant but only illustrates the more general character of pitching statistics: effective pitching means ineffective hitting.

Our examination of hitting in Seventh Games already shows that batters fared not only more poorly than they did in the regular season, as expected, but also more poorly than they did in the first six games of the World Series. But the story does not end there.

The most startling statistic to emerge from the thirty-five Seventh Games of the World Series is the number of shutouts: nine. More than a fourth of all Seventh Games have been shutouts. At first blush, that is an astounding figure. In the light of World Series experience, is it?

If the standard of comparison is the 1905 World Series, a 25 percent shutout rate is puny; for 1905 was when all five games were shutouts, including three by Christy Mathewson. Two standards of comparison may be more meaningful. First, examine all other World Series games, including the games that were not part of a Series that went the distance. That comes to 543 games. Of those games, 97 were shutouts, just under 18 percent. So far the nine shutouts out of thirty-five games seems impressive.

Perhaps a more telling figure is the percentage of shutouts in Games One through Six in the thirty-five years in which there was a Game Seven. That way we are comparing the same pitching staffs. The results are even more dramatic. Of the 211 games preceding Game Seven (we have included the 6–6 tie game in 1912), 33 were shutouts—less than 16 percent.

Nine shutouts out of thirty-five games is indeed remarkable and one indication of how important pitching has been in the Seventh Games of the World Series.

Nine shutouts do not mean nine tense pitching duels. How many great pitching performances have there been? A shutout is, by definition, a great pitching performance. But there have been other stellar mound feats as well. Both Paul Derringer and Bobo Newsom pitched superbly when the Reds edged the Tigers, 2–1, in 1940. Atlanta's John Smoltz pitched brilliantly when the Braves lost to Minnesota, 1–0, in 1991. Even San Francisco's heartbreaking 1–0 loss in 1962 cannot diminish the great work of Giants pitchers Jack Sanford and Billy O'Dell. There have been thirty-five Seventh Games but seventy pitching performances that need to be considered—one for each side.

Assessing a team's mound performance is not easy. Statistics tell only part of the story. Giving up two runs or less is certainly fine work. Three runs or less? That's a good outing, too. Sometimes a team pitches well but only until the eighth or ninth inning. It may have been a great performance that simply ran out of steam. The games are here for you to consider and you can make your own judgment as to how many good pitching performances there were. I am comfortable with concluding that the teams turned in forty-five exceptional pitching efforts, give or take a few. But who has stood out from the crowd?

The nine shutouts deserve special mention, with the number of hits and walks allowed, plus strikeouts, so that you can judge which shutout is the most impressive:

1909: Babe Adams (Pirates) 6 hits, 1 walk, 1 strikeout
1934: Dizzy Dean (Cardinals) 6 hits, 0 walks, 6 strikeouts
1955: Johnny Podres (Dodgers) 8 hits, 2 walks, 4 strikeouts
1956: Johnny Kucks (Yankees) 3 hits, 3 walks, 1 strikeout

1957: Lew Burdette (Braves) 7 hits, 1 walk, 3 strikeouts
1962: Ralph Terry (Yankees) 4 hits, 0 walks, 4 strikeouts
1965: Sandy Koufax (Dodgers) 3 hits, 3 walks, 10 strikeouts
1985: Bret Saberhagen (Royals) 5 hits, 0 walks, 2 strikeouts
1991: Jack Morris (Twins) 7 hits, 2 walks, 8 strikeouts; 10 innings

Bob Gibson of the St. Louis Cardinals never pitched a shutout in a Seventh Game, but he started three games, winning two and losing one on a misplayed fly ball. The most amazing statistic about Seventh Game starts concerns Yankees lefty Whitey Ford. Ford holds the record for most World Series wins (10) and most World Series starts (22). But for all of that, Whitey never took the mound in a Seventh Game.

What about relief pitching? We tend to think of relief specialists as a more modern-day phenomenon but the old-timers were known to enter games as relievers, too. Red Oldham is credited with the first Seventh Game save in 1925. But blown saves seem to capture the attention of baseball fans even more than converted saves. Two blown saves stand out in the history of the Seventh Game—Jose Mesa could not hold a one-run Indians lead against the Marlins in 1997 and Florida won in 11 innings; Mariano Rivera, arguably the greatest reliever in postseason history, blew the save and took the loss against the Diamondbacks in 2001.

Do Hall of Fame credentials make a difference? Many hitters enshrined in Cooperstown went hitless in their Seventh Game appearances, from Ty Cobb to Ted Williams. Have any Hall of Fame pitchers bombed? Not a one. Thirteen have appeared in Seventh Games with a combined ERA of 2.12 and none with an ERA over 4.00. While many pitchers not in the Hall have done well, accounting for seven of the nine Game Seven shutouts, their combined ERA is 3.48. Not bad but not in the same league as their Cooperstown colleagues.

Is there a way to predict the outcome of a Seventh Game? I have tried dozens of variables, from a team's regular-season batting average to a team's earned run average. The only statistic that even comes close to being able to foretell the results of Game Seven is the regular-season ERA of the starting pitcher. Pick the hurler with the lower ERA and you will pick the winner more than three-fourths of the time.

Pitching has been the difference in many games but one other factor needs consideration: defense, the fundamental art of fielding and throwing.

(For the complete pitching records of Seventh Game hurlers, visit this book's companion website, theseventhgame.com.)

Analysis: Defense and the Lack Thereof

It seems so simple: catch the ball, throw the ball. Casual observers of the game often take for granted the skill it takes to play sound defensive baseball but the true fan knows how important defense can be in determining the outcome of any game, especially a World Series Seventh Game.

Sixty three different players have committed a total of 71 errors in the Seventh Games. Seven players have the dubious honor of having committed two errors in the same game and Gil McDougald holds the record for most Seventh Game errors with a pair in 1952 and a single error in 1957.

Defense has two sides, good and bad. Just as the acrobatic catch can save a game, so can a bumbling miscue cost a game and the World Series. Both have figured prominently in a dozen Seventh Games.

- **1912:** It was the most famous error of any Seventh Game. Giants center fielder Fred Snodgrass dropped a routine fly ball to open the bottom of the tenth inning. The Giants compounded their misery when Fred Merkle and Chief Meyers let an easy foul pop drop between them, giving Boston's Tris Speaker a second chance to hit. No error was charged but the mental blunder proved costly.

Speaker and the Red Sox took full advantage and scored two runs to win the game.

- **1925:** Roger Peckinpaugh committed eight errors in the Series and a pair in Game Seven to torpedo the Senators' hopes of repeating as world champions. Poor Roger had made amends for his first error with a home run in the top of the eighth to put Washington into a momentary lead but his second error, a bad throw, gave Pittsburgh their final two runs and the victory.

- **1926:** Everyone remembers the 1926 Seventh Game for Pete Alexander's pitching heroics and Babe Ruth's game-ending unsuccessful steal attempt, but shoddy Yankees defense gave the Cardinals all their runs. Lost in the bad Yankees defense of the day was Cardinals shortstop Tommy Thevenow's leaping catch of Hank Severeid's line drive, ending the fourth inning and saving a run.

- **1946:** If Johnny Pesky hesitated in throwing home to try to nail Enos Slaughter, it was the biggest defensive gaffe in Red Sox history. But the evidence remains inconclusive.

- **1952:** Billy Martin's heads-up play to spear a dying pop-up that the rest of the Yankees' infield lost in the sun saved at least two runs and preserved the New York victory.

- **1955:** Sandy Amoros saved the day for Brooklyn with a running one-handed grab of Yogi Berra's slicing line drive. Two runs likely would have scored and Yogi would have been grinning on second base but for the Amoros catch.

- **1962:** Bobby Richardson did not have to move to spear Willie McCovey's line drive in the bottom of the ninth, ending the game, but the defensive play of the game was the hustle of Roger Maris in preventing Matty Alou from scoring from first on a two-out double.

- **1968:** Bob Gibson deserved better. Curt Flood misplayed Jim Northrup's long fly into a two-run triple.

- **1972:** Bobby Tolan's first-inning error led to an Oakland unearned run that proved to be the margin of victory for the A's.

- **1991:** Both the Twins and the Braves turned sparkling eighth-inning double plays to get out of bases-loaded jams and send the game into extra innings.

- **1997:** Tony Fernandez's error led to the winning run in the eleventh inning. Tony had driven in both Cleveland runs but bitter Indians fans remember only his fielding miscue.
- **2001:** Mariano Rivera's bad throw put runners on first and second with no outs, leading the way to Arizona's ninth-inning comeback.

Defense—good, bad, and ugly—has been a factor in more than a third of all Seventh Games. Who says defense doesn't count for much?

The Greatest Seventh Game Ever Played

You can reduce baseball to numbers. Batting averages, earned run averages, home runs, walks, strikeouts, saves, and countless other statistical measures can be useful benchmarks in comparing players but do not tell the whole story. When it comes to a judgment as to "the best" or "the most exciting" or "the greatest," it is all a matter of opinion. Anyone can tell you who had the highest batting average in 1986 (Boston's Wade Boggs), but does that tell you who was the "best" ballplayer that year? Without intending any slight of Wade Boggs, the answer is no.

Fans of the game can argue until they are red, white, and blue in the face about who the greatest players have been but they will never resolve the issue to everyone's satisfaction. The same applies to individual games. Statistics can tell which is the highest scoring Seventh Game (the 10–9 thriller between the Pirates and Yankees in 1960), the lowest scoring Seventh Game (the 1962 and 1991 games were both 1–0 affairs), or the closest games (twelve games were decided by one run), but statistics cannot decide which is the "greatest" Seventh Game.

Ultimately, determining the greatest Seventh Game ever played is a matter for careful examination of many factors. It is not only a conclusion of the head but also a judgment of the heart.

I have considered every possible factor in evaluating the thirty-five Seventh Games of the World Series. In the final analysis, a great Seventh Game is an exciting, dramatic, and uplifting experience. It values the unexpected over the ordinary, heroism over shame, and character over villainy. It measures nothing but appreciates everything.

The greatest difficulty in rating the Seventh Games is to avoid the inevitable distortions of time. We tend to undervalue the games of long ago in favor of the more recent games that we know better. That is common to all appraisals of cultural phenomena, especially sports. When we have seen the games of recent years, in the vivid sounds and colors that modern technology has given us, they somehow seem "better" than the old games that we can only know from black-and-white photographs and newspaper accounts of the day. It is hard for some to believe, but Walter Johnson, the legendary Washington Senators pitcher, lived his life in color.

Here they are, my humble and ever so subjective ratings of the thirty-five Seventh Games of the World Series. They appear in reverse order, going from worst to best. The first five are what I call "stinkers" because, quite frankly, they were not very good games. They were one-sided blowouts that lacked any dramatic content. Fortunately, there are only five of them.

The next group of fifteen are what I call "good ones" because they were. They were not the most exciting games but I would have gladly paid for a ticket to see any of them. The final group are the "fabulous fifteen" because they are the games that continue to capture our attention and imagination. Rating them has been a challenge and I have drawn upon every tidbit of information about these games in making my judgments. I expect that you will disagree. That's what makes baseball so much fun.

Five Stinkers

35. 1934: St. Louis Cardinals 11, Detroit Tigers 0

One game has to be rated the worst and this one earned its dishonored place. Not only was it out of reach early, the rowdy Tigers fans disgraced themselves by throwing all kinds of garbage at Cardinals left fielder Ducky Medwick. Shame on them! Shame on the game!

34. 1985: Kansas City Royals 11, St. Louis Cardinals 0

This was only marginally better than the 1934 blowout of the same score. At least the fans behaved. It's too bad that George Brett's four hits are lost in the one-sided affair.

33. 1956: New York Yankees 9, Brooklyn Dodgers 0

Four home runs accounted for all the scoring but the Dodgers were clueless from the first pitch. I cannot imagine how painful it must have been for Brooklyn fans to witness the carnage that day at Ebbets Field.

32. 1945: Detroit Tigers 9, Chicago Cubs 3

Five runs in the first made this a tough game for the home crowd to watch. The Cubs banged out more hits than the Tigers did but had little to show for them.

31. 1909: Pittsburgh Pirates 8, Detroit Tigers 0

The Tigers were simply terrible, offensively and defensively. But hats off to Babe Adams, the first rookie to start and win a Seventh Game.

Fifteen Good Ones

30. 1967: St. Louis Cardinals 7, Boston Red Sox 2

Was the outcome ever in doubt after Bob Gibson blew away the Boston hitters in the first few innings? Give Jim Lonborg credit for trying but give the Cardinals even more credit for winning as handily as they did.

29. 1973: Oakland A's 5, New York Mets 2

With Oakland's bullpen and New York's weak hitting, the five-run lead by the end of the fifth meant this game was never in serious doubt.

28. 1957: Milwaukee Braves 5, New York Yankees 0

A great personal effort by Lew Burdette but it was over early, as Milwaukee's four runs in the third inning sealed the Yankees' fate. The Yankees were capable of overcoming the lead but never showed much life in this one.

27. 1964: St. Louis Cardinals 7, New York Yankees 5

Bob Gibson gave up two solo home runs in the ninth inning just to create an illusion of excitement. If one more batter had reached against Gibbie in the ninth, it might have been different. Seeing

Mickey Mantle hit his last World Series home run was worth the price of a ticket.

26. 1931: St. Louis Cardinals 4, Philadelphia A's 2

Again, the score belies how much the Cardinals had this game in control until the very end. Burleigh Grimes pitched a great game until tiring in the ninth but Wild Bill Hallahan saved it for the old spitballer from Wisconsin. What happened to those great A's hitters?

25. 2002: Anaheim Angels 4, San Francisco Giants 1

Coming after six high-scoring games, this one was such a disappointment when the teams finished their run production by the third inning. Give the Giants credit for hammering out hits up until the end. They made it interesting by putting two on in the ninth inning.

24. 1987: Minnesota Twins 4, St. Louis Cardinals 2

There's no place like home, as the Twins won all four games at the Metrodome, capped by this entertaining finale that saw the Cardinals take an early lead only to have the Twins chip away until it was out of reach by the eighth. Frank Viola and Jeff Reardon put the cuffs on the Cards.

23. 1982: St. Louis Cardinals 6, Milwaukee Brewers 3

Closer than the final score reflects, as it was a one-run game until the Cardinals added a pair in the eighth and super-reliever Bruce Sutter shut the door on the Brewers.

22. 1986: New York Mets 8, Boston Red Sox 5

Sure, the Red Sox took an early three-run lead but as soon as the Mets tied it in the sixth and broke through with three in the seventh, the outcome was never in doubt.

21. 1947: New York Yankees 5, Brooklyn Dodgers 2

The Yankees overcame an early Dodgers lead and made Joe Page a Seventh Game legend on the strength of his five-inning, one-hit relief work. The Dodgers were completely helpless against Page and went down with a whimper.

20. 1952: New York Yankees 4, Brooklyn Dodgers 2

Billy Martin's hustling catch of Jackie Robinson's sun-drenched pop-up with the bases loaded was the difference in this exciting game at Ebbets Field. It was tied after five but Casey Stengel's masterful use of his pitching staff overcame the Dodgers.

19. 1979: Pittsburgh Pirates 4, Baltimore Orioles 1

This was a 2–1 game until the ninth, when self-destructed. What a thrill to see Willie Stargell bang out four hits in leading the Pirates to their fifth Seventh Game win without a loss. The Orioles mustered only four hits against three decent but hardly overwhelming pitchers.

18. 1968: Detroit Tigers 4, St. Louis Cardinals 1

This was a superb pitchers' duel between the intimidating Bob Gibson and the portly Mickey Lolich.

17. 1958: New York Yankees 6, Milwaukee Braves 2

Closer than the final score shows—it was 2–2 after seven innings. Lew Burdette came very close to making it two Game Seven wins in a row but Bob Turley, in relief of Don Larsen, was better. Moose Skowron's three-run homer in the eighth made the last two innings particularly brutal for the home crowd.

16. 1972: Oakland A's 3, Cincinnati Reds 2

This game just misses the fabulous fifteen, but not by much. Once the A's took a two-run lead in the sixth, it seemed hopeless for the Reds, especially against Oakland's great bullpen. But they made a game of it, didn't they?

The Fabulous Fifteen

15. 1971: Pittsburgh Pirates 2, Baltimore Orioles 1

What a great effort by Steve Blass in going the distance to beat the Orioles! Roberto Clemente's home run proved to be the difference in this thriller at Baltimore's Memorial Stadium.

14. 1965: Los Angeles Dodgers 2, Minnesota Twins 0

Sandy Koufax dominated the Twins even though he could not count on his curveball—and the Twins knew it. Watching Koufax work was always a treat and this gem was no exception. This game was all the more thrilling because the Twins had beaten Koufax in Game Two, so there was always a chance they would figure out a way to beat him again. A chance? Yes, but not a good one when Sandy was on his game, even with one pitch tied behind his back.

13. 1975: Cincinnati Reds 4, Boston Red Sox 3

The Reds came from behind to pull it out on a bloop single in the ninth inning. Coming right after one of the greatest games ever played, this Game Seven had a tough act to follow but gave the Boston fans hope until the last pitch.

12. 1940: Cincinnati Reds 2, Detroit Tigers 1

This was one of the best pitching duels of all the Seventh Games. Detroit's Bobo Newsom and Cincinnati's Paul Derringer pitched their hearts out but the Reds came from behind with two runs in the seventh. A tense and evenly matched game.

11. 1997: Florida Marlins 3, Cleveland Indians 2 (11 Innings)

Cleveland fans may not like it but this extra-inning nail-biter is one of the fabulous fifteen. Jose Mesa blew the save and Tony Fernandez's error set up the winning hit by Edgar Renteria. The first six games were sloppy but Game Seven was filled with suspense.

10. 1946: St. Louis Cardinals 4, Boston Red Sox 3

Enos Slaughter hustled home from first base in the bottom of the eighth inning to give the underdog Cardinals the win. There's nothing like a little controversy to make a game live forever and Boston fans have kept this one going. Did Johnny Pesky hesitate before throwing home in the unsuccessful attempt to nail Slaughter? Boston made it even more interesting by putting two runners on in the ninth inning.

9. 1962: New York Yankees 1, San Francisco Giants 0

A few feet to the left or to the right and Willie McCovey's line drive out to Bobby Richardson would have won the World Series for the Giants. Ralph Terry pitched a masterpiece and redeemed himself for the infamous Mazeroski home run in the 1960 Seventh Game. Who says we never get a second chance?

8. 1955: Brooklyn Dodgers 2, New York Yankees 0

It may have been a two-run game but no Dodgers fan believed their beloved Bums could beat the Yankees to win the World Series and some still don't believe it. Johnny Podres pitched brilliantly but Sandy Amoros made the finest catch of any Seventh Game to seal the victory.

7. 1926: St. Louis Cardinals 3, New York Yankees 2

This is the stuff that legends are made of. Two moments stand out from this thriller. Pete Alexander came in to strike out Tony Lazzeri with the bases loaded in the seventh inning and Babe Ruth ended the game by being thrown out trying to steal second base. Too bad the Yankees' terrible defense gave the Cardinals their three runs.

6. 1912: Boston Red Sox 3, New York Giants 2 (10 Innings)

The Giants scored a run in the top of the tenth only to have the Red Sox come back with two in the bottom of the tenth to beat the great Christy Mathewson. Two costly defensive lapses by the Giants made the difference—Fred Snodgrass's muff of an easy fly ball and Fred Merkle's inability to catch a simple foul pop-up. The only thing that keeps this game from being rated higher is the way the winning run scored. A sacrifice fly is baseball's equivalent of kissing your sister.

5. 1925: Pittsburgh Pirates 9, Washington Senators 7

What a comeback! The Pirates were down by four runs in the top of the first inning but scratched and clawed their way back to victory. Roger Peckinpaugh almost made up for his terrible fielding with a home run in the eighth to put the Senators into the lead but the Pirates came back with three in the bottom of the inning to complete their heroics.

4. 1960: Pittsburgh Pirates 10, New York Yankees 9

It may not have been the most artful game ever played but it may have been the most fun game to watch. Back and forth, back and forth, with the Pirates jumping out to an early four-run lead and the Yankees coming back not once but twice. New York's ninth-inning rally to tie it after the Pirates rallied to take the lead in the bottom of the eighth only underscores the drama and excitement of the final moment, Bill Mazeroski's game-winning home run in the bottom of the ninth. What would you give to have been in Mazeroski's shoes that day?

3. 1991: Minnesota Twins 1, Atlanta Braves 0 (10 Innings)

Great pitching, timely double plays, and baserunning both good and bad make this game a modern-day classic. Each team had plenty of chances to score but the pitching and defense managed to keep the game scoreless until the bottom of the tenth, when Dan Gladden hustled his way to second base on a bloop base hit and scored on Gene Larkin's single. Jack Morris came through with the grittiest pitching performance of any Seventh Game.

2. 2001: Arizona Diamondbacks 3, New York Yankees 2

A tough choice! How can coming from behind in the last of the ninth to beat the game's all-time best relief pitcher not be the greatest Seventh Game ever played? Good question! After twenty-three straight converted saves, Mariano Rivera was seemingly invincible but the Diamondbacks found a way to beat him, aided in large part by Rivera's own error. Add to the mix a terrific pitching matchup between Roger Clemens and Curt Schilling, both of whom pitched so well, and you have arguably the greatest Seventh Game. And it is a close call, very close. But we have chosen a classic oldie, one that the commissioner of baseball believed was the high point of the game when it was played. . . .

1. 1924: Washington Senators 4, New York Giants 3 (12 Innings)

Only by a thread do we proclaim the 1924 game between the high-flying New York Giants and the tenacious Washington Senators to be the greatest Seventh Game ever played. It took a two-run eighth-inning comeback to get the Senators into extra innings, and a most improbable ending—a bad-hop single over third baseman Fred Lindstrom's head in the twelfth inning—to get this to the top of our list. If any other Washington pitcher had been in there we might have thought otherwise, but the great veteran Walter Johnson gave his all to keep John McGraw's mighty Giants from scoring in the final four innings to give the city of Washington its only baseball championship.

Seventh Game Redux: Reliving the Past

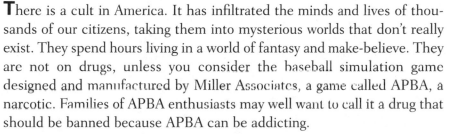

There is a cult in America. It has infiltrated the minds and lives of thousands of our citizens, taking them into mysterious worlds that don't really exist. They spend hours living in a world of fantasy and make-believe. They are not on drugs, unless you consider the baseball simulation game designed and manufactured by Miller Associates, a game called APBA, a narcotic. Families of APBA enthusiasts may well want to call it a drug that should be banned because APBA can be addicting.

APBA may seem like an acronym for something but it is not; it is just "APBA." It is a game that uses the mathematical nature of baseball to allow its legions of fans to act as big-league managers, choosing lineups from batters and pitchers who actually played the game and using their managerial skills to see what these players would do in a world not of grass and dirt but of probabilities and statistics.

They are everywhere, these APBA enthusiasts. Celebrities, politicians, and everyday people play APBA, testing their baseball expertise against each other and against the computer. Even George W. Bush has been known to spend a few hours as a big-league manager in the world of APBA. The premise is simple. Using the statistics that a player generates during a season, APBA creates a probabilistic profile for that player. For example, the model for a player who hit .320 during the season should hit safely 32 percent of the time. A batter's real-life frequency of walks, strikeouts, double plays, etc., becomes part of that profile, as does the distribution of hits (singles, doubles, triples, home runs). The effectiveness of a pitcher influences the outcome of a given batter's performance. Fielding abilities, throwing abilities of outfielders, even the configuration of the ballpark can come into play. Throw in some kind of randomization mechanism (dice or a computer) and one can replay an entire season using APBA. As manager, you can choose to bunt, call for the hit-and-run, intentionally walk a hitter, hold a speedy runner close, play the infield in, and make all the choices that real-life managers make.

APBA was originally played using cards, dice, and game boards. Although many APBA buffs still use cards and dice, many have migrated to the computer to help them in simulating the world of baseball. With the computer, you can even hear the digitized voice of legendary baseball broadcaster Ernie Harwell render a delicious play-by-play of all the action.

APBA has an elegance that is hard to resist. Pitchers who walk a lot of batters in real life will walk a lot of batters in the simulation. Batters who hit lots of home runs will generally hit a lot of homers in the simulation. There are even balks, wild pitches, and injuries. I recall an APBA player who remarked, after attending his first major-league game in many years, "It's amazing how those players on the field really do such a good job in replicating APBA."

Although APBA's true-to-life performance is best achieved over many games, as is the case with all statistical simulations, I wondered how the Seventh Games of the World Series would have turned out as APBA simulations and decided to test this intriguing proposition.

I have imposed a few restrictions to make the simulations as fair and realistic as possible. First, I tried to use the actual starting lineups and starting pitchers. Second, players who were not available in real life (e.g., Jim Rice in 1975, due to injury) were not used. Third, substitutions were made as probably would have been made in real life. I also retained the right to "correct" for real-life managerial errors when I saw them. Ready? Here are the results of my APBA simulations of the thirty-five Seventh Games of the World Series:

1909: Pittsburgh Pirates 1, Detroit Tigers 0

As in real life, the Pirates blanked the Tigers but this time it was a much closer game. The Pirates scored in the fourth when Honus Wagner led off with a bloop single. Dots Miller singled to left center but Davy Jones gunned down Wagner at third. Miller took second on the throw and scored when Bill Abstein singled to left for the only run of the game.

Neither Babe Adams nor Wild Bill Donovan lasted past the fourth inning. Adams plunked Donovan on the leg in the bottom of the fourth and the Tigers' pitcher could not go on. The hit batsman prompted the home plate umpire to eject Adams but the Tigers could do nothing with relievers Ed Summers and Ed Killian. Ty Cobb won the hitting duel with Honus Wagner, two hits to one, but the Tigers could not come through in the clutch, stranding thirteen runners.

1912: Boston Red Sox 4, New York Giants 3

How is it possible for the New York Giants to replicate their unbelievable collapse of the 1912 Seventh Game in a totally random simulated replay? With Christy Mathewson again on the mound for John McGraw's confident troops, there was no way the Giants could fail. We even made sure Fred Snodgrass and Fred Merkle took extra fielding practice before the game.

Matty was brilliant through six innings, scattering four singles. New York reached Boston starter Hugh Bedient for a run in the fourth when Red Murray doubled home Fred Snodgrass. The Giants loaded the bases in both the sixth and seventh innings against Sox reliever Ray Collins but came up empty. Mathewson surrendered his first walk to Heinie Wagner with two gone in the seventh and Hick Cady made him pay with a triple to tie the game.

As he did in the real Seventh Game, Smokey Joe Wood took the mound for Boston late. And as they did in the real Seventh Game, the Giants scored on Wood, not once but twice, aided by a costly Steve Yerkes error and a timely bloop double by Mathewson himself. The Giants were on the verge of winning the Series, leading by two runs with the great Christy Mathewson pitching. Then, as it happened to the Giants in 1912, everything fell apart. Duffy Lewis beat out an infield squib. Jake Stahl ripped a double to left center, moving Lewis to third. Matty was frustrated but he had no bonehead plays to blame.

Heinie Wagner tripled high off the wall in center and the game was tied. Mathewson walked Hick Cady and up came Smokey Joe Wood. The Sox had already used their better pinch hitters but Wood was an accomplished batsman in his own right. And Smokey Joe was the hero, lining a single between short and third. The Giants had blown it again.

1924: Washington Senators 6, New York Giants 3

It started much the same way the real game started, with neither team scoring in the first three innings and the Giants taking a mid-game two-run lead. New York scored a pair in the fourth inning on back-to-back doubles by Frankie Frisch and George Kelly, followed by a Hack Wilson single. Washington stormed back with three in the bottom of the inning on consecutive doubles by Joe Judge, Ossie Bluege, and Tom Taylor, followed by a run-scoring grounder.

The Giants tied it in the fifth when Heinie Groh singled home Travis Jackson. New York almost took the lead but Goose Goslin cut down Groh at home with a perfect throw. Washington reclaimed the lead in the bottom of the inning when Bucky Harris scored on Goslin's single. The Senators added two more in the seventh on hits by Harris and Sam Rice, followed by a costly error by Ross Youngs. Firpo Marberry, baseball's first relief specialist, pitched the ninth inning to save it for George Mogridge.

1925: Pittsburgh Pirates 4, Washington Senators 2

The APBA replay was no kinder to the Senators than was history. Just as in 1925, Washington jumped out to an early lead. Sam Rice led off the game with an infield single. Bucky Harris ripped a drive to deep right, scoring Rice easily. But Bucky got greedy and tried to stretch his triple into an inside-the-park homer—he must have been thinking about the fact that he slammed the first real Seventh Game homer in 1924. The Senators had starter Vic Aldridge on the ropes, as they did in real life, with two more runners but could not score.

Pittsburgh came back, as they did in the actual Seventh Game, but this time they took the lead for good in the early innings. After retiring the first eight Pirates in order, Walter Johnson walked pinch hitter Carson Bigbee in the third. Eddie Moore singled Bigbee to third, the first Pirate hit. Max Carey doubled them both home and the Pirates were in the lead. Pittsburgh added another run in the fourth when Stuffy McInnis drove in Pie

Traynor. Meanwhile, Pirates pitcher Jughandle Johnny Morrison kept the Senators off stride with his sweeping curves.

The Pirates scored their fourth and final run when Kiki Cuyler singled home Max Carey in the sixth. The Senators scored an unearned run in the seventh but could not get through to Morrison or Pirates closer Ray Kremer. Max Carey was the hitting star for Pittsburgh with a pair of doubles. Not bad, but he had three of them back in 1925.

1926: New York Yankees 5, St. Louis Cardinals 1

There were no last-minute heroics by Pete Alexander in this replay of the classic 1926 Seventh Game. Tony Lazzeri came through when the Yankees needed him and the Yankees' defense did not falter. The story of this game was the brilliant pitching of Waite Hoyt, who pitched no-hit ball for five innings as the Yankees coasted to a 5–1 win.

Babe Ruth began the scoring for New York, as he did in the real Seventh Game, with a solo home run. The Yankees scored two more in the third with the help of a walk, a Cardinals error, and only one hit. New York increased its lead in the fifth on a double by Lou Gehrig, a triple by Tony Lazzeri, and a sacrifice fly. The Cardinals scored their only run in the sixth, when Jim Bottomley doubled home Wattie Holm. But St. Louis saw its chance at a big inning go by the boards when Earle Combs nailed Rogers Hornsby at home on a Les Bell fly ball. Lou Gehrig had three of the Yankees' six hits but the story of this replay was Waite Hoyt's complete-game victory.

1931: St. Louis Cardinals 4, Philadelphia A's 3

The Cardinals came from behind to nip the A's in a thrilling seesaw game at St. Louis. The A's scored in the second when Jimmie Foxx doubled and came home on a Bing Miller single. The Cardinals took the lead with a two-out, two-run rally in the fifth, with key hits from Pepper Martin and Ernie Orsatti.

The A's retaliated with a pair in the sixth on Mickey Cochrane's two-run homer. A's starter George Earnshaw was cruising along until the eighth inning. With one out, Ernie Orsatti tripled and Jim Bottomley tied it with a double. After Jimmy Wilson flied to left for the second out, the A's intentionally walked Charlie Gelbert, forcing St. Louis manager Gabby Street to make a tough decision. Old Gabby played to win it and called on Rip Collins to pinch-hit. Collins singled past shortstop Dib Williams and the Cardinals led, 4–3.

Syl Johnson, owner of two saves in the regular season, came in to pitch for St. Louis. Al Simmons and Jimmie Foxx flied out but Bing Miller gave Connie Mack's A's a chance with a double. Jimmy Dykes got hold of a fastball and sent it deep to right field, but not deep enough, as George Watkins grabbed it for the final out.

1934: St. Louis Cardinals 8, Detroit Tigers 1

The incomparable Dizzy Dean was not going to let the real Detroit Tigers beat him in the 1934 Seventh Game and you have to believe that Dizzy wouldn't let them beat him in an APBA replay either. Just as it happened then, the Cardinals routed the Tigers in Detroit. Just as it happened then, Dizzy Dean went the distance and even got two hits himself.

Pepper Martin started the assault with a leadoff double and scored on a sacrifice fly. St. Louis put the game out of reach in the fourth on a Pepper Martin triple and homers by Bill DeLancey and Jack Rothrock. At least Detroit scored a run, which is more than they can say about the real 1934 Game Seven. Joe "Ducky" Medwick had four hits to lead St. Louis and the fans did not pelt him with garbage this time. A rout then, a rout now.

1940: Cincinnati Reds 5, Detroit Tigers 4

The real 1940 Game Seven was a nail-biter and so was our APBA replay. The teams swapped goose eggs through five innings as opposing pitchers Bobo Newsom and Paul Derringer were focused and in control. The Tigers erupted for four in the sixth on a Charlie Gehringer single and home runs by Hank Greenberg and Paul Campbell. The Reds came back with one in the bottom of the inning but Newsom and the Tigers were enjoying a comfortable three-run lead.

With six outs left, the Reds came alive. Late-season acquisition Jimmy Ripple poled an opposite-field two-run homer to cut Detroit's lead to one run. But Newsom got out of the inning and took the one-run lead to the ninth where destiny again turned against him. Lew Riggs doubled to lead off the Reds' ninth and took third on an infield roller. Mike McCormick lifted a fly ball to Hank Greenberg. Riggs tagged and Greenberg uncorked a good throw that seemingly had Riggs beat. Riggs barreled into catcher Birdie Tebbetts, who dropped the ball for a devastating error. The Reds had tied the game.

Junior Thompson kept the demoralized Tigers off the board in the tenth and the eleventh innings. Detroit manager Del Baker stayed with Newsom, who was throwing as hard as he was in the early innings. But with one out in the eleventh inning, Bill Myers stepped to the plate. Myers had hit only .202 during the regular season and only .130 in the real 1940 World Series. Maybe Myers just closed his eyes when he swung but it went a long way, over the left-field wall for the game-winning home run. An unlikely hero? Without question. And even more heartache for Bobo Newsom in the simulated world of APBA.

1945: Detroit Tigers 3, Chicago Cubs 1

Oh, the poor Cubbies! They couldn't do it for real in 1945 and couldn't do it in the make-believe world either. But the game was a lot closer with APBA. Detroit's Hal Newhouser was as razor-sharp as he was before the real crowd at Wrigley but this time Cubs starter Hank Borowy also pitched well. Unfortunately, his mates let him down with bad baserunning and two costly errors by third baseman Stan Hack. Hack's first error put Hank Greenberg on first in the top of the second. Greenberg took second on a walk and scored when the light-hitting Paul Richards singled him home. Déjà vu? In the real Seventh Game, Richards came up big with four RBIs.

The Tigers plated another run in the third when Doc Cramer tripled and scored on Hank Greenberg's two-bagger. The Cubs ran themselves out of a run in the bottom of the third when Roy Cullenbine gunned down Roy Hughes trying to score from second on a single. The Cubs gave Detroit a third run on Stan Hack's wild throw with two out and runners on second and third. In the bottom of the fifth, the Cubs had runners on second and third with only one out when Stan Hack lined a single to left center, but Doc Cramer pegged a perfect strike to Paul Richards to nip Roy Hughes at home. Another wasted chance for the Cubs.

Chicago finally scored on Newhouser when Andy Pafko singled home Don Johnson in the sixth. They had a chance in the bottom of the ninth. Phil Cavaretta and Andy Pafko reached safely and moved into scoring position on a sacrifice bunt, but Newhouser bore down and got Roy Hughes to end the game on a pop fly to short right. Two errors by Stan Hack? How realistic is that? As it turned out, he led all players in the actual 1945 World Series with three miscues.

1946: St. Louis Cardinals 5, Boston Red Sox 4

Everyone knew that the Boston Red Sox were the better team in the 1946 World Series. A statistical simulation of the Seventh Game would surely prove Boston's superiority. One would think. Through the magic of APBA, Boo Ferriss matched up against Murray Dickson for another chance at proving history wrong.

Ferriss must have had the jitters in the first inning, walking Red Schoendienst and hitting Terry Moore. Whitey Kurowski singled home both runners to give St. Louis an early 2–0 lead. Boston threatened in the fourth but Enos Slaughter's diving catch and subsequent throw to double up Johnny Pesky at second snuffed a Red Sox scoring chance. The Sox came back with a run in the fifth on pinch hitter Tom McBride's RBI single to cut the St. Louis lead to one run. Boston reliever Joe Dobson gave it right back by walking three, including Enos Slaughter with the bases loaded. The Red Sox rallied for three runs in the sixth to take the lead; Rudy York's single and Pinky Higgins's double were the key blows.

Joe Dobson settled down in the bottom of the sixth and retired the Cardinals without a run. Harry Brecheen, winner of the actual Game Seven and Boston's nemesis back in 1946, held the Red Sox off the board in the seventh. The Cardinals could do nothing in the bottom of the seventh and Boston was six outs away from the championship. Things looked even brighter for the Sox when Brecheen had to leave due to an injury in the eighth, but Boston could not take advantage of Cardinals reliever Al Brazle and the game moved to the bottom of the eighth, when Boston's one-run lead disappeared on an Enos Slaughter home run.

After failing to score in the top of the ninth, Boston turned the ball over to its 20-game winner, Tex Hughson. Red Schoendienst led off with a single. Terry Moore grounded to Pesky, who flipped to Bobby Doerr for the force as Moore beat the throw back to first by a noodle. Stan Musial drew a walk, bringing Enos Slaughter to the plate.

Slaughter smashed a grounder to Rudy York. York threw to short for the force but Slaugher hustled, as he always did, to beat the return throw from Johnny Pesky. (Did Pesky hesitate on the throw back to York? We'll never know.) With two outs and runners on first and third, Whitey Kurowski singled to cap a dramatic Cardinals comeback.

1947: New York Yankees 3, Brooklyn Dodgers 2

This replay was downright eerie. Just as in the real game, the Dodgers took an early 2–1 lead only to see the Yankees storm back and bring in super reliever Joe Page to shut the door on the Dodgers. Each team scored single runs in the third. Brooklyn pitcher Hal Gregg reached on an error and came home on Pee Wee Reese's single. In the bottom of the inning, New York's Tommy Henrich drove in Aaron Robinson with a two-out single.

Brooklyn took the lead in the fifth, thanks to another Yankees error and a Reese double. Down a run, skipper Bucky Harris lifted hard-luck Yankees starter Spec Shea. Pinch hitter Bobby Brown and Tommy Henrich singled, forcing Gregg from the game. Reliever Hank Behrman retired Yogi Berra but walked Joe DiMaggio to load the bases. Brooklyn manager Burt Shotton brought in his star lefty, Joe Hatten, to face George McQuinn but McQuinn ripped a two-run single. And as it happened in the real Seventh Game, the Yankees brought in Joe Page, who pitched shutout ball the rest of the way to deny the Dodgers their first World Series championship.

1952: New York Yankees 4, Brooklyn Dodgers 3

Just as he did in the actual Seventh Game, star reliever Joe Black took the mound for Brooklyn. The Yankees started their veteran lefty, Eddie Lopat, and it was a classic pitchers' duel for the first three innings. The Dodgers grabbed the lead in the fourth on Roy Campanella's two-hit double scoring Pee Wee Reese.

In the fifth inning, the Yankees' Irv Noren tripled and scored on pinch hitter Ralph Houk's sacrifice fly to tie the game. The Dodgers could do nothing with the new Yankees pitcher, Allie Reynolds. The Yankees took the lead in the sixth when Yogi Berra cracked a two-run homer. New York picked up its fourth run in the eighth when Mickey Mantle doubled and came home on an infield grounder. Allie Reynolds had given the Yankees four brilliant innings and they turned the ball over to Bob Kuzava to nail down the win. It wasn't easy. With one out in the bottom of the ninth, Jackie Robinson and Roy Campanella homered to cut the Yankees' lead to one run. The Dodgers had two outs to go. Kuzava shook off Campy's blast and retired Gil Hodges and Andy Pafko on long fly balls. Once again, Brooklyn could only mutter something about waiting 'til next year.

1955: Brooklyn Dodgers 5, New York Yankees 4

Johnny Podres was the real-life hero for Brooklyn, shutting out the Yankees on eight hits with help from a sensational catch by Sandy Amoros. It did not work out so well for Johnny in the APBA replay. After Phil Rizzuto singled to open the game, Billy Martin ripped an opposite-field two-run homer.

Brooklyn bounced back. In the third inning, Duke Snider doubled home a pair of runs to tie the game. In the bottom of the fourth, the Yankees' Andy Carey singled home a run to send Podres to the showers. Dodger reliever Clem Labine gave up a run-scoring single to Phil Rizzuto before the inning was over and the Yankees were back in front by two. As he did in the real Seventh Game, Bob Grim came in to hold Brooklyn in check.

Brooklyn scored a run in the sixth on Jim Gilliam's sacrifice fly. Pitchers Don Bessent and Roger Craig kept the Yankees from adding to their lead, but Bullet Bob Turley was keeping the Dodgers from tying the game as well. Three outs to go.

Yankees reliever Tom Morgan walked Pee Wee Reese and up stepped Duke Snider. The Duke crushed Morgan's first pitch high and deep to right for a two-run homer. The Dodgers had come back with a bang and now needed only three outs for the win.

Brooklyn's fate was in the hands of Roger Craig. Phil Rizzuto walked to lead off the bottom of the ninth. Billy Martin sacrificed the Scooter to second and the Yankees had two chances to tie—or maybe even win it. Gil McDougald grounded out, leaving it up to Yogi Berra, New York's leading

RBI man in 1955. After fouling off several good pitches, Berra swung at a Roger Craig fastball—and missed. Craig and the Duke had done it. It was finally "next year," not exactly the way it really happened but Dodgers fans in the make-believe world of APBA are not complaining.

1956: Brooklyn Dodgers 3, New York Yankees 1

The baseball world has not forgotten how the Yankees exacted their revenge upon the Dodgers in 1956, shutting them out 9–0. This time there would be an exciting game, simulated as it was, for the fans, simulated as they were. Once again, Johnny Kucks squared off against Don Newcombe and the big Dodger right-hander got off to a shaky start when Mickey Mantle homered to give New York a 1–0 lead. But Newk settled down, and instead of a rout there was a pitching duel at Ebbets Field. The Dodgers struggled against Kucks but tied the score when Sandy Amoros homered in the bottom of the fifth.

Casey Stengel tried to get something going in the eighth inning when he lifted Kucks for a pinch hitter. But the Yankees came up empty and the move ended up costing them the game. Tom Sturdivant came in to pitch and Brooklyn scored two runs; Jackie Robinson's two-out single was the key blow.

Don Newcombe shook off all the old ghosts and sealed the victory to give Brooklyn what it never had in real life, a World Series championship celebrated at Ebbets Field. In the actual Game Seven, Jackie Robinson struck out to end the game and never played another inning in his career. How fitting it is that he used his last at-bat here to win the World Series for the Dodgers.

1957: Milwaukee Braves 10, New York Yankees 4

Lew Burdette got the win for Milwaukee but not exactly the way he got it in real life in 1957. The Braves chased Yankees starter Don Larsen with five runs in the first inning, highlighted by Frank Torre's three-run double. Hank Bauer's leadoff homer in the bottom of the first made quick work of Burdette's shutout aspirations, but the Braves were not through scoring. Eddie Mathews cracked a two-run homer in the fourth and Henry Aaron put it out of reach with a three-run homer in the ninth. Mickey Mantle's solo home run in the fifth was all the Yankee Stadium crowd had for excitement.

Aaron was the hitting star for Milwaukee, with three hits and four RBIs. As for Lew Burdette, it wasn't pretty but his slugging teammates did what they had done all year. The fans in Beer City are just as happy.

1958: Milwaukee Braves 8, New York Yankees 1

Could the New York Yankees exact their revenge on the Milwaukee Braves as they did back in the 1958 Seventh Game at County Stadium? Lew Burdette was trying to make it two in a row and Don Larsen was on the hill for New York. Just as in the actual Seventh Game, the Braves scored a run in the bottom of the first but that is where the similarity between our APBA replay and history ends. Milwaukee scored in each of the first six innings, chasing Larsen in the fourth. The mighty Braves belted out six extra-base hits, including Henry Aaron's two-run homer in the fourth to put the Yankees into a giant hole, 7–0.

Lew Burdette made only one mistake, a solo home run to Bill Skowron (who really did hit one in the 1958 Seventh Game), but was otherwise invincible, giving up only four hits in going the distance. The city of Milwaukee has never seen a world championship won on its own turf so this APBA replay will have to do.

1960: New York Yankees 5, Pittsburgh Pirates 3

It was not the slugfest that took place at Forbes Field in 1960 but a thrilling game nevertheless. The Pirates jumped on Bob Turley for three runs in the fourth inning, with key hits from Smoky Burgess and Don Hoak. New York scratched its way back with a run in the fifth, thanks to an RBI single from Yogi Berra.

The Yankees lifted Turley for a pinch hitter in the sixth and his replacement, little Bobby Shantz, kept the Pirates off the board while the Yankees pecked away. A passed ball set up a seventh-inning sacrifice fly to narrow the Pittsburgh lead to 3–2, and the Pirates turned the ball over to their ace reliever, Roy Face, in the eighth. The move backfired when Bill Skowron homered in the eighth to tie it. In the ninth inning, Roger Maris cracked a two-run homer to win it for New York. There were no last-minute heroics from the Pirates at Forbes Field this time.

1962: New York Yankees 3, San Francisco Giants 1

Ralph Terry and Jack Sanford treated the fans to another thrilling game and once again Terry came out on top. Roger Maris, defensive hero of the real Game Seven, put the Yankees on the board with a solo home run in the fourth inning, New York's first hit off Sanford. The Giants tied it in the bottom of the sixth without a hit, on a walk, a sacrifice bunt, a wild pitch, and a passed ball.

Mickey Mantle put the Yanks on top for good with a seventh-inning monster clout to right center. New York added its third and final run when Bill Skowron tripled home Roger Maris in the ninth inning. But just as it happened in real life, the Giants put the tying run aboard in the bottom of the ninth and challenged Ralph Terry to shake off his ghosts of autumns past. With two gone, Harvey Kuenn doubled and Terry hit pinch hitter Ed Bailey. Felipe Alou was at the plate, representing the winning run. Alou hit the ball sharply but right at—who else?—Bobby Richardson, and the Yankees survived a scare not unlike the one they really faced back on October 7, 1962.

1964: St. Louis Cardinals 8, New York Yankees 7

The real 1964 Seventh Game was good, but the APBA replay was even better. Phil Linz and Mickey Mantle homered—again—but Bob Gibson was nowhere to be found at the end of the game.

Five New York hits plated three in the second inning and it was clear that Gibson did not have his best stuff. St. Louis came back with two in the third but the Yankees ripped Gibbie for three more in the fourth, thanks to a three-run homer off the unlikely bat of Phil Linz. It looked bleak for the Cards, down 6–2 after four innings and with the Yankees threatening for more in the fifth. Barney Shultz relieved Gibson and pulled St. Louis out of a bases-loaded jam and the Cards began to claw their way back. Bill White doubled home Curt Flood in the bottom of the fifth to cut the Yankees' lead to three runs.

The Cards tied the game on back-to-back doubles by Flood and Lou Brock, followed by a two-run homer by White that chased Yankees starter Mel Stottlemyre. The first two Yankees went out quietly in the eighth against reliever Roger Craig. Then came Mickey Mantle and there went the St. Louis lead on a prodigous blast to deep center. The Cardinals could do nothing with reliever Al Downing in the eighth and St. Louis entered the bottom of the ninth in desperate need of a run. Down to their last out, Brock doubled to keep hope alive. Bill White then looped a single to right. Roger Maris fielded the ball cleanly and rifled a perfect throw to Ellie Howard but not in time to stop the speedy Brock from scoring the tying run. To compound matters for New York, White took second on the throw home.

Yankees manager Yogi Berra brought in Pete Mikkelsen, the team's save leader during the season, to try to send the game into extra innings. Ken Boyer singled sharply into the left-field corner and Bill White raced home with the winning run.

1965: Los Angeles Dodgers 2, Minnesota Twins 0

This replay was downright scary, as if APBA had just cloned the Seventh Game of the 1965 World Series and fed it into my computer. Koufax was unhittable, the Dodgers scored two early runs, and the game was never in any doubt, even with just a two-run lead. The only differences were in the way the Dodgers scored and the fact that the Twins got four hits instead of three. Other than that, hats off to Sandy Koufax.

In the first inning, Jim Gilliam scored on Lou Johnson's sacrifice fly. The Dodgers' second and final run came when Maury Wills drove home Wes Parker with a single to right in the second inning. Jim Kaat pitched well for Minnesota, as he did in the real deal, but the Twins' hitters could not keep up with Koufax. Sandy struck out ten, just as he did in the actual 1965 Seventh Game. It was déjà Koufax.

1967: Boston Red Sox 5, St. Louis Cardinals 1

Okay, Red Sox fans, you can rejoice now, even if it is only in the world of APBA "what if?" In the great Gibson-Lonborg rematch of the Seventh Game, the Boston ace stymied the Cardinals on four hits and Boston won the 1967 World Series by taking Game Seven, 5–1. Mike Andrews, who hit only eight home runs all season, hit a friendly Fenway fly over the Green Monster to give Boston an early 1–0 lead. The Sox came back with two more in the second on Rico Petrocelli's RBI triple and a fluke bad-hop single by Jim Lonborg. Meanwhile, the Cardinals could do nothing with Lonborg. They finally tallied a run in the eighth on Julian Javier's single. (Boston fans will remember that it was Javier who broke up Lonborg's no-hit bid in the eighth inning of the real Game Two.)

Boston put the game out of reach on Ken Harrelson's two-run home run in the bottom of the eighth and the Cardinals went quietly in the ninth. It was the Jim Lonborg that Boston fans had seen so many times during the 1967 season. You can almost hear Tom Yawkey weeping with joy.

1968: Detroit Tigers 5, St. Louis Cardinals 3

The simulated 1968 Cardinals took a 2–0 lead on single runs in the fourth and sixth innings, both a direct result of Lou Brock's speed and Curt Flood's timely hitting. But just as they did in real life, the Tigers scored three in the seventh, and Jim Northrup's bat was again Detroit's big weapon. Northrup's two-run homer tied the game and Bill Freehan followed with a round-tripper to give the Tigers the lead.

St. Louis came back to tie the game in the bottom of the seventh on Dal Maxvill's RBI single. Starters Mickey Lolich and Bob Gibson battled as long as they could but eventually gave way to the bullpen when neither team could win in regulation. The teams did not score again until Detroit plated two in the top of the fourteenth inning on Norm Cash's solo home run and Bill Freehan's run-scoring single. The Cardinals put the tying run aboard in the bottom of the inning but were unable to score against Pat Dobson, the Tigers' fourth pitcher of the day.

1971: Pittsburgh Pirates 7, Baltimore Orioles 3

The original 1971 Seventh Game was a tense pitchers' duel between Steve Blass and Mike Cuellar, with Blass pitching a four-hit complete game. The APBA replay started out as a wild slugfest. Pittsburgh scored four in the top of the first as Manny Sanguillen's two-out single scored Roberto

Clemente and Willie Stargell followed with a tape-measure home run to stun the Orioles. But the O's stormed back with a trio of runs in their half of the first inning. Frank Robinson, Merv Rettenmund, and Brooks Robinson tallied three of Baltimore's five hits to account for the Orioles' scoring. It looked as if neither pitcher would last very long, but one did.

Clemente gave Pittsburgh another run in the third when he singled, stole second, and came home on Manny Sanguillen's single. Meanwhile, the Orioles were getting nothing off Steve Blass. Pittsburgh increased its lead to 7–3 on Bob Robertson's two-run homer in the fifth and the Pirates never looked back. Blass never looked better, pitching no-hit ball for the rest of the game. After a two-out walk to Frank Robinson in the third inning, Blass retired the last nineteen Orioles in order.

1972: Cincinnati Reds 2, Oakland A's 1

It was a replay worthy of the 1972 World Series, tight until the last out. Dennis Menke put the Reds on top with a solo homer in the second inning but the A's tied it in the sixth on Sal Bando's RBI single. Catfish Hunter relieved Blue Moon Odom in the sixth and kept the Reds off the board until Tony Perez singled home Bobby Tolan in the eighth with what proved to be the winning run.

Pedro Borbon picked up the win in relief for the Reds, who won despite being outhit by the A's, nine to five. The A's may not have missed the injured Reggie Jackson in the real 1972 Seventh Game but they sure missed him in the computer replay.

1973: New York Mets 2, Oakland A's 0

Mets fans have always known that when Jon Matlack was on, he was as tough to hit as anyone in the game. He may not have had his best stuff in the real 1973 Seventh Game, but in our APBA replay the Oakland A's thought they were facing Sandy Koufax in his prime.

Jon Milner's second-inning solo homer to right was all that Matlack needed. The only Oakland player to reach base through six innings came aboard courtesy of Matlack's own error. Joe Rudi broke up the no-hitter in the sixth and Deron Johnson collected the only other hit for the A's, an eighth-inning double. Jerry Grote's ninth-inning bloop single gave New York its second run and Jon Matlack was the master. He walked Sal Bando in the ninth but retired Reggie Jackson and Gene Tenace to end the game. Ken Holtzman pitched well for Oakland, but Matlack struck out eleven and faced only five batters over the minimum. Another Mets miracle!

1975: Cincinnati Reds 5, Boston Red Sox 4

This computer replay was too close for comfort. George Foster doubled home the first run of the game in the fourth but Boston answered with a Rick Burleson sacrifice fly in the fifth. The Reds replied with a run in the sixth, an RBI single by Johnny Bench, and two more in the seventh, thanks to a Rico Petrocelli error and a Pete Rose single.

The Red Sox refused to fold. They came back with two unearned runs in the bottom of the seventh inning when Pete Rose booted two tough grounders. Boston tied it in the eighth on Carlton Fisk's two-out RBI double. Reliever Jim Burton walked the first batter he faced in the ninth, just as he did in the ninth inning of the real Seventh Game. And as he did in the real finale, Joe Morgan singled home the winning run. And as they did in the real Seventh Game, the Red Sox went out in order in the bottom of the ninth. Ouch!

1979: Pittsburgh Pirates 4, Baltimore Orioles 2

Once again it was a case of too much Willie Stargell. The Pirates struck for a run in the first when Bill Robinson singled home Dave Parker. The difference in the game, though, was Stargell's two-run homer in the third.

Baltimore's John Lowenstein narrowed the lead back to one run with a two-run dinger in the fourth. Omar Moreno's solo homer in the seventh inning gave Pittsburgh the final run of the game and Kent Tekulve pitched a scoreless ninth to pick up the save for Jim Bibby.

1982: St. Louis Cardinals 5, Milwaukee Brewers 3

No one really expected the Brewers to win the World Series. Getting to a Seventh Game was miracle enough thought the multitudes, but they almost pulled it off back in 1982. And they almost knocked off the Cardinals in the APBA replay. The Brewers missed an opportunity to score a run in the first when Lonnie Smith nailed Paul Molitor at home on a close play. But they scored an unearned run in the second thanks to pitcher Joaquin Andujar's throwing error. Milwaukee starter Pete Vuckovich returned the favor with an error of his own that gave St. Louis a run to tie the score after two innings.

The Brewers took the lead in the third on Cecil Cooper's RBI double. The Cards answered in the fourth on Willie McGee's solo round-tripper. It looked like a pitcher's duel between two tough righties until the Cardinals took the lead in the sixth on Lonnie Smith's two-out RBI single. St. Louis put the game out of reach with two more in the eighth in typical Cardinals fashion—two bloop singles to drive home the clinching runs. Bruce Sutter recorded the save but not before Ben Oglivie made things interesting with a solo homer in the ninth. Of course, Benjie really did hit one in the actual Seventh Game, too.

1985: Kansas City Royals 3, St. Louis Cardinals 2

There was no blowout for the home team at Royals Stadium in our APBA replay of the 1985 Seventh Game. To the contrary, it looked downright grim for Kansas City, as St. Louis starter John Tudor scattered three hits and held the Royals scoreless through seven innings. Meanwhile, the Redbirds picked up a run in the fifth on Ozzie Smith's two-out RBI double and added one more in the sixth on Andy Van Slyke's solo homer.

With two gone in the bottom of the eighth, John Tudor and the St. Louis Cardinals were four outs away from avenging their real Seventh Game loss when Willie Wilson doubled to the gap in right center. George Brett then singled to right, just beyond the diving Tommy Herr, and the shutout was gone. Tudor looked sharp but he hung a curveball to Frank White and—WHACK!—White parked it over the left-field fence for a two-run homer and a one-run Royals lead. Dan Quisenberry saved it for Saberhagen with a perfect ninth.

1986: New York Mets 8, Boston Red Sox 3

Some things will never change, including a second try to win Game Seven of the 1986 World Series after the most heartbreaking loss in the history of the Boston Red Sox. Just as in real life, Boston jumped to an early 3–0 lead only to see the Mets storm back with a bunch of runs in the late innings.

Boston tallied single runs in the second, third, and fourth innings. New York got one back on a Darryl Strawberry homer in the fourth (he hit one in the real game) but Bruce Hurst shut down the Mets into the seventh inning. That's when the Mets tied the real Seventh Game and that's when they tied it in the replay, on Danny Heep's pinch two-run double.

After Hurst gave up a bloop single to lead off the bottom of the eighth, Sox skipper John McNamara brought in Calvin Schiraldi to try to keep the Mets from scoring. Schiraldi was Boston's best reliever in 1986 and a computer simulation should reflect his fine year (a 1.41 ERA). But as they did in the real Seventh Game, the Mets teed off on poor Calvin, this time ripping him for four hits and a walk, aided by a Wade Boggs throwing error with the bases loaded. When the inning was over, five Mets had crossed the plate and it was all over for Boston.

1987: Minnesota Twins 7, St. Louis Cardinals 1

It was no contest, as the Minnesota Twins throttled the St. Louis Cardinals behind another masterful performance by the Twins' real Game Seven winner, Frank Viola. Tom Brunansky gave Frankie V. all the runs he needed with a two-run homer in the second inning.

The Cardinals drew to within a run on Ozzie Smith's RBI single in the sixth but the Twins salted it away with five runs in the bottom of the inning. A walk, an error, and a few well-placed singles did the damage and the Minnesota Twins were again Seventh Game winners.

1991: Minnesota Twins 2, Atlanta Braves 1

Jack Morris did it again, a complete-game extra-inning win against a tough Atlanta team that put up another great fight. The Braves scored a run in the top of the first on Sid Bream's bases-loaded sacrifice fly, but after that Morris was invincible.

Minnesota tied the game in the bottom of the third when Dan Gladden's single scored Mike Pagliarulo. After that, it was a classic pitchers' duel between Morris and Atlanta's John Smoltz. Smoltz weakened in the tenth when he loaded the bases but Alejandro Pena bailed him and the

Braves out of the jam. Jack Morris remained untouchable through twelve innings, allowing only four singles, though he did walk six. In the bottom of the twelfth, Minnesota's Al Newman led off with a single and took second on Gladden's sacrifice bunt. Chuck Knoblach drove in the winning run with a single to right and Jack Morris was again the hero.

1997: Cleveland Indians 6, Florida Marlins 5

Leave it to those Indians of 1997—their ace reliever blew the save in the real Seventh Game and almost blew it in our APBA replay. But this time the city of Cleveland can cheer about something, even if it's only make-believe.

Tony Fernandez doubled home Omar Vizquel in the first for a quick Cleveland lead but Moises Alou tied it with a homer in the second for Florida. With the bases full, Sandy Alomar Jr. gave the Indians a three-run lead with a bases-clearing double in the third. Cleveland rookie starter Jared Wright had no problems with Florida until the bottom of the seventh, when pinch hitter Gregg Zaun knocked in one run and another scored on a Manny Ramirez error. The Indians brought in their star reliever, Jose Mesa, in the eighth inning and he set down the Marlins without incident. Cleveland padded their slim one-run lead with a pair in the ninth and it looked hopeless for Florida. In the bottom of the ninth, Craig Counsell walked and Kurt Abbott tagged Jose Mesa for a two-run homer and the lead was back to one run. When Devon White singled, it seemed as if Mesa was about to blow it again. But Edgar Renteria, the hero of the real Game Seven, grounded out and Gary Sheffield ended the game with a high foul pop to Sandy Alomar Jr.

2001: New York Yankees 3, Arizona Diamondbacks 2

Even in a computer-simulated replay of the Seventh Game of the 2001 World Series, the blood rushes and the adrenalin flows. As in the real game, Curt Schilling squared off against Roger Clemens. But New York scored a pair of runs early. Tony Womack booted a Tino Martinez grounder and Jorge Posada followed with a homer to right.

The Yankees stretched their lead to three on a fifth-inning single. Roger Clemens was slicing through the Arizona lineup until the eighth inning, when Tony Womack cracked a solo home run. Clemens gave way to Mario Mendoza, who retired the first two batters he faced but gave up a single to Matt Williams. That brought the tying run to the plate and the Yankees called for super lefty reliever Mike Stanton to pitch to Steve Finley. Stanton got Finley on a comebacker and the Yankees were up by two runs, three outs away from victory.

The Yankees failed to score in the top of the ninth and brought in Mariano Rivera to save it. Could the Diamondbacks score off Rivera as they had done in real life? Danny Bautista opened the inning with a double and there was a ray of hope in the Arizona dugout. As he had done against Rivera in the actual game, Mark Grace singled, sending Bautista to third. Rivera was struggling. He uncorked a wild pitch to score Bautista and move the tying run, pinch runner Junior Spivey, into scoring position with no outs. The Diamondbacks were seemingly poised for another improbable comeback. But Rivera shut the door, as he had done so many times, with a strikeout and two harmless grounders to the infield. This time the Yankees held on to nip the Diamondbacks, 3–2.

2002: Anaheim Angels 9, San Francisco Giants 3

It started well for the Giants as they scored three in the top of the first to silence the home crowd. Starter John Lackey walked a pair and Barry Bonds ripped a two-run double, followed by a sacrifice fly by Benito Santiago. But the Angels came right back in the bottom of the inning, thanks to a three-run homer by the real-life Seventh Game star, Garrett Anderson.

As in real life, the APBA 2002 Angels had no trouble with Giants starter Livan Hernandez. David Eckstein's run-scoring single through a drawn-in infield in the fourth inning put the Angels ahead to stay. Hernandez was gone by the end of the fifth inning as Anaheim kept pouring it on. Garrett Anderson's second homer, a two-run shot in the sixth, sealed the victory for the Angels.

Rookie John Lackey picked up the victory, with late-inning help from Brendan Donnelly and Troy Percival. Just as they did in real life, the Anaheim Angels handled the San Francisco Giants with relative ease. As for

Barry Bonds, he singled once (as he did in the real game) and walked twice (once for real) but it was too much Anaheim, especially Garrett Anderson.

So how did the APBA computer simulation do compared with real life? Here are the results:

Year	Actual	APBA Simulation
1909	Pirates 8, Tigers 0	Pirates 1, Tigers 0
1912	Red Sox 3, Giants 2 (10 inn.)	Red Sox 4, Giants 3
1924	Senators 4, Giants 3 (12 inn.)	Senators 6, Giants 3
1925	Pirates 9, Senators 7	Pirates 4, Senators 2
1926	Cardinals 3, Yankees 2	Yankees 5, Cardinals 1
1931	Cardinals 4, A's 2	Cardinals 4, A's 3
1934	Cardinals 11, Tigers 0	Cardinals 8, Tigers 1
1940	Reds 2, Tigers 1	Reds 5, Tigers 4 (11 inn.)
1945	Tigers 9, Cubs 3	Tigers 3, Cubs 1
1946	Cardinals 4, Red Sox 3	Cardinals 5, Red Sox 4
1947	Yankees 5, Dodgers 2	Yankees 3, Dodgers 2
1952	Yankees 4, Dodgers 2	Yankees 4, Dodgers 3
1955	Dodgers 2, Yankees 0	Dodgers 5, Yankees 4
1956	Yankees 9, Dodgers 0	Dodgers 3, Yankees 1
1957	Braves 5, Yankees 0	Braves 10, Yankees 4
1958	Yankees 6, Braves 2	Braves 8, Yankees 1
1960	Pirates 10, Yankees 9	Yankees 5, Pirates 3
1962	Yankees 1, Giants 0	Yankees 3, Giants 1
1964	Cardinals 7, Yankees 5	Cardinals 8, Yankees 7
1965	Dodgers 2, Twins 0	Dodgers 2, Twins 0
1967	Cardinals 7, Red Sox 2	Red Sox 5, Cardinals 1
1968	Tigers 4, Cardinals 1	Tigers 5, Cardinals 3 (13 inn.)
1971	Pirates 2, Orioles 1	Pirates 7, Orioles 3
1972	A's 3, Reds 2	Reds 2, A's 1
1973	A's 5, Mets 2	A's 2, Mets 0
1975	Reds 4, Red Sox 3	Reds 5, Red Sox 4
1979	Pirates 4, Orioles 1	Pirates 4, Orioles 2
1982	Cardinals 6, Brewers 3	Cardinals 5, Brewers 3
1985	Royals 11, Cardinals 0	Royals 3, Cardinals 2
1986	Mets 8, Red Sox 5	Mets 8, Red Sox 3

1987	Twins 4, Cardinals 2	Twins 7, Cardinals 1
1991	Twins 1, Braves 0 (10 inn.)	Twins 2, Braves 1 (12 inn.)
1997	Marlins 3, Indians 2 (11 inn.)	Indians 6, Marlins 5
2001	Diamondbacks 3, Yankees 2	Yankees 3, Diamondbacks 2
2002	Angels 4, Giants 1	Angels 9, Giants 3

The APBA computer simulation came up with the same Seventh Game winner 77 percent of the time (twenty-seven out of thirty-five). How many big-league hitters can boast of a .770 average? Even with the benefit of computer replay, the Giants remained winless, but the Red Sox erased the "Curse of the Bambino." To top it all off, the Dodgers successfully defended their world championship at old Ebbets Field.

Sweet. In real life and in make-believe, the Seventh Games of the World Series are oh so sweet.

Appendix

The Seventh Games at a Glance

October 16, 1909

	1	2	3	4	5	6	7	8	9	R	H	E
PITTSBURGH (NL)	0	2	0	2	0	3	0	1	0	8	7	0
DETROIT (AL)	0	0	0	0	0	0	0	0	0	0	6	3

PITCHERS: PGH: Adams (W); DET: Donovan (L), Mullin
DOUBLES: Abstein, Delahanty, Gibson, Leach, Moriarty, Schmidt
TRIPLES: Wagner
HOME RUNS: None
ATTENDANCE: 17,562
TIME OF GAME: 2:10

October 16, 1912

	1	2	3	4	5	6	7	8	9	10	R	H	E
NEW YORK (NL)	0	0	1	0	0	0	0	0	0	1	2	9	2
BOSTON (AL)	0	0	0	0	0	0	1	0	0	2	3	8	5

PITCHERS: NYG: Mathewson (L); BOS: Bedient, Wood (W)
DOUBLES: Gardner, Henriksen, Herzog, Murray (2), Stahl
TRIPLES: None
HOME RUNS: None
ATTENDANCE: 17,034
TIME OF GAME: 2:37

October 10, 1924

	1	2	3	4	5	6	7	8	9	10	11	12	R	H	E
NEW YORK (NL)	0	0	0	0	0	3	0	0	0	0	0	0	3	8	3
WASHINGTON (AL)	0	0	0	1	0	0	0	2	0	0	0	1	4	10	4

PITCHERS: NYG: Barnes, Nehf, McQuillan, Bentley (L); WAS: Ogden, Mogridge, Marberry, Johnson (W)

DOUBLES: Goslin, Leibold, Lindstrom, McNeely, Ruel

TRIPLES: Frisch

HOME RUNS: Harris

ATTENDANCE: 31,667

TIME OF GAME: 3:00

October 15, 1925

	1	2	3	4	5	6	7	8	9	R	H	E
WASHINGTON (AL)	4	0	0	2	0	0	0	1	0	7	7	2
PITTSBURGH (NL)	0	0	3	0	1	0	2	3	X	9	15	2

PITCHERS: WAS: Johnson (L); PGH: Aldridge, Morrison, Kremer (W), Oldham (SV)

DOUBLES: Bigbee, Carey (3), Cuyler (2), J. Harris, Moore, Smith

TRIPLES: Traynor

HOME RUNS: Peckinpaugh

ATTENDANCE: 42,856

TIME OF GAME: 2:31

October 10, 1926

	1	2	3	4	5	6	7	8	9	R	H	E
ST. LOUIS (NL)	0	0	0	3	0	0	0	0	0	3	8	0
NEW YORK (AL)	0	0	1	0	0	1	0	0	0	2	8	3

PITCHERS: STL: Haines (W), Alexander (SV); NYY: Hoyt (L), Pennock
DOUBLES: Severeid
TRIPLES: None
HOME RUNS: Ruth
ATTENDANCE: 38,093
TIME OF GAME: 2:15

October 7, 1931

	1	2	3	4	5	6	7	8	9	R	H	E
PHILADELPHIA (AL)	0	0	0	0	0	0	0	0	2	2	7	1
ST. LOUIS (NL)	2	0	2	0	0	0	0	0	X	4	5	0

PITCHERS: PHI: Earnshaw (L), Walberg; STL: Grimes (W), Hallahan (SV)
DOUBLES: None
TRIPLES: None
HOME RUNS: Watkins
ATTENDANCE: 20,805
TIME OF GAME: 1:57

October 9, 1934

	1	2	3	4	5	6	7	8	9	R	H	E
ST. LOUIS (NL)	0	0	7	0	0	2	2	0	0	11	17	1
DETROIT (AL)	0	0	0	0	0	0	0	0	0	0	6	3

PITCHERS: STL: D. Dean (W); DET: Auker (L), Rowe, Hogsett, Bridges, Marberry, Crowder

DOUBLES: D. Dean, DeLancey, Fox (2), Frisch, Rothrock (2)

TRIPLES: Durocher, Medwick

HOME RUNS: None

ATTENDANCE: 40,902

TIME OF GAME: 2:19

October 8, 1940

	1	2	3	4	5	6	7	8	9	R	H	E
DETROIT (AL)	0	0	1	0	0	0	0	0	0	1	7	0
CINCINNATI (NL)	0	0	0	0	0	0	2	0	X	2	7	1

PITCHERS: DET: Newsom (L); CIN: Derringer (W)

DOUBLES: Higgins, M. McCormick, F. McCormick, Ripple

TRIPLES: None

HOME RUNS: None

ATTENDANCE: 26,854

TIME OF GAME: 1:47

October 10, 1945

	1	2	3	4	5	6	7	8	9	R	H	E
DETROIT (AL)	5	1	0	0	0	0	1	2	0	9	9	1
CHICAGO (NL)	1	0	0	1	0	0	0	1	0	3	10	0

PITCHERS: DET: Newhouser (W); CHI: Borowy (L), Derringer, Vandenberg, Erickson, Passeau, Wyse

DOUBLES: Johnson, Mayo, Nicholson, Richards (2)

TRIPLES: Pafko

HOME RUNS: None

ATTENDANCE: 41,590

TIME OF GAME: 2:31

October 15, 1946

	1	2	3	4	5	6	7	8	9	R	H	E
BOSTON (AL)	1	0	0	0	0	0	0	2	0	3	8	0
ST. LOUIS (NL)	0	1	0	0	2	0	0	1	X	4	9	1

PITCHERS: BOS: Ferriss, Dobson, Klinger (L), Johnson; STL: Dickson, Brecheen (W)

DOUBLES: Dickson, DiMaggio, Kurowski, Metkovich, Musial, Walker

TRIPLES: None

HOME RUNS: None

ATTENDANCE: 36,143

TIME OF GAME: 2:17

October 6, 1947

	1	2	3	4	5	6	7	8	9	R	H	E
BROOKLYN (NL)	0	2	0	0	0	0	0	0	0	2	7	0
NEW YORK (AL)	0	1	0	2	0	1	1	0	X	5	7	0

PITCHERS: BKN: Gregg (L), Behrman, Hatten, Barney, Casey; NYY: Shea, Bevens, Page (W)

DOUBLES: Brown, Jorgensen

TRIPLES: Hermanski, Johnson

HOME RUNS: None

ATTENDANCE: 71,548

TIME OF GAME: 2:19

October 7, 1952

	1	2	3	4	5	6	7	8	9	R	H	E
NEW YORK (AL)	0	0	0	1	1	1	1	0	0	4	10	4
BROOKLYN (NL)	0	0	0	1	1	0	0	0	0	2	8	1

PITCHERS: NYY: Lopat, Reynolds (W), Raschi, Kuzava (SV); BKN: Black (L), Roe, Erskine

DOUBLES: Cox, Rizzuto

TRIPLES: None

HOME RUNS: Mantle, Woodling

ATTENDANCE: 33,195

TIME OF GAME: 2:54

October 4, 1955

	1	2	3	4	5	6	7	8	9	R	H	E
BROOKLYN (NL)	0	0	0	1	0	1	0	0	0	2	5	0
NEW YORK (AL)	0	0	0	0	0	0	0	0	0	0	8	1

PITCHERS: BKN: Podres (W); NYY: Byrne (L), Grim, Turley

DOUBLES: Berra, Campanella, Skowron

TRIPLES: None

HOME RUNS: None

ATTENDANCE: 62,465

TIME OF GAME: 2:44

October 10, 1956

	1	2	3	4	5	6	7	8	9	R	H	E
NEW YORK (AL)	2	0	2	1	0	0	4	0	0	9	10	0
BROOKLYN (NL)	0	0	0	0	0	0	0	0	0	0	3	1

PITCHERS: NYY: Kucks (W); BKN: Newcombe (L), Bessent, Craig, Roebuck, Erskine

DOUBLES: Howard, Mantle

TRIPLES: None

HOME RUNS: Berra (2), Howard, Skowron

ATTENDANCE: 33,782

TIME OF GAME: 2:19

October 10, 1957

	1	2	3	4	5	6	7	8	9	R	H	E
MILWAUKEE (NL)	0	0	4	0	0	0	0	1	0	5	9	1
NEW YORK (AL)	0	0	0	0	0	0	0	0	0	0	7	3

PITCHERS: MIL: Burdette (W); NYY: Larsen (L), Shantz, Ditmar, Sturdivant, Byrne
DOUBLES: Bauer, Mathews
TRIPLES: None
HOME RUNS: Crandall
ATTENDANCE: 61,207
TIME OF GAME: 2:34

October 9, 1958

	1	2	3	4	5	6	7	8	9	R	H	E
NEW YORK (AL)	0	2	0	0	0	0	0	4	0	6	8	0
MILWAUKEE (NL)	1	0	0	0	0	1	0	0	0	2	5	2

PITCHERS: NYY: Larsen, Turley (W); MIL: Burdette (L), McMahon
DOUBLES: Berra, McDougald
TRIPLES: None
HOME RUNS: Crandall, Skowron
ATTENDANCE: 46,367
TIME OF GAME: 2:31

October 13, 1960

	1	2	3	4	5	6	7	8	9	R	H	E
NEW YORK (AL)	0	0	0	0	1	4	0	2	2	9	13	1
PITTSBURGH (NL)	2	2	0	0	0	0	0	5	1	10	11	0

PITCHERS: NYY: Turley, Stafford, Shantz, Coates, Terry (L); PGH: Law, Face, Friend, Haddix (W)

DOUBLES: Boyer

TRIPLES: None

HOME RUNS: Berra, Skowron, Nelson, Smith, Mazeroski

ATTENDANCE: 36,693

TIME OF GAME: 2:36

October 16, 1962

	1	2	3	4	5	6	7	8	9	R	H	E
NEW YORK (AL)	0	0	0	0	1	0	0	0	0	1	7	0
SAN FRANCISCO (NL)	0	0	0	0	0	0	0	0	0	0	4	1

PITCHERS: NYY: Terry (W); SFG: Sanford (L), O'Dell

DOUBLES: Mays

TRIPLES: McCovey

HOME RUNS: None

ATTENDANCE: 43,948

TIME OF GAME: 2:29

October 15, 1964

	1	2	3	4	5	6	7	8	9	R	H	E
NEW YORK (AL)	0	0	0	0	0	3	0	0	2	5	9	2
ST. LOUIS (NL)	0	0	0	3	3	0	1	0	X	7	10	1

PITCHERS: NYY: Stottlemyre (L), Downing, Sheldon, Hamilton, Mikkelsen; STL: Gibson (W)

DOUBLES: K. Boyer, White

TRIPLES: None

HOME RUNS: C. Boyer, Mantle, Linz, K. Boyer, Brock

ATTENDANCE: 30,346

TIME OF GAME: 2:40

October 16, 1965

	1	2	3	4	5	6	7	8	9	R	H	E
LOS ANGELES (NL)	0	0	0	2	0	0	0	0	0	2	7	0
MINNESOTA (AL)	0	0	0	0	0	0	0	0	0	0	3	1

PITCHERS: LAD: Koufax (W); MIN: Kaat (L), Worthington, Klippstein, Merritt, Perry

DOUBLES: Fairly, Roseboro, Quillici

TRIPLES: Parker

HOME RUNS: Johnson

ATTENDANCE: 50,596

TIME OF GAME: 2:27

October 12, 1967

	1	2	3	4	5	6	7	8	9	R	H	E
ST. LOUIS (NL)	0	0	2	0	2	3	0	0	0	7	10	1
BOSTON (AL)	0	0	0	0	1	0	0	1	0	2	3	1

PITCHERS: STL: Gibson (W); BOS: Lonborg (L), Santiago, Morehead, Osinski, Brett

DOUBLES: McCarver, Brock, Petrocelli

TRIPLES: Maxvill, Scott

HOME RUNS: B. Gibson, Javier

ATTENDANCE: 35,188

TIME OF GAME: 2:23

October 10, 1968

	1	2	3	4	5	6	7	8	9	R	H	E
DETROIT (AL)	0	0	0	0	0	0	3	0	1	4	8	1
ST. LOUIS (NL)	0	0	0	0	0	0	0	0	1	1	5	0

PITCHERS: DET: Lolich (W); STL: Gibson (L)

DOUBLES: Freehan

TRIPLES: Northrup

HOME RUNS: Shannon

ATTENDANCE: 54,692

TIME OF GAME: 2:07

October 17, 1971

	1	2	3	4	5	6	7	8	9	R	H	E
PITTSBURGH (NL)	0	0	0	1	0	0	0	1	0	2	6	1
BALTIMORE (AL)	0	0	0	0	0	0	0	1	0	1	4	0

PITCHERS: PGH: Blass (W); BAL: Cuellar (L), Dobson, McNally

DOUBLES: Hendricks, Pagan

TRIPLES: None

HOME RUNS: Clemente

ATTENDANCE: 47,291

TIME OF GAME: 2:10

October 22, 1972

	1	2	3	4	5	6	7	8	9	R	H	E
OAKLAND (AL)	1	0	0	0	0	2	0	0	0	3	6	1
CINCINNATI (NL)	0	0	0	0	1	0	0	1	0	2	4	2

PITCHERS: OAK: Odom, Hunter (W), Holtzman, Fingers (SV); CIN: Billingham, Borbon (L), Carroll, Grimsley, Hall

DOUBLES: Bando, Morgan, Perez, Tenace

TRIPLES: None

HOME RUNS: None

ATTENDANCE: 56,040

TIME OF GAME: 2:50

October 21, 1973

	1	2	3	4	5	6	7	8	9	R	H	E
NEW YORK (NL)	0	0	0	0	0	1	0	0	1	2	8	1
OAKLAND (AL)	0	0	4	0	1	0	0	0	X	5	9	1

PITCHERS: NYM: Matlack (L), Parker, Sadecki, Stone; OAK: Holtzman (W), Fingers, Knowles (SV)

DOUBLES: Holtzman, Millan, Staub

TRIPLES: None

HOME RUNS: Campaneris, Jackson

ATTENDANCE: 49,333

TIME OF GAME: 2:37

October 22, 1975

	1	2	3	4	5	6	7	8	9	R	H	E
CINCINNATI (NL)	0	0	0	0	0	2	1	0	1	4	9	0
BOSTON (AL)	0	0	3	0	0	0	0	0	0	3	5	2

PITCHERS: CIN: Gullett, Billingham, Carroll (W), McEnaney (SV); BOS: Lee, Moret, Willoughby, Burton (L), Cleveland

DOUBLES: Carbo

TRIPLES: None

HOME RUNS: Perez

ATTENDANCE: 35,205

TIME OF GAME: 2:52

October 17, 1979

	1	2	3	4	5	6	7	8	9	R	H	E
PITTSBURGH (NL)	0	0	0	0	0	2	0	0	2	4	10	0
BALTIMORE (AL)	0	0	1	0	0	0	0	0	0	1	4	2

PITCHERS: PGH: Bibby, D. Robinson, Jackson (W), Tekulve (SV); BAL: McGregor (L), Stoddard, Flanagan, Stanhouse, T. Martinez, D. Martinez

DOUBLES: Stargell (2), Garner

TRIPLES: None

HOME RUNS: Stargell, Dauer

ATTENDANCE: 53,733

TIME OF GAME: 2:54

October 20, 1982

	1	2	3	4	5	6	7	8	9	R	H	E
MILWAUKEE (AL)	0	0	0	0	1	2	0	0	0	3	7	0
ST. LOUIS (NL)	0	0	0	1	0	3	0	2	X	6	15	1

PITCHERS: MIL: Vuckovich, McClure (L), Haas, Caldwell; STL: Andujar (W), Sutter (SV)

DOUBLES: Gantner, L. Smith (2)

TRIPLES: None

HOME RUNS: Oglivie

ATTENDANCE: 53,723

TIME OF GAME: 2:50

October 27, 1985

	1	2	3	4	5	6	7	8	9	R	H	E
ST. LOUIS (NL)	0	0	0	0	0	0	0	0	0	0	5	0
KANSAS CITY (AL)	0	2	3	0	6	0	0	0	X	11	14	0

PITCHERS: STL: Tudor (L), Campbell, Lahti, Horton, Andujar, Forsch, Dayley; KCR: Saberhagen (W)

DOUBLES: L. Smith

TRIPLES: None

HOME RUNS: Motley

ATTENDANCE: 41,658

TIME OF GAME: 2:46

October 27, 1986

	1	2	3	4	5	6	7	8	9	R	H	E
BOSTON (AL)	0	3	0	0	0	0	0	2	0	5	9	0
NEW YORK (NL)	0	0	0	0	0	3	3	2	X	8	10	0

PITCHERS: BOS: Hurst, Schiraldi (L), Sambito, Stanley, Nipper, Crawford; NYM: Darling, Fernandez, McDowell (W), Orosco (SV)

DOUBLES: Evans

TRIPLES: None

HOME RUNS: Evans, Gedman, Knight, Strawberry

ATTENDANCE: 55,032

TIME OF GAME: 3:11

October 25, 1987

	1	2	3	4	5	6	7	8	9	R	H	E
ST. LOUIS (NL)	0	2	0	0	0	0	0	0	0	2	6	1
MINNESOTA (AL)	0	1	0	0	1	1	0	1	X	4	10	0

PITCHERS: STL: Magrane, Cox (L), Worrell; MIN: Viola (W), Reardon (SV)
DOUBLES: Puckett, Pena, Gladden
TRIPLES: None
HOME RUNS: None
ATTENDANCE: 55,376
TIME OF GAME: 3:04

October 27, 1991

	1	2	3	4	5	6	7	8	9	10	R	H	E
ATLANTA (NL)	0	0	0	0	0	0	0	0	0	0	0	7	0
MINNESOTA (AL)	0	0	0	0	0	0	0	0	0	1	1	10	0

PITCHERS: ATL: Smoltz, Stanton, Pena (L); MIN: Morris (W)
DOUBLES: Pendleton, Hunter, Gladden (2)
TRIPLES: None
HOME RUNS: None
ATTENDANCE: 55,118
TIME OF GAME: 3:23

October 26, 1997

	1	2	3	4	5	6	7	8	9	10	11	R	H	E
CLEVELAND (AL)	0	0	2	0	0	0	0	0	0	0	0	2	6	2
FLORIDA (NL)	0	0	0	0	0	0	1	0	1	0	1	3	8	0

PITCHERS: CLE: Wright, Assenmacher, Jackson, Anderson, Mesa, Nagy (L); FLA: Leiter, Cook, Alfonseca, Heredia, Nen, Powell (W)

DOUBLES: Renteria

TRIPLES: None

HOME RUNS: Bonilla

ATTENDANCE: 67,204

TIME OF GAME: 4:11

November 4, 2001

	1	2	3	4	5	6	7	8	9	R	H	E
NEW YORK (AL)	0	0	0	0	0	0	1	1	0	2	6	3
ARIZONA (NL)	0	0	0	0	0	1	0	0	2	3	10	0

PITCHERS: NYY: Clemens, Stanton, Rivera (L); ARZ: Schilling, Batista, Johnson (W)

DOUBLES: O'Neill, Bautista, Womack

TRIPLES: None

HOME RUNS: Soriano

ATTENDANCE: 49,589

TIME OF GAME: 3:20

October 27, 2002

	1	2	3	4	5	6	7	8	9	R	H	E
SAN FRANCISCO (NL)	0	1	0	0	0	0	0	0	0	1	6	0
ANAHEIM (AL)	0	1	3	0	0	0	0	0	X	4	5	0

PITCHERS: SFG: Hernandez (L), Zerbe, Rueter, Worrell; ANA: Lackey (W), Donnelly, F. Rodriguez, Percival (SV)

DOUBLES: Snow, Anderson, Molina (2)

TRIPLES: None

HOME RUNS: None

ATTENDANCE: 44,598

TIME OF GAME: 3:16

Index